THE EVERYTHING®

GUIDE TO
ANGER MANAGEMENT

Dear Reader,

We live in an increasingly hectic, fast-paced society. The level of stress and anger that people experience can cause them enormous pain, but it doesn't have to be this way. Learning to manage, control, and prevent anger has profound implications for your life.

While anger may not sound like the most exciting topic, think of how many areas of your life anger can impact: your work, your relationships, even your physical and mental health. For those who are able to avoid the serious negative consequences associated with anger (divorce, unemployment, and incarceration) there are still the more chronic, "low-level" problems that diminish your quality of life. When problematic anger follows you from place to place and from year to year, it is hard to experience true happiness.

It is not easy to master your anger. It takes time and effort. But many people have done it, and so can you. We all know the stories: the former violent gang member who now travels to schools giving inspirational speeches about community and nonviolence; the irascible "Scrooge" who learned to surrender his hostility and develop kindness and compassion. No matter how much you have struggled in the past, there is every reason to believe that you can transform your life as well.

Managing anger is about learning to become a more controlled, assertive, and interpersonally effective person. We welcome you on this journey. If you are like most people, the most difficult part of anger management will be convincing yourself you need to make an effort. The second most difficult part will be establishing consistency. By applying the principles of anger management, you will find that these challenges become easier with time. Each success propels you forward. In the end, it is our hope that you find that this effort not only reduced the role of anger in your life, but also increased your sense of joy and spontaneity. Find out for yourself.

Robert Puff, PhD   *James Seghers, PhD*

Welcome to the EVERYTHING® Series!

These handy, accessible books give you all you need to tackle a difficult project, gain a new hobby, comprehend a fascinating topic, prepare for an exam, or even brush up on something you learned back in school but have since forgotten.

You can choose to read an Everything® book from cover to cover or just pick out the information you want from our four useful boxes: e-questions, e-facts, e-alerts, and e-ssentials.

We give you everything you need to know on the subject, but throw in a lot of fun stuff along the way, too.

We now have more than 400 Everything® books in print, spanning such wide-ranging categories as weddings, pregnancy, cooking, music instruction, foreign language, crafts, pets, New Age, and so much more. When you're done reading them all, you can finally say you know Everything®!

QUESTION

Answers to
common questions

FACT

Important snippets
of information

ALERT

Urgent
warnings

ESSENTIAL

Quick
handy tips

PUBLISHER Karen Cooper

MANAGING EDITOR, EVERYTHING® SERIES Lisa Laing

COPY CHIEF Casey Ebert

ASSISTANT PRODUCTION EDITOR Alex Guarco

ACQUISITIONS EDITOR Pamela Wissman

DEVELOPMENT EDITOR Eileen Mullan

EVERYTHING® SERIES COVER DESIGNER Erin Alexander

THE
EVERYTHING®
GUIDE TO
ANGER
MANAGEMENT

Proven techniques to understand and control anger

Robert Puff, PhD, and James Seghers, PhD

Featured by MSNBC, WebMD.com, and *Psychology Today*

Adams Media
New York London Toronto Sydney New Delhi

Dr. Seghers: I dedicate this book to my wife, Helen Berlin.
Dr. Puff: I dedicate this book to my father, Robert Puff, Sr.

Adams Media
An Imprint of Simon & Schuster, Inc.
57 Littlefield Street
Avon, Massachusetts 02322

An Everything® Series Book.
Everything® and everything.com® are registered trademarks of Simon & Schuster, Inc.

ADAMS MEDIA and colophon are trademarks of Simon and Schuster.

For information about special discounts for bulk purchases, please contact Simon & Schuster Special Sales at 1-866-506-1949 or business@simonandschuster.com.

The Simon & Schuster Speakers Bureau can bring authors to your live event. For more information or to book an event contact the Simon & Schuster Speakers Bureau at 1-866-248-3049 or visit our website at www.simonspeakers.com.

Manufactured in the United States of America

9 2021

Library of Congress Cataloging-in-Publication Data has been applied for.

ISBN 978-1-4405-7226-5
ISBN 978-1-4405-7227-2 (ebook)

Contents

Acknowledgments

Dr. Seghers: Without the love and support of my wife, Helen, this project never would have been completed. I would like to express my deepest gratitude to my mother, Ralda Singer, who offered so much love and wisdom over the years; to my stepfather, Nick Singer, the best "buddy" I can imagine having, and who always encouraged me to write; to my father, Jimmy Seghers, who taught me how to think critically and to live a values-driven life; and to my stepmother, Michelle, who has been an incredible inspiration. In addition, I would like to acknowledge the support of Ronnie Yeh, Frank Chen, Mike and Tracy Baas, Richard and Laurice Nahas, and Seta Nahas.

In addition, my PhD advisor, Nancy Docherty, played a major a role in my career; she taught me so much about how to do real scholarship. I would like to thank Josh Bregman, a true friend of the heart. I would like to thank my coauthor, Robert Puff, for a very rewarding partnership. Finally, I would like to thank my brother, Steven Seghers, whom I admire greatly, and who has shared so much of this life's journey with me.

Dr. Puff: This book came into being because of my colleague, James Seghers. I knew my schedule was too busy to tackle this project alone. Dr. Seghers is an excellent writer, a caring psychologist, and a gifted communicator. If you benefit from this book, please let Dr. Seghers know.

Top Ten Telltale Signs of an Anger Problem

1. Do you experience or express your anger in a manner that is out of proportion with the triggering event?

2. Have you ever hurt yourself, in any way, with your temper?

3. Do you feel angry when you think about certain times, events, or significant people in your life?

4. Have you noticed that you always have this feeling of anger, tension, or irritability?

5. Do people "walk on eggshells" around you?

6. Do you feel (or fear) being out of control when you are angry?

7. Have you lost or damaged a relationship, job, or something else important because of your anger?

8. Do you take out your anger on someone or something else rather than the person or situation that is bothering you?

9. How many people have you alienated with your temper?

10. Has anyone ever told you that you have an anger problem? Have you heard it more than once and from different people?

Introduction

IF YOU'RE READING THIS introduction, you probably have an anger problem, or know someone who does. You're not alone. Most people have struggled with anger at some point in their lives. Many great leaders in human history, from Alexander the Great to Steve Jobs, have struggled with issues of temper and rage. Having an anger problem doesn't mean you are bad person, are "weak," or that your character is flawed. But it is a problem worth addressing. Anger problems can have serious, even fatal consequences.

You have probably seen how destructive out-of-control anger can be. Perhaps you've frightened yourself, or those you love, with episodes of rage. The aggressive, rageful feeling that anger brings can be both intoxicating and frightening. People sometimes convince themselves that anger "helps"—that it makes them stronger, more capable, and more respected—but the realities are hard to ignore. In the wake of protracted anger problems, you'll find a trail of broken relationships, shattered careers, health problems, and a lot of unhappiness. Uncontrolled anger destroys lives.

Anger can inspire people to do great things, as in the case of Martin Luther King Jr., who used his anger about injustice to pursue positive social change. Anger can also be quite dangerous. Anger is the hottest of the "hot" emotions, and has the power to induce otherwise kind and respectable people to behave very badly. Consider what you know of history and world events from the perspective of anger. How many wars, atrocities, and injustices have been committed under the banner of rage? On a more personal level, think of how anger has played out in your life, and in the lives of people you know. It isn't always a pretty picture.

Today, more than ever, people look around and find many reasons to get upset. Economic problems, school violence, partisan politics, the pressures of an increasingly fast-paced society, even urban drift. If you talk with other people about this, you will likely find a consensus that anger problems are getting worse. In addition, the level of stress people experience—one of the important causes of anger—is getting worse, not better.

The good news is that anger problems are solvable. You don't have to struggle with anger for the rest of your life, and you certainly don't have to reinvent the wheel. Psychologists know considerably more about anger than they did even a generation ago. The current scientific understanding of what anger is, what causes it, and the associated risks has reached a highly developed level. At the same time, a tremendous amount of work has been done to figure out what works and what doesn't from the perspective of *managing* and *preventing* problematic anger. Bringing you this information in a coherent, easy-to-use manner is the central purpose of this book.

The *Everything® Guide to Anger Management* is shaped by four key areas of emphasis:

Emphasis on psychological science: Wherever possible, an effort has been made to present the most up-to-date scientific information.

Emphasis on practicality: The book was written so that you can engage in a self-directed anger management program, as opposed to requiring direct guidance. Much of the material is presented progressively, so that more advanced techniques on anger control and prevention build on more basic concepts and strategies. This allows you to apply techniques very quickly while continuing to learn.

Emphasis on breadth: Many topic areas are discussed, providing a comprehensive picture. Common difficulties and stumbling blocks are anticipated and addressed. Most importantly, a great variety of approaches are presented for learning the actual management, control, and prevention of anger.

Emphasis on flexibility: This book affords considerable flexibility regarding the implementation of an anger management program. Most of the techniques can be used on their own, but they can also be combined with other principles and techniques. You have all the information necessary to design an anger management program that fits your unique needs, situation, and personality.

Learning to manage anger is a challenge, but it is very achievable, and very rewarding. There is no area of your life that will not be improved by learning to better manage and control your own emotions. In taking this journey, you will find that the benefits extend well beyond a reduction of problematic anger. In the bigger picture, you will find that you grow as a person, that your life is more peaceful, and that you are more effective in your relationships.

CHAPTER 1

Anger Is Important

You may consider anger to be an all-around negative emotion, but this is not true. Anger is a protective emotion that helps people defend themselves against physical and psychological threats. Considered a "whole-person" phenomenon, anger is expressed emotionally, cognitively, physically, and behaviorally. While anger can occur for many different reasons, it always involves three factors: a triggering event, characteristics of the individual's personality, and a particular interpretation of the situation. Because anger can be very subjective, it can also be controlled.

This Emotional Life

Emotions allow you to experience the highs of excitement, joy, and love, and the depths of anguish, guilt, and sorrow. In a word, emotions are visceral. They convey a sense of immediacy and truth. Your emotions reflect you as an individual, who you are and where you've been, and they mirror your unique relationship with the world, incorporating the information you receive (and your *processing* of that information) moment by moment. Emotions exert a powerful influence on behavior. Strong emotions can cause you to act in a way that you might not normally or to avoid situations that you generally enjoy. So much of what makes life wonderful and poignant and frustrating is reflected in your emotional experience.

In fact, emotions color the entire fabric of human experience. Imagine a life without emotion. No anger, no sadness—but also, no joy. No love, no affection, a life of numbness, devoid of color or quality. Would you want to live this life? Who would you be with no emotion? You might just be unrecognizable.

Emotions Are Important for Survival

At one point, emotions were so inseparably connected with the sense of what it means to be human that it was difficult to imagine other species sharing in this experience. Now, however, there is good evidence to suggest that emotions are linked with all complex life on the planet. The reason is simple: basic survival.

Naturalist Charles Darwin conceptualized emotions as adaptations that allow both humans and animals to survive and reproduce. Subsequent studies supported and expanded on this view. Researchers have learned that emotions act as signals, alerting organisms to what is happening in their environment. Emotions also guide and direct reactions to those signals: *run away* from the crocodile, *attack* this man, *show affection* toward this child. While emotions are not equivalent to this action or that action (you can be quite angry, for example, without displaying any overt behaviors whatsoever), they carry definite action tendencies. When you are angry, you are likely to attack the source of your irritation. When you experience fear, you are more likely to flee. When you feel love, you may engage in altruistic behavior. Thus, emotions convey information (what is happening), direction (what to do), and motivation (the impulse to take action). Emotions serve an adaptive role in human life by motivating people to act quickly and to take actions that will maximize opportunities for success.

Emotions Are Important for Decision-Making

Recently, neuroscientist Antonio Damasio made a discovery as he studied a group of people who had a damaged prefrontal cortex, the part of the brain where emotional information is synthesized with conscious thought. Damasio noticed that although these people appeared normal in many respects and showed intact reasoning capacity, they exhibited a singular impairment: They struggled to make even the most basic decisions. They could clearly describe possible actions they might take and readily weigh the logical consequences of a given alternative. Yet choosing an appointment date or even deciding what to eat was incredibly difficult.

Damasio's research shows that emotions have a major influence not only on the kinds of decisions people make, but, more fundamentally, on the ability to make decisions. Some decisions are obvious: Do you drive straight ahead and hit the stalled car in front of you, or do you swerve to avoid the collision? In real life, however, decision-making is often far less clear. Even many seemingly mundane decisions are not so clear-cut when examined more closely. What shirt do you wear today? What toaster do you buy? What school do you send your child to? Emotion greatly facilitates these kinds of decisions.

FACT

Emotions have three constituents: a subjective component (how you experience the emotion), a physiological component (how your body reacts to the emotion), and an expressive component (how you behave in response to the emotion).

Emotions Signal Information to Others

In an environmental context, emotions convey important information about how others should behave toward you, and also about how you should behave toward them. For example, if you encounter a growling animal, you may infer that the creature is angry and defensive, motivating you to back off and avoid possible danger. In much the same way, human emotional displays provide information, or cues, about how others need to respond to them. In some cases, these cues are transmitted through body language, facial expression, or tone of voice. In other cases, the person may just say how he feels. Conveying this information to others gives them cues they can then use to take action.

Just as your emotions provide valuable information to others, their emotional expressions offer you a wealth of information as well. Social communication is an important part of daily life, and being able to interpret and react to the emotions of others is essential. This information allows you to respond appropriately and to build close relationships with friends, family, and loved ones. It also allows you to communicate effectively in a variety of social situations, from dealing with an irate customer to managing a challenging employee.

Primary Versus Secondary Emotions

What are primary and secondary emotions? The initial response you have to a pleasant or unpleasant event is a primary emotion. These feelings arise quickly. They originate as a direct result of an external cue and occur close to the triggering event. For example, if you receive a large pay raise, you will likely have an instant emotional response of joy or surprise. On a sadder note, if a loved one passes away, you will probably quickly feel a powerful emotion of sadness. Primary emotions provide information about your current situation and prepare you to act in some way.

Secondary emotions are an emotional reaction to your primary emotions; that is, they are feelings in response to feelings. If, for example, you yell at your child for forgetting to put the dishes away, your primary emotion of anger comes on quickly, but then you may begin to feel guilty (the secondary emotion) for having lost your temper. The relationship between primary and secondary emotions can be quite complex.

Secondary emotions can arise in response to not recognizing or expressing a primary emotion, as, for example, when an emotion is actively suppressed. A secondary emotion is likely to occur when you don't value, listen to, or respond to your primary emotions. When you ignore or suppress a primary emotion, it does not simply disappear. Instead, it is re-expressed in covert form. A classic case is the tendency for repressed anger to be "turned inward" and re-expressed as depression.

Secondary emotions can also have a primarily defensive function. A common example is the use of anger to defend against feelings of hurt. Some people are so armored against experiencing vulnerable emotions that they bury these feelings with anger almost immediately. In fact, although statistics are not available, many experts believe that most anger experienced in modern society is defensive and secondary in nature, protecting against the experience of vulnerable emotions such as hurt, rejection, and shame.

FACT

Conducting cross-cultural research in locations as diverse as Papua New Guinea, and San Francisco, psychologist Paul Ekman discovered that a core subset of emotions is recognized throughout the world. He classified the following six "basic" emotions: anger, disgust, fear, happiness, sadness, and surprise.

Anger Is a Three-Stage Process

Anger is experienced as a unified phenomenon. People don't typically think about "components" or "stages." Something triggers you, and you get angry. Just like that.

In reality, anger is a process that unfolds in stages. This perspective incorporates up-to-date research findings that have demonstrated the complexity of anger as a phenomenon that is influenced by many factors simultaneously. Beyond the triggering event, anger is significantly determined by personality characteristics, temperament, life history, and personal beliefs. Recognizing anger as a three-stage process provides an actionable framework against which anger can be utilized, controlled, and prevented.

The first stage in the anger process is the trigger event. It's the "something happened and I got mad" stage. The event can be internal, such as a thought, or external, such as a particular situation that you experience. Internal events usually refer to an earlier external event. For example, you recall a recent incident when a friend broke your trust, with the result that you move from a state of calm to one of anger based on a recollection alone.

The second stage in the anger process is interpretive. It is controlled by how you think about the event that triggered your anger. For example, you tell a friend that you were irritated by what someone said and then you snapped at that person. But was it really so simple? In reality, perhaps you interpreted the person's behavior as condescending, decided you did not like being addressed that way, decided the other person should be punished for doing so, and snapped back on that basis. This kind of processing can unfold in seconds. Interpretation, or appraisal, of events is facilitated by the fact that, as an adult, you have already internalized a network of beliefs and rules of behavior that direct how you respond to situations (e.g., "disrespectful behavior from others is unacceptable!").

ESSENTIAL

Anger serves a purpose, even when it goes wrong, as it has and does for so many people. The experience of anger can be useful in terms of understanding yourself better and becoming aware of issues that you need to address.

The interpretive component of anger is particularly obvious in situations where a triggering event produces different reactions in different people. For example, think of the different reactions that occur when people are confronted with a mundane irritant such as a stoplight that quickly turns red. Some people calmly accept the situation, others are mildly irritated, and some become furious. In each case, the nature of the reaction reveals something important about that person's state of mind over and above the immediate context that appeared to "cause" the anger in the first place.

The third and final stage in the experience of anger is behavioral. How do you act based on your anger? Do you slam the door? Do you swallow your anger? Do you decide to wait until you can express your anger more indirectly, such as by not showing up at the person's birthday party? The behavioral-response stage of anger affords many opportunities for either resolving or exacerbating a difficult situation.

Why People Get Angry

People become angry because of a broad range of experiences that are *not* necessarily threatening or dangerous. Often, anger is aroused when things do not go in accordance with a person's desires. Thus, it is helpful to distinguish between a real threat, which is anything that threatens your sense of self or that which you love, and an instrumental threat, which might better be expressed as frustration.

For example, your spouse didn't put the dishes away . . . again. You find yourself trapped in bumper-to-bumper traffic. The weather is unseasonably hot and humid. People can, and do, get angry over these kinds of things all the time. You probably have as well. This kind of anger emerges as a response to feelings of frustration, which in turn arise whenever you are met with unpleasant circumstances. Any time you are prevented from fulfilling your wishes or forced into a situation you dislike—in short, whenever you have to put up with something you would rather avoid—your mind tends to react with aversion, which can quickly develop into anger.

In modern life, anger most often develops in response to the unwanted actions of another person. For example, another person is perceived as being disrespectful, demeaning, or neglectful. This kind of interpersonal anger is associated with certain styles of thinking, such as "My boss criticized me in front of my colleagues. Now I'm pissed. She shouldn't be so disrespectful!" or "That guy is going twenty miles over the speed limit. Who does he think he is!" Anger energizes you not only to defend yourself, but also to retaliate. Research indicates that about 25 percent of anger incidents involve thoughts of revenge. Anger often emerges during interactions with loved ones, such as relatives, spouses, and close friends.

Anger As a Defense

One very important reason that people become angry is to protect themselves from feeling vulnerable. Anger is an active, attack-oriented emotion. When you feel angry, you feel powerful, confident, and capable. Contrast this with allowing yourself to feel hurt or afraid; then you feel vulnerable, exposed, and insecure. As a result, people often experience anger as a secondary emotion within the context of the primary emotions of hurt and fear. How many times, in real life or in film, have you seen someone display anger in the face of rejection or betrayal? This jump to anger is a defensive move that typically occurs outside conscious awareness. For many, this move is so strongly conditioned that the anger appears to arise immediately as a primary emotional response.

How do I know if my anger is defensive?
Anger is often experienced as a secondary emotion to protect yourself from feeling vulnerable. Ask yourself what it is about what happened that upset you. If you recognize that you are experiencing another emotion alongside anger, that other emotion is likely to be your primary emotion.

Common Anger-Provoking Situations

Research has shown that certain situations are more likely to produce anger. In one landmark study by Sanford Mabel, a questionnaire was administered to participants based on an initial review of 900 anger-triggering stimuli. Following a number of iterations, the resulting analysis produced the following list of the ten situations most likely to elicit anger:

1. Interruption of goal-directed behavior when time is important
2. Experiencing personal degradation or unfair treatment and being powerless to stop it
3. Being treated unfairly, unkindly, or in a prejudicial way, whether or not one is present
4. Being the object of dishonesty or broken promises, being disappointed by others or oneself
5. Having one's authority, feelings, or property disregarded by others
6. Being ignored or treated badly by a significant other
7. Experiencing harm because of one's negligence toward oneself
8. Being shown by others' behavior that they do not care
9. Being the object of verbal or physical assault
10. Being a "helpless victim"

A quick glance through these situations highlights the self-protective nature of anger. Indeed, all but one (the first, interruption of goal-directed behavior) readily conform to an overarching experience in which one's person or sense of self is threatened in some way.

A Model for How People Get Angry

In 1996, Dr. Jerry Deffenbacher of Colorado State University offered a simple model for the development of anger that synthesized a broad range of research findings. In terms of this model, anger results from three distinct factors that work together. These factors are the trigger event, the qualities of the individual, and the individual's appraisal of the situation.

The Trigger Event

Consider the simplest part of this formula: the trigger event. As discussed earlier, there is always some event, internal or external, that triggers the initial anger. This is not a new idea. An important point of Deffenbacher's model, however, is that the trigger event only explains *some* of the anger that people experience but not all of it. This point bears emphasizing, because it runs contrary to how most people think about anger. People tend to explain their anger exclusively in terms of the situation that provoked it. If the trigger event could explain everything, then everyone would respond in the same manner to a certain situation. For example, everyone would react the same way when they are cut off in traffic or insulted. This is not the case, of course. People's reactions to these situations can be quite varied, and the reasons for this variability are explained by the other two factors.

Individual Characteristics

The phrase *individual characteristics* is very general. A more accurate, but unwieldy, description would be "the condition of the individual at the time and place of the trigger event." This phrasing shows that the individual characteristics encompass both the established, solidified qualities of the individual (e.g., personality), as well as her fluid state of mind. Solidified qualities include personality, memories, beliefs and values, and physiological status. For example, if you have the personality trait of competitiveness, you may be more likely to be angered by a colleague's boasting. Or, if your sister is struggling with drug addition, you may react more negatively to someone stating that "drug addicts are all a bunch of losers."

The particular state of mind, or pre-anger state, that was present immediately before the trigger event is also an important determinant. For example, if you are stressed or worried immediately before a trigger event, you will more likely react angrily. On the other hand, if you are in a good mood, you will more likely react with calm. Pre-anger states have a strong effect on emotional reactions.

Appraisal of the Situation

Ultimately, whether you get angry in response to a particular situation has a lot to do with how you appraise or interpret the situation. Generally speaking, when you interpret a situation negatively, you experience a negative emotional reaction: hurt, anger, fear. The reverse is true as well. This phenomenon is generally referred to as cognitive appraisal, and it is the cornerstone of many contemporary models of stress and anger. The underlying idea is very simple: Your emotions parallel and reflect the content of your thoughts.

Some people tend to interpret things negatively as a matter of habit. They may believe someone's error had malicious or unkind motives, for example. They may take one negative event as a sign that more negative events are to come, which can further contribute to anger and stress. Remember, an anger-evoking interpretation of an event can be either accurate or inaccurate. You will be just as angry, and feel every bit as "justified," even when your perspective on the event is mistaken or distorted.

The modern understanding of the role that appraisal plays in anger owes an enormous debt to earlier research on stress. It was once believed that certain events, such as losing a job, were uniformly upsetting for all people. Research that began in the 1960s showed that this was not the case. People can have very different emotional reactions to events merely as a result of their differing judgments about them.

Anger Is an Embodied Experience

People sometimes speak about anger as if it were a psychological phenomenon —something that occurs only in the mind. In reality, the experience of anger has a strong sensory quality, and the immediate expression of anger is decidedly physical. A key point that bears repeating is that anger has evolved to protect you from danger—real, actual, physical danger. In modern life, very few of the things that arouse anger in people pose an immediate physical threat. You feel your spouse is being unsupportive. You receive an unfair performance evaluation. A driver gives you a mean look. Nevertheless, the physiological mechanisms through which anger is expressed cause you to react physically with the same rapidity and intensity as if you were in danger. This is an important point because it speaks to the real difficulty people face in learning to manage and control their anger.

The Physiology of Anger

Anger keeps your body and mind stimulated and ready for action. When you become angry, your sympathetic nervous system—the body's *threat system*—becomes activated to contend with the threat. Think back to the last time you were really mad. You probably felt as if your body was preparing for a fight. Once you've hit that first step in the anger process, your heart is beginning to race, your breathing is becoming fast and shallow, and you're sweating or shaking. Other common symptoms include tensing your muscles, grinding your teeth, and reddening of your face.

At the level of your brain and body, a cascade of reactions occurs to produce these symptoms. The body's threat system is associated with the fight-or-flight response. You are on red alert. You are anticipating physical harm, and you are preparing to take decisive action to counter any threat.

Researchers have found that anger results in more sympathetically aroused sensations than any other emotion, except fear. In other words, anger enables you to work very hard physically and mentally to right a perceived "wrong." The amygdala, an almond-shaped structure located deep in the brain's temporal lobe, plays an important role in this process. The amygdala performs a number of functions (including a role in memory formation), but when it comes to fear and anger, the amygdala is primarily responsible for identifying threats and alerting other parts of the brain to take action. The process can be quite rapid and intense, such that you will often react before the reasoning part of your brain, the prefrontal cortex, is able to establish control. This is an important point: The human brain is wired in such a way that anger induces you to act *before you can consciously weigh the rationality of your anger or the consequences of your actions*. The threat system activates rapidly because anything less could be insufficient to protect you from an immediate physical danger. That is why it often feels as if anger emerges instantaneously. This does not mean that the situation is hopeless, or that you are excused from behaving poorly when you are upset. With effort, even the most intense anger reactions can be moderated and controlled. What it does mean, however, is that you have to make that effort. Learning to manage anger means taking the time to master a set of skills and techniques.

Once you've hit that first stage in the anger process, things move quickly. Your brain releases neurotransmitters known as catecholamines, which in turn produce a surge of energy. This energetic surge is highly motivating, producing a temporary elevation of self-confidence and an immediate desire to take action. These reactions are paralleled by physiological changes, such as accelerated heart rate and breathing. Blood pressure increases, resulting in flushing (redness) of the extremities and face. In quick succession, additional neurotransmitters and hormones, including adrenaline, are released, which trigger a lasting state of arousal and aggressiveness. You are ready to fight.

The Effects on Thinking and Attention

During the arousal of any kind of anger, your attention narrows and becomes locked onto the target of your anger, inhibiting higher-order reasoning. You become "captured" in your own point of view, such that it is increasingly difficult to view the situation objectively, or to separate the other party from your emotional reaction to her. Because the purpose of anger is to be protective, it focuses your attention on the worst aspects of the situation. As a result, anger tends to reinforce itself. By focusing primarily on threats, anger generates a state of mind where the anger is readily justified, not examined or questioned. The motive impulse is to neutralize the threat. It's an "attack first, ask questions later" state of mind. Furthermore, because anger (as well as stress and fear) impairs the encoding of long-term memories, the self-reinforcing nature of anger is carried forward in time. Important contextual and moderating information is lost, while the most threatening observations and impressions are retained and remembered.

FACT

Anger can alter brain function at the cellular level. Researchers at the Hotchkiss Brain Institute in Calgary discovered that anger impairs neurons in the hypothalamus, the brain's command center for the stress response. This is one of the reasons anger management can be so challenging: The angrier you get, the harder it is to control your anger.

The Moderating Role of "the Executive"

Powerful emotions such as anger can challenge your thinking and judgment in any number of ways, but they do not have to cause you to lose control. The part of your brain responsible for conscious reasoning is the prefrontal cortex. It is sometimes referred to as "the executive," and for good reason: It allows you to moderate and control the powerful action tendencies generated by more primitive brain regions such as the amygdala. The left prefrontal cortex, in particular, has the ability to switch off emotions. It serves an executive role in decision-making and analysis.

With all this in mind, imagine asserting control over your anger as helping your prefrontal cortex gain the upper hand over the amygdala so you can control how you react to angry feelings. The many ways to facilitate this process include behavioral strategies, relaxation techniques, meditative practices, and the use of cognitive interventions.

The Wind-Down Phase

As the saying goes, "what comes up, must come down." As more time separates you from the event that triggered your anger, or as the person who is the target of your anger no longer poses an immediate threat, you begin to relax. This is the beginning of the wind-down phase.

Just as the sympathetic nervous system—your body's threat system—facilitates the activation of anger, now the parasympathetic nervous system takes over, helping to create a sense of calm. The parasympathetic nervous system counters the flood of arousal produced in anger, releasing a neurotransmitter, acetylcholine, that neutralizes the stress hormones and allows the body to settle down.

An important point here is that this winding-down process can be slow and difficult. It can be further complicated by the tendency some people have to marinate in their anger, which can sustain arousal over long periods. Even as you begin to cool down, moreover, your anger threshold will remain lowered from some time. The result is that, following a bout of anger, you are at greater risk for becoming angry again, and will be more likely to overreact to minor irritations. You will likely also find that your memory and concentration are variably impaired in the aftermath of acute anger.

CHAPTER 2

Anger Gone Awry

Anger can be healthy, but it can also be a serious problem for many people. Unhealthy anger is discernible in a number of ways, chiefly by how it affects a person's life: It creates more problems than it solves. Many factors come into play in terms of understanding why some people develop anger problems while other do not, but common causes include genetics, family background, stress, and low frustration tolerance.

When Anger Becomes a Problem

Anger can be a powerful ally. It is one of the most cathartic emotions, and it can be a very effective cleanser of the emotional system. However, when anger becomes a habit, it loses its power to transform and becomes an obstacle.

America seems to be in the midst of an anger epidemic. From traffic jams to computer glitches to friends who don't show up when they say they will, there's never been a shortage of things to get mad about. Recently, fall-out from the economic crisis—lost jobs, shrunken nest eggs—seems to be amplifying the overall level of arousal. The pressures of modern-day life put enormous stress on families, relationships, individuals, and organizations. The result is that people are increasingly witnessing and experiencing greater levels of anger, frustration, irritability, and stress.

The Societal Context

Statistics demonstrate a high prevalence of anger in modern society. According to a study led by Ronald Kessler, more than 7 percent of the U.S. population have met criteria for intermittent explosive disorder (IED), a particularly severe form of chronic anger. A recent *USA Today*/Gallup poll reported that 53 percent of Americans were angry about the economy. In another poll conducted by the American Psychological Association, 60 percent of Americans reported feeling angry or irritable—up from 50 percent in 2007. Anger problems are not limited to the United States, though. A recent survey in the United Kingdom, for example, found that 12 percent of respondents had trouble controlling their anger, 28 percent worried about how angry they sometimes feel, and 64 percent agreed that people in general are getting angrier.

FACT

People spend, on average, three-and-a-half years of their lives being angry. Although work problems, money worries, and family issues all play a part, various customer service issues, and other societal horrors, such as "Dog Mess" and "Public Displays of Affection" also cause distress.

Healthy Versus Unhealthy Anger

Feelings of anger can generate positive or negative behavior, depending on the situation and the individual's manner of dealing with the emotion. Healthy anger is differentiated from unhealthy anger in terms of how successfully the emotion serves the person's basic needs. For example, if you made a quirky, somewhat angry response to a coworker's rude comment that positively resolved the situation, the anger response would be considered healthy. However, if you punched your coworker, thus endangering employment and violating another person's integrity, the anger response would be considered unhealthy.

Healthy anger motivates you to stand up for yourself, address problems, and correct injustices. When you manage anger well, it prompts you to make positive changes. Mismanaged anger, on the other hand, is counterproductive, creating more problems than it solves. Here are some of the core characteristics of unhealthy anger:

- It is too frequent.
- It is too intense.
- It lasts too long.
- It masks other feelings.
- It disturbs family and/or work relationships.
- It begins a destructive cycle that often cannot be controlled.
- It hurts people.

Anger that exhibits these core characteristics can lead to poor decision-making and problem-solving, can create problems with relationships at home and at work, and can directly affect your health.

Anger, Hostility, and Aggression

Anger, hostility, and aggression are frequently used terms that have significant differences in meaning. *Anger* is a normal emotion; despite its adaptive benefits, however, it is considered a negative emotion because most people would generally prefer not to feel angry.

Hostility is the pervasive attitude that anticipates aggression in others and justifies aggression toward others. It is a characteristic of chronically angry people who tend to ignore their own contributions to frustrating situations, which they view as intolerable, unjustified, and intentionally caused.

Aggression is a behavior intended to cause harm. Often, it reflects a desire for dominance and control. Aggressive behavior can be measured on a continuum ranging from pushy and controlling behavior to violence and rage. Aggressive behavior can involve either covert or overt behavior. *Covert aggression* expresses anger in an indirect, manipulative, or passive-aggressive manner, including subtle behaviors such as withdrawal, sabotage, or sarcasm. *Overt aggression* expresses anger in a direct, controlling, or domineering manner, including more obvious behaviors such as arguing, yelling, or violence.

Since anger is typically expressed through loud verbalizations, aggression is usually the driving point behind cases that wind up in the criminal justice system. Research shows that about 90 percent of aggressive incidents are preceded by anger. However, only 10 percent of anger experiences are actually followed by aggression. People often want to act aggressively when they are angry but, fortunately, most do not actually take aggressive actions.

Situational Anger

Situational anger is experienced as an immediate response to an event. For example, your boss unfairly blames you for a late project; you're running late for work, only to find that an accident has shut down the highway; you discover that your child has been cheating at school. Not taking into account an underlying chronic anger problem, the most challenging form of situational anger is overreactive anger, in which either the intensity or the expression of anger is disproportionate to the triggering event. Situational anger aroused by these kinds of events is time-limited by definition.

Chronic Anger

You likely know someone who seems to carry a chip on his or her shoulder. You may even be this person. Chronically angry people are always angry or upset about something. They complain about and criticize the boss, their children, their spouse, the economy, the government, the phone company, the quality of produce at the supermarket. They wake up full of complaints. They spread criticism and negativity throughout the day and go to bed unhappy and still complaining. They are not fun to be around.

Whereas some forms of dysfunctional anger are situation-dependent, acute chronic anger is self-sustaining. These people are unable to deal with stress appropriately and are therefore easily frustrated, which inevitably leads to increased anger. They may become angry in situations where it is not useful or appropriate, and they have difficulty resolving interpersonal ruptures. Chronically angry people tend to become angry quicker than others and to remain angry for longer periods.

This condition affects adults, teenagers, and children, often causing rage or ill temper on a regular basis. In most cases, the person becomes easily upset, even over trivial circumstances. The causes of chronic anger vary, but many experts believe one cause is neglect or abuse in childhood. Many people with anger issues risk alienating close friends and loved ones, who may find it uncomfortable or even frightening to be around the chronically angry person.

Anger as a Habitual Response

The more that you engage in anger, the more likely you are to become angry in the future. The physiological pathways to anger become primed with frequent use. Over time, aggressive displays of anger can become a habit that is hard to break. By their very nature, habits have a repetitive quality, and are initiated readily, with little thought. Because of this, people with anger management problems tend to turn to anger as their preferred problem-solving and coping technique, with little consideration of adverse consequences.

Why Are Some People Angrier Than Others?

Some people really are angrier than others. They get angry more easily and more intensely than other people. Sometimes they don't show their anger in loud spectacular ways but are chronically irritable and grumpy. Easily angered people do not always curse and throw things; they may just withdraw, sulk, or even get physically ill.

People who are easily angered generally have a low tolerance for frustration, aggravation, and everyday hassles. They seem to overreact to the many problems of daily living and believe they should not be subjected to frustration, inconvenience, or annoyance. They find it difficult to take things in stride and are particularly exasperated if the situation seems unreasonable or unfair.

Anger Risk Factors

There are a number of risk factors that increase a person's chance of developing an anger problem. How you deal with anger is something that you learn throughout your life. If you do not have healthy coping or anger management techniques, you will be more prone to having difficulty controlling anger. In addition, anger control issues can be observed in families, so if a parent had anger issues, you will be more likely to experience similar problems. It's not set in stone, but the probability is increased.

Common risk factors for developing anger management issues include the following:

- **Genetics.** Some children are born irritable, touchy, and easily angered, and these signs are present from a very early age. There are babies who are crankier than others, and in some cases these tendencies continue through adolescence and into adulthood.

Scientists have been able to disentangle the influence of genes and the environment on behavior by studying twins. A study in Denmark looked at similarities among identical twins who had been adopted as infants and raised separately. According to *www.sciencemag.com*, overall, there was a 12.9 percent concordance between twins' aggressive behaviors as adults, suggesting that genetics makes a small but significant contribution to aggression.

- **Witnessing poor anger management.** Family background is an established source of anger problems. People who are easily angered often come from families that are disruptive, chaotic, and unskilled at emotional communication. Children learn how to behave and regulate their emotions by watching their parents. If one or both parents have anger management problems, their children are more likely to believe that losing their temper is an acceptable and normal reaction to anger.

- **Impaired processing of social information.** This is a major cause for anger problems and often serves as an immediate trigger for combative interactions. Social information processing occurs over multiple stages. A deficit at any one of these steps can give rise to persistent problems in the experience and management of anger. For example, some people tend to believe that others' actions are malevolent, a cognitive distortion known as the hostile attribution bias. Others may exhibit distortions in interpreting their own behaviors. While they may exaggerate the hostility in others' actions, they may underestimate the impact of their own aggressive behavior. Such people will tend to react strongly to situations that are generally perceived as only mildly irritating and feel justified in assigning blame to others for their own aggressive responses.

- **Experiencing abuse or trauma.** Witnessing or experiencing any kind of abuse as a child or an adult is a risk factor for developing anger management issues. For some, anger feels like the safest emotion to experience. They believe that if they are angry, they are safe from further abuse. For others, depending on the extent of the abuse, changes in brain chemistry can result in difficulty regulating anger and other emotions. Anger outbursts are common amongst people who experience post-traumatic stress disorder.

- **Mismanaging stress.** Stress due to a job, an unhappy relationship, or even the death of a loved one can lower the threshold for feeling overwhelmed. When stress surpasses this lowered threshold, anger emerges as a natural response. In more severe situations, when the stress becomes chronic or is not managed properly, expressions of anger tend to become more frequent and may turn into a "go-to" habit for coping with feeling overwhelmed.

- **Being taught that expressing emotions is unacceptable.** Some families have low tolerance for expressing certain emotions in front of anyone. This teaches children that they should not feel or show these emotions. Because emotions are a necessary and natural part of life, this kind of teaching can be quite harmful. Suppressing negative emotions does not allow the child to learn healthy emotion management techniques. Instead, everything is bottled up inside, which creates a pressure-cooker environment in which blowups become almost inevitable.

- **Low self-esteem.** People with low self-esteem tend to misinterpret events as threatening to themselves, their goals, or their needs. Even a calm, rational request—"Don't forget to pay the phone bill before you leave"—can be interpreted as an attack. Because people with low self-esteem are sensitized to communications from other people that might implicate or degrade their own self-worth, ability, or competence, they are more likely to misinterpret everyday comments in a threatening manner.

- **Low frustration tolerance.** Everyone has experienced lowered frustration tolerance at some points in his or her life. For some, this low-tolerance level is not temporary and they generally cannot tolerate moderate levels of frustration. The reaction to feeling extra-frustrated is to lash out.

- **Hiding vulnerable emotions.** Sometimes emotions are too hurtful or overwhelming to express, and become overshadowed by defensive expressions of anger. In these situations, the primary emotions of vulnerability such as hurt, sadness, loneliness, or grief are suppressed in favor of anger. This kind of emotional substitution can be effective in the short term in terms of protecting people from hurt and energizing them to stand up for themselves. The problem is that once anger takes center stage, it tends to hog the spotlight while deeper, underlying issues are hidden from view.

- **Authoritative personality.** People with an authoritative personality have inflexible ideas about how things should, and should not, be done. Chiefly, they expect others to bend before their will. They prefer to be the authority on any matter they bring up and are generally intolerant of other people's opinions. It is easy to see how people with these traits would be more likely to experience anger. Almost anything that goes against their wishes is grounds for an angry confrontation.

- **Impulsive temperament.** People with impulsive temperaments are distinguished by a combination of emotional reactivity and poor decision-making. Their motto is "Act first, ask questions later." As it happens, anger is very much an "act first, ask questions later" emotion. When anger and impulsivity combine, there is an increased likelihood for outbursts, escalations, misunderstandings, and long-term interpersonal damage.

- **Perfectionism.** The pursuit of excellence is a prized value in Western cultures and has produced many notable achievements. For some, however, this pursuit is becoming contaminated with intolerance and unrealistically high standards. Any failure is unacceptable. Any setback, real or perceived, triggers anxiety and anger. Nothing is ever good enough. The resulting toxic combination of pervasive dissatisfaction and critical-mindedness is a breeding ground for problematic anger.

QUESTION

If being angry gets me what I want, is that considered healthy anger?
Most of the time, no. Coercive anger is not considered healthy because it tends to create larger problems. When people use anger manipulatively, they inflict unnecessary damage to their relationships. They also tend to struggle with self-control.

- **Pain and suffering.** If two animals are hurt and put close to each other, they will frequently start to fight. This behavior is so common and occurs across so many species that it is believed the pain-aggression relationship may be unlearned—that is, it is built-in. Exposure to unpleasant stimuli increases the possibility of aggressive tendencies in humans. These stimuli include foul odors, high room temperatures, cigarette smoke, disgusting scenes, unpleasant interactions with others, fear, depression, and general discomfort.

Anger Styles

People tend to exhibit their anger around consistent patterns of expression known as *anger styles*. Habitually angry people tend to use anger styles that are dysfunctional, including physical and verbal assaults, heated arguing, displaced aggression, suppressed emotion, and other negative behaviors. Angry people also use fewer adaptive anger expressions, such as time-outs and reciprocal communication.

Although people use each style at different times in their life, one of these styles is probably more dominant than the others. The source of anger styles is a mix of environmental experiences and genetic influences. Certain temperament types are more likely to demonstrate one or more of these styles than others. At the same time, learning through experience plays a major role in the development of these styles of expression, particularly during childhood. Cultural and societal influences play a role as well.

Aggressive

The aggressive anger style conforms to the typical image of an angry person. For aggressors, anger is externalized or "turned loose." This pattern can include everything from swearing when you stub your toe to road rage, yelling, punching a wall, or breaking something. Without taking time to think or calm down, aggressors are highly reactive and likely to respond in an extreme manner. If perceived insults or everyday frustrations send you into a rage, this is your anger style.

People with aggressive styles freely and uncontrollably express their angry feelings. They have no mercy in the heat of the moment. Anyone and everyone can be a target. Aggressors often describe themselves as feeling "flooded" by their emotions, which can result in out-of-control behavior. They may feel guilty and remorseful for their behavior afterward and promise to change; however, doing so is often more challenging than they realize. Moreover, these people have learned that anger is a quick and effective way to control others or get what they want; as a result, their aggressive displays are sometimes rewarded. Aggressive behaviors are typically learned and reinforced as children. For example, a young child may learn that temper tantrums will get her the candy or toy or attention that she desires.

A need for power and control is often a central concern for people with an aggressive anger style. Conversely, these people often feel insecure and powerless in their lives unless they are venting at others. Aggressors tend to suffer interpersonally more than they realize, especially when they are younger. As other people avoid them more and more, they become isolated and alone. This, too, may result in more venting.

Passive-Aggressive

The passive-aggressive anger style is distinguished by a combination of superficial agreeableness and indirect expressions of anger. If you use indirect attacks and digs to express your anger but try to avoid direct confrontation, this describes your anger style.

Passive-aggressive individuals may be unable or unwilling to acknowledge their anger, yet they leave no doubt in the minds of those around them. They are masters of sarcasm, door slamming, guilt trips, and pouting. Passive-aggressiveness can be the most complicated style of anger to unravel, because people with this anger style tend to be invested in denying their angry feelings.

Passive-aggressive behavior was first defined during World War II by Colonel William Menninger. Menninger described soldiers who were neither openly defiant nor readily compliant toward their superiors. Instead, they expressed covert defiance through "pouting, stubbornness, procrastination, inefficiency, and passive obstructionism." These "passive measures" were initially attributed to "immaturity" and the effects of "routine military stress."

In some cases, passive-aggressive people will hold their true feelings in over long periods and then explode along the spectrum of yelling, screaming, cursing, threatening, throwing things, punching holes in walls and, at the most extreme end, being physically violent toward others. In other cases, they will displace their anger onto a weaker or more convenient target that happens to be in the wrong place at the wrong time.

Avoidant

The avoidant anger style is characterized by pretending everything is okay, when in reality you're burning with fury. It is synonymous with suppressed and repressed anger. With suppression, angry feelings are deliberately pushed away and ignored. With repression, angry feelings are denied—you don't even admit them to yourself.

People with avoidant anger styles have learned that anger is bad and must be eliminated. Anger is therefore internalized or "locked up." Because they avoid facing the anger itself, nothing ever gets resolved. Instead, the underlying anger is bottled up until it reaches a boiling point. At this stage, avoidant people are likely to explode over the smallest, most insignificant situation.

People who exhibit this anger style are worried about what others might think or say if they were to express their anger openly. They might also have grown up in a family with a venting parent. As a result, they might have learned to suppress their anger for fear of retaliation or they might have made a personal vow never to be like their parent.

Avoidance of anger can lead to a sense of something "eating away" at you. In some cases, angry feelings are covertly expressed through physical symptoms such as headaches and fatigue. In other cases, avoidant individuals turn their anger against themselves in a psychological sense, becoming chronically depressed. They may not know they are angry, but they know, for sure, that they are unworthy failures, shameful losers, and the sole source of every problem in their life. They may turn to drugs, alcohol, pornography, and other addictions in an effort to turn off the shame and depression.

Assertive

The assertive anger style is associated with healthy anger. This is the anger style you actually want to have. Assertive individuals are willing and able to talk through their feelings, negotiate a change in a relation-ship, and take constructive action to solve a problem. They don't pop off immediately nor do they hold their feelings inside. Instead, they form a rational argument and express their feelings directly with the person who is the focus of their anger. Alternatively, they will acknowledge their emotion and use that energy to create a positive change in their lives. The key is to pick battles wisely, maintain a sense of respect for others, and keep communication skills sharp.

CHAPTER 3
Anger Dangers

Anger can be dangerous, and not always in the ways you might think. There is a large, and growing, body of research demonstrating a significant connection between anger and a broad range of physical, psychological, interpersonal, and functional difficulties. Studies have tied anger to diseases linked with weakened immune systems, heart problems, cancer, suicide, and even increased workplace injuries. Every single form of chronic anger—whether aggressive, passive-aggressive, or avoidant—has been associated with a broad range of negative outcomes.

The Anger-Stress Relationship

The idea that emotions impact health is not new. Even the conservative Centers for Disease Control and Prevention (CDC) has stated that 85 percent of all diseases appear to have an emotional element. The actual percentage is likely to be even higher.

The anger-stress relationship is real. If you are angry, you are in a state of stress by definition. Moreover, although not all stress leads to anger, people who are in a state of stress are far more likely to exhibit anger, to overreact to annoyances, and to experience prolonged anger problems than those who are not. Not surprisingly, the effects of chronic anger on health, psychological well-being, and relationships significantly overlap the detrimental effects of chronic stress.

ALERT

Just because you're not aware of stress in your life doesn't mean it isn't there. Many people are oblivious to their stress, even though they experience it physiologically, because they've become so accustomed to it. Small stresses accumulate and impair mental and emotional clarity. People adapt to these changes, and it begins to seem normal.

The General Adaptation Syndrome

Stress researcher Hans Selye coined the term *general adaptation syndrome* to describe a common biological response pattern to prolonged or excessive stress. Selye pointed out that the human body responds similarly to many kinds of unpleasant stressors, whether the source is an invasion of microscopic disease organisms, a divorce, or the aftermath of a flood.

The general adaptation syndrome consists of three stages: the alarm reaction, the adaptation stage, and the exhaustion stage. Let's say your spouse criticizes you; your perception of this immediate stressor triggers an alarm reaction, also known as the fight-or-flight response. This response mobilizes your body to prepare for an emergency. With the alarm process in full motion, your adrenal glands begin to release cortical steroids and stress hormones that mobilize your body's defenses. You're ready for action.

If the stressor is persistent, you will eventually progress to the adaptation stage. Endocrine and sympathetic system responses (the release of stress hormones, for example) remain at high levels, but not as high as during the alarm reaction. During adaptation, your body tries to renew spent energy and repair damage. But when the stressors continue or new ones occur, you may progress to the final stage—exhaustion. Although individuals differ in their capacity to resist stress, everyone will eventually exhaust their bodily resources. If the stress persists to the point of exhaustion, you may develop what Selye termed diseases of adaptation, which range from allergic reactions to heart disease and even death.

Health Dangers

Anger is a form of stress. It can take a serious toll on your body. When anger is experienced often, or with great intensity, the excessive demands on your nervous system can have harmful health consequences that are felt for many years.

One of the key players in this process is cortisol, the stress hormone. Cortisol provides a ready surge of energy that helps you when you need to deal with a challenging situation. In small, periodic releases, the adverse effects of cortisol are minimal. However, higher and more prolonged releases of the hormone can disrupt the production of antibodies that are vital for fighting off sickness and disease. Prolonged cortisol elevation produces many undesirable effects: It can create a blood-sugar imbalance, decrease bone density, suppress the immune response, inhibit metabolic functioning, and elevate blood pressure.

Uncontrolled anger can cause health problems in other ways as well, some of which you might not expect. Remember that when you are angry, your body is in survival mode. In order to help protect you against blood loss from being wounded, chemicals are released prophylactically in order to clot the blood. This results in an increased risk of experiencing a stroke or heart attack caused by a blood clot. Highly intense anger can also trigger a stroke in another way, by causing the bursting of an artery in the brain. Circulation is impeded, lung function is reduced, and chest pain can result from lack of oxygen. With chronic anger, moreover, your metabolism slows down, potentially resulting in weight gain. This can be further exacerbated by eating binges, which are more likely to occur when you are angry. Anger also directly impacts your gastrointestinal system through the release of acids that can lead to ulcers and acid reflux disease. Another very common outcome is headaches, including severe migraine headaches, which can be triggered by the extreme muscle tension associated with intense anger.

Heart Disease and the Type A Personality

Heart disease is the most well-established disease outcome associated with chronic anger, especially for the hostile, hypercompetitive, and aggressive form of anger that defines the Type A personality. The evidence from numerous studies is clear: Chronic anger, hostility, and aggression raise the risk of developing various deadly forms of heart disease by as much as two to five times the normal rate. The more hostility a person expresses, the more prone to heart disease he or she is likely to be.

Type A personality behavior was first linked with heart disease in the 1950s by cardiologists Meyer Friedman and Ray H. Rosenman. They found that type A behavior doubled the risk of coronary heart disease in otherwise healthy individuals.

According to recent analysis of findings from forty-four studies published in the *Journal of the American College of Cardiology*, chronic anger and hostility are significantly associated with more heart problems in initially healthy people, as well as worse outcomes for patients already diagnosed with heart disease. The same study showed that chronically angry or hostile adults with no history of heart trouble are significantly more likely than their calmer peers to develop heart disease. Among patients already diagnosed with heart disease, those with angry or hostile temperaments were 24 percent more likely than other heart patients to have a poor prognosis. Overall, in a survey of nearly 13,000 adults, those with the highest levels of anger had twice the risk of coronary artery disease and three times the risk of heart attack as compared to participants with lower levels of anger.

Immune System Suppression

Anger suppresses the immune system, increasing susceptibility to illness and disease, through a couple of key mechanisms. First, anger destroys T cells, in particular the so-called natural killer cells that have the ability to destroy tumor cells. One study, for example, showed that high-hostility-scoring students (e.g., type A students) had fewer natural killer cells present during their high-stress exam periods than did their low-hostility-scoring peers.

Second, anger suppresses the antibody IgA (immunoglobulin A), which serves as the immune system's first line of defense. The result is an impaired ability to cope with bacteria, viruses, and toxins, leaving people more vulnerable to respiratory problems such as colds or the flu. Just how powerful is this connection? One study titled, "The Power to Change Performance," found that simply *recalling* an angry experience caused a six-hour suppression of the immune system. On the other hand, feelings of care or compassion were found to improve immune functioning.

Cancer

The link between chronic anger and the development of cancer is not as well established as the findings regarding heart disease, but there is definite cause for concern. One particular form of anger, chronic *repressed* anger, has been associated with cancer across a number of studies. Evidence shows that habitually suppressed anger can be a precursor to the development of cancer and can also exacerbate the disease's progression following diagnosis.

Stroke

Anger increases the risk for experiencing stroke. In one large multi-state study with more than 13,000 participants, trait anger was associated with a significant increase in the risk for stroke, especially ischemic stroke (a stroke triggered by an obstruction within a blood vessel supplying blood to the brain), among younger men and women. Younger participants ($\leq$ 60 years) who reported having high trait anger had nearly three times greater risk for ischemic stroke than those who reported having low trait anger. In another study, patients were found to be more likely to have experienced anger during the two hours before their stroke than during other times. This study addresses the dangers of acute transient anger, since the researchers did not measure trait anger or cumulative risk over extended periods of time.

The association with ischemic stroke is caused by anger's ability to arouse the sympathetic nervous system and activate neuroendocrine cells, impacts associated with the general adaptation syndrome. Over time, this arousal and subsequent exhaustion can lead to the initiation and progression of atherosclerosis (hardening of the arteries), a direct risk factor for stroke. Anger is also believed to increase arterial pressure, triggering a disruption in the blood supply to the brain that can lead to a stroke.

Headaches

Researchers at St. Louis University have shown that people who suppress their anger may be more likely to suffer from chronic headaches. The scientists examined how angry the subject was, how much he or she internalized their anger, and the severity and frequency of the headaches. Results showed that holding in anger was the biggest predictor of headaches among a group of 422 patients. The researchers also considered whether patients were anxious or depressed, but they found that repressed anger was significantly more likely to cause headaches than either of these emotions.

Other studies have found associations between anger and the occurrence of individual headaches. Given how powerfully anger is expressed in the body, this association is not surprising. Anger can cause the muscles in the head, neck, and scalp to contract and tense sharply. If a person stays angry for too long, those muscles will fatigue, increasing the risk of a tension headache.

Chronic Pain

People who restrain or suppress anger have been described as pain-prone and are uniquely susceptible to experiencing chronic pain. Evidence also shows that expressed forms of anger, such as aggressive anger, are also associated with physical pain. People with high-trait anger exhibit heightened sensitivity to pain stimuli. In addition, the behavioral expression of anger has been associated with subsequent chronic pain intensity.

Death

Researchers have gathered a wealth of data suggesting that chronic anger is so damaging to the body that it ranks with, or even exceeds, cigarette smoking, obesity, and a high-fat diet as a risk factor for early death. One recent study found that people who scored high on a hostility scale as teenagers were much more likely than their more cheerful peers to have elevated cholesterol levels as adults. This finding suggests a link between unremitting anger and heart disease.

QUESTION

Do anger problems affect men and women in the same way?
The overall constellation of health and psychological dangers is the same for men and women, but there are differences in terms of which gender is more likely to have a certain kind of outcome. Women are more likely to show symptoms of psychological distress, while men are more likely to report health problems.

In another study, researchers analyzed the effects of chronic anger on women over a period of eighteen years. The women who had answered initial test questions with obvious signs of long-term suppressed anger were three times more likely to have died than those who did not harbor such hostile feelings. If that weren't enough, reports show that chronically high anger linked to relationship stress increases the chances of dying before age fifty by five times.

Other Health Outcomes

Long-term, intense anger is associated with poorer overall physical health and has also been linked to the following conditions:

- Arrhythmia (irregular heartbeat)
- Asthma
- Colds and flu
- Gastrointestinal distress
- Glaucoma
- Insomnia
- Memory lapses
- Skin disorders (eczema, psoriasis, hives)
- Teeth grinding
- Weight gain

Cognitive and Psychological Dangers

The health dangers associated with chronic anger are frightening enough on their own, but the bigger picture is even more sobering. Chronic anger can cause a plethora of emotional and psychological issues that diminish quality of life, compromise day-to-day functioning, and elicit poor choices.

Long-term, intense anger has been linked with mental health problems such as feelings of hopelessness and helplessness, depression, anxiety, self-loathing, low self-esteem, eating disorders, sleep disorders, and addictions. People with long-term anger problems tend to have poor decision-making capabilities, take more risks, and are more reckless and impulsive. Anger is closely linked to violent and aggressive behavior, the potential negative consequences of which are numerous. Common outcomes include legal problems, incarceration, physical injury, loss of employment, destruction of relationships, and long-term shame and regret.

Chronic anger can directly harm the functioning of your brain. For example, research out of Calgary's Hotchkiss Brain Institute shows that neurons in an important brain structure called the hypothalamus can be directly compromised by frequent anger activation. Because the hypothalamus is a key control point in the anger response, this results in an impaired ability to regulate your own anger. It becomes harder and harder to slow yourself down. Even more seriously, studies show that stress and anger can block the growth of neurons in important areas of the brain, such as the hippocampus, creating an increased risk for depression and post-traumatic stress disorder. Increased stress hormones produced by anger can also lead to memory impairment, information processing deficits, and learning difficulties. Your overall ability to think clearly and logically is diminished.

These effects directly impact your ability to function effectively across a range of contexts, from work to family life. Completing tasks is more challenging, attention wanders, and distraction sets in. The most basic everyday tasks—listening, learning, problem solving—become far more difficult. Chronic anger and hostility also introduce biases in decision-making that can have serious consequences. Angry people are more likely to interpret information in an unrealistically negative manner, resulting in distorted thought processes and inappropriate choices.

Relationship Dangers

Anger is the emotion most likely to cause problems in relationships with family, coworkers, and friends. There are very few places where aggression is an appropriate response. This is particularly true in the more public parts of life, including workplace interactions. Verbally assaulting the boss is likely to result in termination, while a pattern of hostile interactions with coworkers and customers can damage your career in any number of ways.

Anger is particularly destructive in close relationships. Hostile, angry people are less likely to have healthy supportive relationships. Chronically angry people have fewer friends because they are also likely to become verbally and physically abusive toward others. Chronic anger reduces the intimacy within personal relationships; partners and other family members tend to be more guarded and less able to relax in their interactions with hostile people.

Angry people frequently exaggerate misunderstandings and minor grievances. They are inclined to end relationships, even with close friends, rather than work to resolve problems. Their demeanor and mood are unpleasant to be around. In addition, their emotional patterns can create a cycle of guilt and regret, leading to more anger. The impact is both immediate and long term, from hampering success at work to damaging their children's ability to succeed in school and make friends. Consequently, angry people often alienate themselves—even from their own families. It is quite common for angry people to have trouble being effective parents and spouses.

Anger is not always bad for relationships. Interpersonal anger is typically a sign that someone's needs are not being met. When this information is used constructively to address an underlying problem, it can provide the catalyst for a relationship to grow in closeness and maturity.

Angry people are frequently cynical and are unable to recognize or utilize support when it is available. Because they don't realize the impact their behavior has on others, they don't realize that they are pushing people away. They also tend to drink, smoke, and eat more than their less angry counterparts. Without a social network of people to dampen these tendencies, the probability of serious health consequences is high.

Apparent Short-Term "Payoffs"

The inappropriate expression of anger may have some apparent "payoffs" in your relationships with others. One payoff is the ability to manipulate and control others through aggressive and intimidating behavior; others may comply with your demands because they fear verbal threats or violence. Another payoff is the feeling of power and self-confidence that can accompany aggressive behavior.

These initial payoffs are short-lived, and are purchased at great cost. When a parent, for example, habitually obtains compliance from his children through aggressive and even violent measures, the "payoff" is the children's obedience, and perhaps, as well, a sense of satisfaction that derives from being able to "control" or "dominate" a situation. However, these behaviors are neither loving, nor kind, nor constructive. They are coercive. They communicate very clearly to the children that they will be mistreated if they fail to comply with parental dictates. Thus, in the long-term, there is a strong probability that they will learn to fear and dislike their father. They may also suffer long-term emotional and psychological damage. In an example like this, the apparent rewards of angry behavior are offset by the greater harm that is ultimately produced.

Vicious Cycles

One of the most insidious aspects of chronic anger is the creation of vicious cycles of behavior. In a vicious cycle, the outcome of an event strengthens the original cause of that event, creating a cyclical pattern that reinforces and strengthens itself over time. The result can be likened to a snowball effect. Problems get bigger and bigger. In practice, a cycle like this can feed on itself for a long period.

Say, for example, your spouse behaves in a manner that you feel is demeaning. Rather than assertively sharing your hurt feelings, and risk feeling vulnerable, you may react with anger and strike back. You could be directly aggressive, criticizing him for forgetting to put something away, or for a past mistake that compromised the family budget—in short, launching whatever verbal attack comes to mind. Or you could opt for a passive-aggressive response, using sarcasm, being passively noncompliant, or subjecting him to the "silent treatment." In such instances, you're endeavoring to retaliate.

And what about your spouse? Now he is on the receiving end of the hurt and anger you've just managed to shake off. You have "transferred" your negative feelings to him. At the most primitive level, by experiencing himself as the object of your anger, he will quickly grasp that you harbor hostile feelings toward him. If he steps back from you, it's not because he is providing you with more space to vent. It's that he's feeling an urgent need to distance himself. Or, he may retaliate. His defensive reaction is likely—in "counter retaliation," as it were—to be one of blaming you right back. This behavior can escalate the conflict with lightning speed. It's an undeclared, largely unrecognized, game of tit for tat.

The opposite of a vicious cycle is a *virtuous cycle*. A virtuous cycle develops when a person does something positive that produces a satisfying result, which has the effect of encouraging her to make additional positive choices, which produces more satisfying results, and so on. As people learn to better manage their anger, they can begin to benefit from virtuous cycles.

People with chronic anger problems likely have participated in any number of vicious cycles whereby their aggressive behaviors elicited responses in people that appeared to justify their original anger, which resulted in more anger, leading to further aggressive behaviors, and so on. One of the great traps of chronic anger is the tendency to create a complex network of vicious cycles, which locks the person into an ongoing state of hostility and hyperarousal.

CHAPTER 4

How Anger Problems Develop

The roots of an anger problem can often be traced to childhood—that vulnerable period when personalities are formed, beliefs and values develop, and the basic "rules" of how to function in the world are adopted. The beginning of emotional difficulties can arise in infancy, when very young children first learn to regulate their feelings. In later childhood, the dynamics become more complex. As children interact with and observe the adults and children around them, they are powerfully influenced by what they experience.

The Context of Human Development

The environment in which you grow up has a powerful and pervasive influence on your life. Personality and character, emotional functioning, and habits, beliefs, and preferences are all shaped during childhood. Family members, particularly parents, play a crucial role in every area of a child's growth, especially emotional development. Your first emotional experiences (good and bad) were with your family. You were exposed to models of emotional expression, coping, and behavior, and received direct instruction about how to recognize and label emotions, and how to act based on what you were feeling. If you struggle in managing anger, there is a good chance the roots of that difficulty can be traced back to your youth.

Early Attachment

As an infant and young child, you were reliant on your caregivers, typically your parents, to regulate your painful emotions. The next time you observe a parent comforting and soothing an infant, know that it was precisely through such experiences that you first began to learn to manage your own upsetting emotions. It is at this very early stage that things can begin to go wrong.

Consider the attachment theory. When an infant's emotional needs are met, the baby will more than likely exhibit the behavior pattern known as secure attachment. He will exhibit a high degree of behavioral flexibility and will be capable of soothing himself in the absence of a caregiver. However, if the infant's emotional needs are not met during this period, he is likely to struggle under the weight of her emotions and to adopt compensatory strategies that can set in place lifelong patterns of emotional mismanagement and relationship chaos. The general term for this condition is insecure attachment.

There are two primary forms of insecure attachment: avoidant and resistant. Avoidant children deactivate distress through suppression. As a result, anger is more likely to be expressed in indirect ways. Resistant children, in contrast, are hyperactivated. They are more likely to be chronically angry, to behave aggressively, and to express other emotions through their anger (i.e., defensively employing anger as a secondary emotion). Secure children become angry as well, of course, but they are more likely to express that anger directly to others. When the source of the anger is not available, secure children can rely on mental representations for self-soothing and for returning toward a state of emotional well-being. Insecure children lack a positive mental representation of soothing, and as a result, their mental representations (ideas, thoughts, etc.) are likely to contribute to more anger rather than less.

While there is not a simple one-to-one association between childhood attachment style and adult emotional functioning, important analogies can be drawn between early attachment and adult anger styles. Secure attachment is analogous to the assertive anger style, avoidant attachment to the avoidant anger style, and resistant attachment to the aggressive anger style. Finally, both insecure attachment types have some overlap with the passive-aggressive anger style, which combines avoidant and resistant behaviors.

In the 1970s, psychologist Mary Ainsworth expanded on John Bowlby's formulation of attachment theory. Using an experiment called the "Strange Situation," she observed different behaviors in infants as they were left alone briefly and then reunited with their mothers. Ainsworth found that these behaviors clustered into distinct patterns, which helped to establish the modern understanding of secure and insecure attachment "styles."

Overall, researchers have found that there is strong link between childhood attachment patterns and adult attachment patterns. This means that the earliest strategies you learn for dealing with anger are likely to persist, in some form, into adulthood. Some expressions of these strategies may become more sophisticated, whereas some may not be too dissimilar from a child's expression of anger. However, for a large percentage of people, the generalized pattern of deactivation, hyperactivation, and flexibility persist in adolescence and adulthood.

Talking about Emotions

When parents and other adults take the time to discuss emotions with their children, this can have a potent effect in teaching them emotional competence. This beneficial impact is observed both in children's ability to understand themselves and others, and in terms of their ability to manage their own emotions. Research shows that children who receive this kind of instruction are more likely to be kind and caring toward others. In fact, this association is so strong that children's awareness and sensitivity toward other people's emotions at age six can be directly predicted by the amount of emotion-focused discussions experienced at the age of three.

By the time children reach school-age, emotions are most effectively discussed most frequently with respect to behavioral and interpersonal issues. As children grow, their development of social competence is directly associated with a parental discussion style that is open, nondirective, and accepting. Parents who interact with their children in this way are able to acknowledge and validate their children's experience, helping them to understand themselves better while also highlighting broader principles about choices and emotional consequences. There are many advantages to this style of parenting. Children show greater maturity and moral sophistication, improved social and communication skills, and more positive peer relationships. Children who do not receive this kind of parental nurturing and guidance are more likely to have difficulty managing their emotions as adults and are at an increased risk of experiencing problematic anger.

Empathy and Emotional Coaching

In families, emotional socialization of children occurs in a number or ways. From the child's perspective, family members may be the *cause* of emotional experiences, they provide *models* of emotional expression and resolution, and they also provide *direct instruction*. Regardless of whether or not they intend to do so, or are even aware of doing so, all parents play a role in emotionally socializing their children. The implications are profound. Emotional socialization impacts children's ability to understand other people, to recognize and self-regulate their own emotions, and to resolve emotionally heated interpersonal situations. By the time children are in preschool—still very young indeed!—individual differences in these areas are readily apparent.

One of the most crucial areas of emotional socialization has to do with learning to cope with the distress and physiological arousal that accompanies intense negative emotional states such as anger, fear, and sadness. Interestingly, one of the most important factors in facilitating a child's ability to regulate aversive emotions is parental empathy. Empathy is more than "feeling sorry" for someone; it is the ability to accurately understand and reflect another person's subjective emotional experience. Parents' ability to display empathy with their children, combined with their overarching ability to help their children work through painful emotions, plays an important role in shaping their children's emotional competence. Empathic children with good emotional self-regulation skills are far more likely to have been reared by parents who are themselves empathic, engaged, and lovingly responsive.

An important factor here is balance. The optimal rearing environment is one in which parents provide a moderate level of coaching their children through negative emotions. Given a more permissive, "laissez-faire" approach in which negative expressions are allowed, children may fail to develop self-control. On the other hand, when parents rigidly discourage any negative emotional expressions, children are more likely to remain aroused and upset over abnormally long periods, and may also develop maladaptive compensatory strategies (e.g., bullying other children). Prolonged physiological arousal has many of the same drawbacks for children as it does for adults, including impaired reasoning and information processing ability, social withdrawal, interpersonal aggression, and ongoing emotional distress.

What do constructive parental reactions to children's negative emotionality look like? These responses can take on many forms, depending both on the situation and the unique characteristics of the people involved. Broadly speaking, however, these reactions will involve providing comfort and reassurance, encouraging children to express and talk through their emotions, and helping them to analyze and problem-solve different ways of responding. These kinds of loving and skillful interventions help children to feel better, cope better, and behave better.

Behavior Modeling

It started with a Bobo doll. Picture a large inflatable toy, painted to look like a clown and weighted at the bottom so that after falling over it would immediately lift back to a standing position. In a series of experiments conducted in 1961 and 1963 by Albert Bandura, children were divided into three groups. In one group children observed adults behaving aggressively toward the doll; in another, adults were observed playing peacefully with the doll; and in the third group, no adult was present. Once the children were given the opportunity to play, results showed that those exposed to the aggressive model were more likely to imitate what they had seen and to behave aggressively toward the doll.

This basic finding, along with many related findings, has a very important implication: People learn through observation. Known as *observational learning*, or *modeling*, this type of learning can be used to explain a wide variety of behaviors. For example, a child using her parent's favorite curse words is a simple example of childhood modeling. The negative side of children modeling adult behavior is fairly predictable: Some behaviors are best not imitated, such as aggression, violence, and substance use. Many parents are unaware of how children observe and learn from their behavior and may unwittingly model behavior for their children when they are unaware that young eyes are watching.

ESSENTIAL

Behavior modeling isn't just for kids. Modeling is a widespread phenomenon in which people modify their behavior based on observations of others. If people observe someone behaving selflessly, they are more likely to behave similarly—and vice versa.

Childhood modeling encompasses interpersonal relationships, communication, problem-solving, conflict resolution, and emotional expression—including anger management. Children who are raised in an environment with frequent exposure to unhealthy expressions of anger are likely to mimic those behaviors and to exhibit similar behaviors as adults. In fact, recent research has shown that exposure to a range of negative family behaviors—such as negative commands, dependency, destructiveness, humiliation, noncompliance, and being ignored—can reinforce aggressive behavior in children.

Other Factors That Influence Modeling

There are many other factors that are involved in understanding how modeling affects the development and learning of a child. For instance, children will look up to those of the same gender and imitate their behavior. The role models could be anyone from their parents to their teachers, to a character on television. These role models can exert a powerful influence. By imitating the behavior of this role model, children will learn what is deemed appropriate for society. When children learn what their peers approve of, they are likely to adhere to that standard.

Peers and Mass Media

Other important sources of modeling include peers and the mass media. Peer influence becomes increasingly important as children reach adolescence, but it is also evident in early childhood. The desire to fit in and feel like part of "the group" is powerful. As a result, children are strongly influenced by their same-age peers, particularly those whom they look up to or whom they perceive to possess a higher status.

The influence of the mass media, such as movies and television, gives modeling particular social importance. By the time the average teenager graduates from high school, he or she will have spent more time watching television than any other activity, except sleeping. The impact of television content on society is significant, which leads to concerns with issues such as violence on television. The average viewer may see several acts of violence each day, and television shows and movies often increase violence in competition with each other. It is well established that viewing aggression can increase aggressive behavior. Most experts agree that media exposure influences child development and can contribute to long-standing emotional and behavioral difficulties.

Parental Conflict

Marital discord is significantly associated with child dysfunction. Conflict between parents, whether in intact or divorced families, is a risk factor for later behavior problems, low achievement, and low social competence.

In one study done in 1981, children as young as ten months already exhibit distressed behavioral reactions to adult anger, such as through crying or negative facial expressions. By the toddler and preschool years, children almost invariably react with distress to adult anger. They do things like freezing, running away, distraction (often by "acting out"), reassurance-seeking, and attempting to resolve the adult conflict. Preschoolers, in particular, are more likely to show delayed reactions of anger and irritability, and are more likely to behave aggressively toward peers in the aftermath of a parental conflict. When children are exposed to frequent displays of parental conflict, even when it does not involve them directly, they tend to become sensitized to adult anger. They look for it more, and are more greatly affected by it. They will often inappropriately assume responsibility for adult anger, similar to the well-known phenomenon of children blaming themselves for their parents' divorce.

FACT

It is not only confrontational parental fighting that can harm children. Research shows that kids feel distressed when the parents give each other the "silent treatment" in the hope their children won't notice that something is wrong. These children are still able to pick up on the fact that their parents are unhappy with each other, and they report feeling more fearful, angry, and sad.

This vulnerability extends well into adolescence. Just like younger children, teenagers display more intense emotional reactions as adult conflicts escalate. Feelings of anger, fear, sadness, and shame are quite common in these situations. The above might sound frightening. You may be (or plan to be) a parent who occasionally has conflicts with your spouse (which seems awfully likely). Keep in mind, not all adult conflicts have detrimental effects on children. In fact, many experts believe that adult and interparental conflicts can actually provide a helpful teaching example for children . . . *when they are handled well.*

When conflicts are handled assertively and respectfully, when they are meaningfully resolved (as opposed to swept under the rug), and when the parties involved conclude with a display of positive emotion, there is a double benefit: First, children will more readily return to a state of emotional calm; and second, the effective handling of the conflict provides an example from which they can learn how to better respond to the conflicts that will inevitably arise in their own lives.

Parent-Child Conflict

Conflict with the family is extremely common throughout a child's lifetime.

Research has shown that preschool-aged children confront their parents with three to four mildly unpleasant events *every hour*, on average. Perhaps even more striking, mothers have been found, on average, to issue a command or criticism to their young child once every three minutes. That's a lot of potentially stressful provocation going in both directions. Far less surprising, the teenage years have been highlighted as a second peak period for parent-child conflict. During this time, 15–20 percent of families report severe levels of parent-child conflict. As you might expect, everyday concerns such as chores, homework, hygiene, and getting along with others tend to provide the trigger for most parent-child conflicts. Such frequent events allow children to learn negotiation and conflict-resolution skills through modeling, direct interactions, parental instruction, and various combinations of reinforcement and punishment.

During conflicts, parents and children directly influence one another, and as a result, there tends to be a matching of emotion and behavior. One of the hallmarks of healthy families is the ability to work through interpersonal conflicts in an atmosphere of respect and calm. They show genuine concern for the other party, they are cooperatively engaged, they weigh alternative possibilities, and they work to establish a consensus directed toward reasonable solutions. The picture is very different in more dysfunctional family environments. Here, common conflict resolution strategies include mutual avoidance, stonewalling, criticism, aggressive expressions of anger, triangulation strategies (e.g., parental coalitions against the child, or one parent conspiring with the child against the other parent), and coercive parental attempts at control.

The manner in which families address conflicts is directly related to the skillfulness with which children are able to negotiate conflicts in other contexts. This should not be surprising, as the family provides the fundamental crucible in which children develop (or fail to develop) these skills. At a more global level, family conflict resolution styles are also directly related to children's overall psychological adjustment. This holds true across the entirety of childhood, including adolescence, where the ability to listen, problem-solve, and compromise during conflicts with their parents is associated with a significantly lower rate of emotional and behavioral problems and greater academic achievement.

Coercive Family Processes

Coercive family process is a well-supported theory that explains how parents and children influence each other's behavior. Children learn how mildly negative behaviors, such as running around, attract reprimand and attention from a parent. The child recognizes that escalating the behavior will reap more attention from the parent, even if it is delivered via a sterner reprimand. The negative spiral continues, leading the parent to inadvertently reinforce the child's poor behavior.

Consider a simple example: A mother asks her young son to get up from the TV and get ready for bed. Timmy throws a small temper tantrum and says he wants to watch the show. His mother does not say anything further. Timmy stops whining.

In this simple interaction, Timmy learns that if he throws a tantrum, he will not have to go to bed. His mom learns that if she backs off from her requests, Timmy will stop whining. Both of these events are examples of negative reinforcement. In this example, if whining gets Timmy out of having to go to bed, he is more likely to whine in the future.

This is coercive family process in action. *Coercion* means "to control." Timmy is learning that he can control (or influence) other people's behavior by acting out.

Children learn to behave this way when their parents routinely yield to their negative and disruptive behaviors. Every time parents acquiesce in this manner, they are essentially "rewarding" their child for behaving inappropriately. The effect of this is to increase the probability that these kinds of behaviors will be repeated in the future; the child learns that *this* is how I can get what I want. As time goes by, coercive behaviors may become the primary means for influencing other family members.

It is no coincidence that children with emotional and behavioral problems are often raised in coercive environments. These environments are breeding grounds for psychological difficulties. Often, but not always, the child emerges as the victor in coercive family interactions; that is, they are able to attain something that they want. At the same time, parents in these families can be inconsistent and unpredictable. They may give in to their child's nagging one day, and fall back on explosive and violent disciplinary techniques the next. Parents in these families often "give in" when they should be firm, and yet are stubbornly punitive when empathic engagement is the optimal response. These problems are compounded by the fact that they often spend little engaged time with their children, neglect to reward their children's positive behaviors, and poorly monitor their children's activities.

QUESTION

How do I avoid coercive processes in my life right now?
The most important rule in avoiding coercive processes is twofold: (1) Don't use aggression to get what you want, and (2) be vigilant in refusing to reward negative or inappropriate behaviors. When pressured in this way, you must firmly and calmly hold your ground.

The difficulties experienced by coercive children can extend beyond the home. In some instances, these children are positively influenced by peers and teachers. They learn more healthy, adaptive ways to interact with and persuade others, and these serve to counteract some of the negative influences coming from home. In many cases, however, these children experience real and ongoing interpersonal problems with other children and adults. They are likely to be rejected by peers and avoided by teachers. Self-esteem and motivation suffer. They may become bullies or loners, and may even identify with an antisocial peer group that further reinforces maladaptive and socially inappropriate behaviors. At this point, problems can begin to snowball in a big way.

Social Information Processing Deficits

Just as with adults, when a child is in the grip of angry thoughts and feelings, some measure of thought is required before a decision is made to respond in a particular way. Experts actually prefer to use terms such as "cognitive processing" or "social information processing," because much of this processing activity occurs outside the arena of conscious (i.e., aware) thought (for example, think of automatic reactions learned from past experiences). Socially competent children are more skilled at social information processing. They are better able to inhibit aggressive impulses, analyze a situation objectively, weight contextual factors, listen to other points of view, and find reasonable points of compromise. On the other hand, children with deficits in social information processing are prone to anger, can easily be "captured" by their own point of view (they can't see anything else), and are more likely to act out in an aggressive, disruptive, or immature manner across a range of situations.

There are two distinguishable patterns of social information processing deficiencies that are closely associated with aggressive children. The first has to do with biases in the way that social information is interpreted. Quite simply, these children tend to interpret other people's behavior in a negative and threatening manner. They look for mistreatment, and they find it. This is especially true in cases where social information is ambiguous, or where multiple sources of information (e.g., words, social context, prior history, tone of voice, etc.) must be synthesized in order accurately understand another person's meaning or intent.

Because of this interpretive bias, aggressive children are more likely to view others in oppositional framework, as "the enemy," which further incites their aggressive behaviors. Other children and adults take exception to such behaviors, and respond negatively to them. Here, there is a great irony, because these negative reactions from others only serve to "confirm" the aggressive child's initial false interpretation. A vicious cycle is set in motion.

The second pattern of information processing deficits has to do with how chronically angry children respond to interpersonal challenges. When gauging a response, children, like adults, will consider different response options and the anticipated outcomes for each. They choose the response that has the best anticipated outcome. Because coercive children have learned that they can get what they want by behaving aggressively, they are confident that this approach will work for them again in the future. This positive assessment increases the likelihood that they will use such aggressive strategies. If the strategies are effective, which they very well can be, that will reinforce the child's aggressive, coercive behavior.

In summary, aggressive children have poor social problem-solving skills. They often fail to attend to social cues, interpret peer intentions incorrectly and assume hostile intent, are the targets of aggression more often than their peers, and interpret their own aggressive behaviors as leading to positive outcomes.

Interestingly, social information processing deficits showed by aggressive children extend, as well, into the arena of explicitly friendly and positive behaviors from others. You might think that these children would "respond well" when on the receiving end of some kindness, but this expectation fails to account for the likely impact of being raised in a coercive family environment. These children are often distrustful and wary with respect to other people's intentions, and are unsure how to interpret friendly behaviors. They may, for example, suspect an ulterior motive, or that if they let their guard down they may get hurt. Thus, they are likely to show surprise and even hostility when receiving praise from a peer.

Anger in Your Family

Now that you have learned about the development of anger problems from the perspective of contemporary theory and research, it is time to apply this knowledge directly. When you have the time to sit and reflect, ask yourself the following questions. If you happen to be married or have a close relationship in which anger has caused problems, consider initiating a conversation based on these questions in which you compare how conflict, anger, and emotions in general were handled in your respective families of origin. This kind of conversation can be very beneficial in terms of improving mutual understanding, patience, and caring.

- How would you describe the anger styles of your mother, father, grandparents, siblings, or other close family members?
- How did your caregivers (or important adults in your life) express their anger?

- What are the similarities and differences between how your caregivers managed their anger and how you manage your anger? Do you see any patterns?
- In what ways did their anger styles affect you?
- How has your anger style affected your children?

CHAPTER 5

Deciding to Work on Your Anger

Having an anger management problem is not a life sentence. The fact that you are reading this book is positive, because it implies that you have passed the first step in "anger management," namely, the willingness to take responsibility for your emotions. In so doing, you are ahead of the majority of people who prefer to blame everything and everyone for their anger and aggressive behaviors.

You Are in the Driver's Seat

Effective anger management begins with you. Controlling anger can be viewed from two perspectives: managing your anger and learning to respond effectively to anger in others. You don't have to be a victim of anger, yours or someone else's. People often think that emotions happen to them, but that's not necessarily the case. Emotional problems—including anger problems—tend to become habitual, but any habit can be undone. The work is not always easy, but it is worthwhile.

The best way to approach learning to control your anger is as a process—a task that extends forward in time. You will need to look closely in the mirror, rethinking your assumptions about others and the ways you respond to frustration and conflict. You will need to accept a level of personal responsibility that might feel uncomfortable at first, but is ultimately liberating. You will need to take the time to master new approaches and techniques, learning how to harness the power of thought and committed action to gain a new level of self-mastery and interpersonal effectiveness. These objectives are realistic and achievable. Many people have succeeded in improving their anger management skills, and there is absolutely no reason you cannot do the same. The primary requirements are discipline, consistency, and a structured approach.

Taking Responsibility

Taking responsibility for your anger is the essential first step in anger management, and it is challenging. People often prefer to blame other people or situations, because it seems easier than taking responsibility for their own lives. The problem is twofold. First, when you externalize responsibility for your anger to circumstances outside your control, you're stuck. You'll be angry forever unless things change. You're like a puppet on a string—and you've handed the string to someone else. People are sometimes very resistant to this concept, because it means there is no one else to blame for their bad behavior. However, when you take responsibility for your own feelings, you begin to take control over your life. You can choose to be explosive or calm. Choice is the ultimate freedom, and it is empowering.

Second, the externalization of anger is based on a false premise: It is simply untrue that other people (or situations) cause your anger. Anger is a choice. Although the first step in the experience of situational anger is largely automatic and reactive, in a very short time, typically seconds, you have the opportunity to evaluate, regulate, and control your anger through adaptive behaviors and your innate ability to think. This element of personal responsibility is most evident at the level of chronic anger, where people actively nurture and protect their anger by ruminating repeatedly over perceived grievances, slights, and injustices.

ALERT

People are sometimes afraid of taking personal responsibility. Don't be. In taking responsibility, you choose freedom. You choose to stop being pushed around by past conditioning, by fears and beliefs, and by the gusts of present circumstances. You decide to take conscious control of your life. That's the real meaning of personal responsibility.

She *Made* Me Mad

For most people, the blame game starts as children. "Kristen *made* me mad." "Alex *made* me hit him because he wouldn't stop teasing." "It *got* me upset!" This is the viewpoint of a child. Adults often know better, and yet they still often speak in similar terms, especially people with anger problems. Always remember that other people's actions can never make you feel a certain way. Emotions are warnings. Your emotions result from whether *your* needs and desires are being met.

The most common form of anger, interpersonal aggression, results from focusing attention on what that person "should" or "shouldn't" do and then judging them as "wrong" or "bad." Yet, these are your judgments and your feelings, and it is important to own them. Even when your assessment of the situation is accurate, you are still responsible for how you respond. You don't have to lash out or seethe with repressed anger when someone behaves disrespectfully toward you. You don't have to react with anger at all.

You might calmly respond as you would to a child's thoughtlessness by recognizing that this behavior is consistent with a level of maturity and experience. You can refuse to "receive" or "personalize" their aversive behavior. Instead, try to understand what led them to act in this way. For example, you might recognize that the person has psychological issues, is weighed down and compromised by considerable stress in his life, or is simply acting out based on a misunderstanding.

Further, when your attention shifts to identifying which of your needs isn't being satisfied in a situation, your feelings will also shift. When you realize that you didn't receive treatment that met your need for respect, you might feel hurt, or scared, or disappointed—but you won't need to lash out. Instead, many creative possibilities for resolution can emerge. When your feelings have served their purpose—when your attention is fully focused on your needs and values—anger melts away. This transformation is not the same as repression, and it's not the same as simply "calming down." The emotions you feel when you are in touch with your needs may be intense and painful, but they will be different emotions than anger.

The Power of Self-Determination

In many ways, your life is the sum of your choices and actions. Your total existence is determined by the daily choices you make—in essence, you choose your way through life. A transformed mind leads to a transformed life. Anger management is about self-determination. It's about transforming your life through your choices and actions and developing the skills for making decisions that lead to positive personal growth and development.

Stages of Change

People go through a predictable set of stages while working through major changes such as learning to manage and control their anger. Progress through these stages takes a combination of motivation, technique, and dedication. Major life changes are rarely a linear process of steady improvements, so it is important to realize that challenges and setbacks are a normal and anticipated part of the process.

There's a well-known saying that the only certainties in life are death and taxes, but there's another certainly that far exceeds these two: *change*. Life is an unending series of changes. Some of these happen without conscious control or effort, and some are made deliberately by you, in order to achieve a valued goal. As you read through the following stages of change, try to map these stages onto real experiences you've had in your life. You've been there, there's little doubt about that. Going one step further, think about how you might approach each stage from the perspective of improving your anger management skills. What obstacles are you likely to face? What will help you to increase your level of motivation and commitment?

Precontemplation Stage

This is the "not ready" stage. At this stage, people are not actively considering making serious changes in their life and may be unaware of a need to do so. They tend to underestimate the benefits of change while simultaneously overestimating imagined difficulties and inconveniences.

Caroline Schroeder, a religious studies professor, is credited with an observation that speaks to the experience of any practicing psychotherapist: "Some people change when they see the light, others when they feel the heat." People often don't make the decision to seriously work on their anger, and other serious personal issues, until after experiencing severe social, legal, and employment consequences.

Contemplation Stage

This is the "getting ready" or "awareness" stage. People at this stage typically intend to embark on integrating healthier behaviors in the near future, often defined as within the next six months. Some degree of ambivalence is common, in the sense that individuals are likely to vacillate between emphasizing either the anticipated pros or cons of change.

For someone with an anger problem, awareness is reflected in attempts to learn about anger and about how it can better be managed. Notice that this falls short of an actual commitment to work on your anger. That comes next.

Preparation Stage

Commitment marks the beginning of the preparation stage: You actively commit yourself to making changes to the way you experience and express anger. Once you've taken that key step, the preparation stage calls for planning out how you will approach enacting change in your life, including the marshalling of available resources to support you in your efforts. One important step is sharing the intent to change with trusted friends and loved ones. This step of "going public" tends to deepen the level of commitment, while providing for sources of support and accountability with the important people in the individual's life.

Action Stage

This is the stage when people start making real changes. They progress by learning effective behaviors, modes of self-expression, and coping techniques. They actively look for opportunities to substitute positive behaviors for unhealthy ones, they reward themselves for making good choices, and they avoid people and situations that tempt them to revert to bad habits. Because motivation tends to fluctuate, it is important for people at this stage to continuously monitor and nourish their level of commitment.

Maintenance Stage

The maintenance stage has no defined end point. Maintenance is about ensuring that you don't slide backwards with respect to hard-won changes you have achieved. Given that slip-ups and setbacks are commonplace for everyone, maintenance is also about getting back on track when these mistakes occur, or when novel challenges are presented. With time, as you learn that you can recover from lapses and mistakes that inevitably take place, you develop greater confidence and skill. And you learn that these course corrections along the way can serve to strengthen and solidify your accomplishments.

Making the Commitment

You have seen how anger problems can negatively impact almost every area of your life. Given the far-reaching effects of chronic and uncontrolled anger, making the commitment to work on this problem may be one of the more important decisions you make in your life. It's a big deal.

Commitment is about more than "wanting" something. People want things all the time. If wanting were sufficient to produce the desired outcomes in life, everyone would be healthy, wealthy, and wise. This is manifestly not true.

Commitment encompasses wanting, but at its heart it has to do with *deciding*. A commitment is like a promise: You are putting your character and integrity on the line. When you truly commit to something, you voluntarily choose to honor a set of choices and values regardless of how you may be feeling. When you commit to working on your anger, you are stating your intention to pursue this work when it is easy and when it is hard, on days when you feel like it and on days when you do not.

Commitment, alongside motivation, is the secret sauce for any notable achievement. In the extreme, imagine the accomplishments of a great athlete, such as Joseph Jordan or Martina Navratilova. Can you imagine them having even remotely approximated their achievements if they had allowed the effort they put into developing their skills to be dictated simply by what they "felt" like doing on a given day? Commitment, based on a foundation of personal responsibility, is essential for great accomplishments.

The Role of Motivation

Motivation can be a serious challenge for people who want to work on an anger problem. Consider what you already know about anger: It constricts attention, it is self-justifying, and it is associated with many illusory payoffs (such as a temporary spike in energy and self-confidence). It is therefore no surprise that many people are not naturally inclined to improve themselves in this area. The reality is that people often have to experience major adverse consequences—sometimes repeatedly, over years—before they are willing to accept that they have an anger problem that merits serious and sustained attention. Sometimes the pain simply becomes too great, or they frighten themselves with their own out-of-control behavior, and it becomes clear that they need to make a change. Sometimes it is the loss of a relationship or a job that finally does it.

FACT

The power of commitment was illustrated in a recent study at a hotel. Guests were asked to hang their towels after use, but a subset of guests were asked to make a brief verbal commitment that they would do so. For this group, the number of towels hung increased by 40 percent. The implication is profound: Even a small commitment can have a significant impact on behavior.

In the commitment process that occurs at the preparation stage of change, a person has the opportunity to transform anger-generated problems by using them as motivation for making, and maintaining, a full-blooded commitment to change. This is an ongoing process. Even when there are powerful reasons for change, a person's motivation can wax and wane over time. It is common for angry people to stop attending an anger management program before finishing it or never actually apply the techniques they read in a book. Once a person has begun the process of accepting responsibility for anger problems, and has committed to taking corrective action, nurturing intrinsic motivation becomes a vital and ongoing task.

Exploring and Nurturing Motivation

From the most mundane activities of day-to-day life to the most extreme examples of human perseverance and achievement, motivation is an essential outgrowth of human emotion that empowers a person to take action. Take, for example, Mark Inglis, a mountaineer from New Zealand. In 1982, Mark suffered severe frostbite during a blizzard and subsequently had to have both legs amputated below the knee. Instead of giving up, Mark found the motivation to pursue his dreams. Twenty-four years later, at the age of forty-seven, Mark successfully reached the summit of Mt. Everest using two prosthetic limbs.

For Mark Inglis, the motivation was both personal and altruistic. Mountaineering was a lifelong passion, and he was determined not to let his disability prevent him from realizing his dreams. At another level, Mark was motivated by his compassion for others. He used his exploits to raise money for charity, as well as to inspire other people with disabilities to believe in their potential to overcome limitations. Doing so gave Mark a tremendous sense of meaning and purpose, and it allowed him to persevere under the most dire and challenging circumstances.

What is your motivation? What are the pros of changing and the cons of not changing? When you're gasping on that metaphorical mountainside, struggling to take just one more step, how are you going to push yourself to keep going? These are important questions. The more you can solidify your commitment to resolving your anger with a sense of purpose, importance, and meaning, the more likely you will be to succeed.

Motivation and the Illusion of Proximity

Try an exercise. Hold your hand directly over your eyes. What do you see? Probably not much more than your hand. It might literally obscure the much larger painting that hangs on the wall across from you. Now move your hand away to arm's length; note how much "smaller" the hand appears and how much more (besides your hand) you are able to see. Your hand is now clearly smaller than the painting on the opposite wall. Now imagine if you were able to look at your hand in the same position, but from 10 feet back, side by side with the painting. Their relative, apparent sizes keep changing.

This is the illusion of proximity, and it has much to do with the day-to-day struggles people experience with motivation. Imagine the kind of obstacles you are likely to face as you seek to manage your anger. You might be having a stressful day at work and are struggling not to behave irritably. You might be short on sleep and just don't *feel* like working on your anger right now. Someone might have done something that *really* got under your skin. Assuming you've already done the work to develop your motivations for working on anger, it is likely that, if you were to place these obstacles alongside your motivations on a level playing field, the motivations for change would win every time. But this is not what happens in real life.

In real life, because of the illusion of proximity, whatever you are experiencing in the moment tends to appear large and important—much like the hand over your eyes—and easily overwhelms your awareness of and connection with the more important priorities that are, at that moment, further removed from your point of view. The hand has obscured the painting. This is how even people with big motivations can be tripped up by relatively trivial events; they lose focus.

To succeed in a challenging endeavor such as anger management, you need to nourish your motivation by actively and regularly giving it a prominent position in your conscious mind. Returning to the earlier illustration, this means that if your hand represents a situational obstacle, and the painting on the wall represents your motivation, you must deliberately set out each day to move the hand away from your eye, while bringing the painting closer and closer within your field of vision. One very effective way to do this is through the use of an intention statement.

ALERT

If you continue to struggle to find the motivation for change, think about the meanings that this change has for you. Don't just think about the positive meanings, but also about what you might be losing or giving up by altering your behavior. Attachments to the "old" way of doing things can hold you back more than you realize.

Using an Intention Statement

An intention statement sums up your intention to take responsibility for and manage your anger. Intention, as used here, can be understood as the marriage of motivation, commitment, and focus—the key engines of success in the pursuit of personal growth. Intention is about what you personally *own* and what you personally *will* to make happen.

In the tumult of daily life, people find that the power of their "intention engines" can be quite variable. In fact, research shows that these engines of change diminish and recede when they are not actively nourished. Even the best intentions fade when they are not consistently reinforced and solidified. This is where an intention statement can be helpful.

The purpose of an intention statement is to maintain your commitment, motivation, and focus at a sufficiently high level to produce the results you want. An intention statement summarizes *the most important changes, values, ideas, and goals you want to actualize in your life right now.* It summarizes, in written form, a personal commitment that you are going to renew on a daily basis. While the focus here is on anger management, any meaningful and significant change that you want to make in your behavior *right now* is fair game for inclusion. Leave out goals or changes that you are planning to work on. Remember to update your statement continually to reflect your current progress and priorities. Remember these three key points:

1. The strength of intention increases when you write it down.
2. The strength of intention increases when you share it with others.
3. The act of reading an intention statement daily is powerfully reinforcing.

To maximize the potential of the statement, you must take the time to write it thoughtfully and in a personal manner. It should reflect the values, goals, and priorities that you want to *work on now.* An intention statement is not the same as a behavior modification plan or an anger control plan, although it may encompass overlapping ideas or points of emphasis. An intention statement is more fundamental than a plan, because it is motivational in nature. It summarizes the essential goals for how you want to change your day-to-day behaviors, the motivations for pursuing these changes, the ideas or points of emphasis you want to keep in mind throughout the day, and the anticipated obstacles that you might encounter.

Your intention statement should be concise. You should be able to read through it in a minute or two. Once you've crafted the statement, commit to reading it daily, preferably in the morning. Intention statements are best read at the start of the day because they enable you to embark on the day's activities with an optimally focused mindset.

Finally, reading the statement should be *an active, not a passive, process.* Every time you read your intention statement, you are making and reinforcing a *personal commitment.* In composing the statement, you want to address these four areas:

1. **Changes you want to focus on.** What are the changes you would like to commit to making in your life right now? What are the primary ideas, values, and activating goals that you want in your life? As succinctly as possible, write these changes in a series of concrete intentional statements, moving from the general to the concrete. Overall, try to be as specific as you can.

2. **Key motivations.** What are the most powerful reasons or motivations for making these changes? Why are these changes important to you right now? What are the benefits of making these changes, and what would be the consequences of *not* making these changes?

3. **Points of emphasis.** These could be ideas that you want to keep at the forefront of your imagination, such as quotations or inspirational sayings. Don't allow this section to become too lengthy. Focus on a manageable handful, and then, as these become more ingrained, you can swap them out for new ideas.

4. **Anticipated obstacles.** If you know that there are certain friends, situations, beliefs, self-doubts, personal characteristics, and patterns of thinking that are likely to impede the changes you wish to make, address these issues by developing thoughtful counter-responses and/or counter-tactics for each obstacle.

Finally, signing the intention statement is a way of providing structure and support; both are important for your success. Print out your statement and sign it. If practical, get one or more people who want to support your anger management progress to sign as witnesses. You may even consider posting the statement in a public place so that people you interact with on a regular basis become aware of your commitment. Going public with your intention to change is not always practical, or may need to be limited to only certain trusted people, but doing so—to the extent possible—will strengthen your commitment.

CHAPTER 6
Basic Awareness

Awareness is essential for changing any ingrained habit. By bringing awareness to your anger, you are empowered to anticipate problems and to take corrective action. One of the most important areas for developing awareness is what triggers your anger—the things that consistently make you angry. Very often, these triggers connect with important past experiences. As you become more aware of your triggers, you will be able to prepare for challenging situations and to resolve past issues.

Becoming Aware of Anger

Awareness is a powerful ally. It is, to put it mildly, difficult to take control of an anger problem when you are unaware of the kinds of situations most likely to upset you, or of the warning signs of an escalating anger response. The more awareness you can develop through observation and self-reflection, the more empowered you will be to forestall, minimize, and resolve anger problems before they get out of control.

It is important to recognize the events, circumstances, and behaviors that can trigger your anger. Awareness also involves monitoring your emotional state so you quickly know when you are becoming angry and can recognize when your anger is escalating. This means that you are aware of, and attuned to, the warning signs (or cues) that signal the progression of your anger.

Just Noticing

In the heat of the moment, it is easy to remain angry and not recognize what is occurring. When you are in an emotionally aroused state, it is as though you are helpless to act differently than the emotion wants you to act. Lacking basic awareness, you are vulnerable to taking actions you will later regret.

As your awareness grows, you are able to notice anger as it is occurring. Noticing anger allows you to step back from it and to witness it as though it were happening to someone else. Noticing anger provides you with the space to recognize what is happening, to make an objective assessment of the situation, and to form judgments as to how best to respond. A self-aware person is conscious of what he is feeling and can use this understanding to change how he acts.

FACT

There are many benefits to awareness that go beyond anger management. These benefits include the ability to act consciously instead of reacting to people and events, a greater depth of experience and enjoyment of life, the ability to redirect negative thoughts and emphasize positive ones, and the ability to respond more critically to difficult or unexpected circumstances.

Using an Anger Meter

One technique that is helpful in increasing an awareness of anger is learning to monitor it quantitatively. Anger is a multifaceted experience that has emotional, psychological, and physiological aspects. Measuring anger requires devising subjective anger ratings, which can be accomplished through a conceptual device known as an *anger meter*.

Imagine a thermometer that indicates the degree of emotional heat, or anger, that you are feeling at any given moment. When you are mildly irritated or experiencing a low degree of frustration, the mercury rises visibly from the base of the thermometer. As this anger builds, the mercury moves toward the halfway mark. Here, you are acutely conscious of feeling angry, but are still in control of yourself. Another rise in the mercury indicates that you are approaching the point where you might lose control. Your anger is approaching the "boiling point," and some sort of emotional explosion is just around the corner. Once your anger has reached the top of thermometer, all bets are off.

This imaginary "anger thermometer" can also be referred to as an anger meter. Imagine a series of anger levels between 0 and 10. Zero on the anger meter means you are in a state of complete calm, while 10 indicates that you have reached the saturation point where self-control is compromised. The points between represent gradations of anger.

Using an anger meter provides a clear, easy mechanism for monitoring the escalation of anger. This method helps you recognize that anger operates on a continuum, that it moves smoothly up and down between calmness and rage. People with anger problems sometimes don't recognize the continuous nature of anger, because they experience their own anger as an "either/or" experience. They are either "fine" or "furious." Often, and this is especially the case for people with aggressive anger styles, it seems as if the anger happens "all at once"—from 0 to 10, with no intermediary steps. In fact, the intermediary steps are always there, but explosive anger can become such a strong habitual response that it seems to happen instantly. With sufficient practice, you can learn to distinguish the finer shades of anger and calmness.

Anger ratings provide feedback about how likely you are to lose control or explode at any given moment. By training yourself to recognize when your anger is escalating, you improve your chances of being able to maintain control by taking steps to reverse the trend. Thus, you are able to intervene before you reach the state in which you generate negative consequences for yourself or others. There is always time, provided you have learned effective coping skills (read on!), to stop anger from escalating to a 10.

Common Difficulties

When describing the anger meter, it is often difficult to define what a 10 means. In fact, the criteria are strict. It is reserved only for instances where your anger has caused you to either lose control or to experience negative consequences. For example, you become so enraged that you yell at a coworker, resulting in a reprimand from your boss. Someone with an avoidant anger style, however, may forcefully suppress or repress her anger, resulting in future difficulties such as increased emotional reactivity to stressful events or lingering feelings of depression.

What may be a 6 on the meter for one person may be an 8 for someone else. Such differences are acceptable. When you use an anger meter, the person to whom you are comparing yourself is you. You are your own yardstick.

The Anger Meter in Practice

The best way to begin using an anger meter is first to establish benchmarks (or ratings qualifications) at both extremes and then at the midpoint. These benchmarks provide clear points of reference against which other ratings can be interpreted. A rating of 0 for complete calm is easy to understand and define for most people; for reference, simply take the time to define this anger level in terms of a particularly relaxed experience that you can remember. A definition for a rating of 10 is subjective, but it is helpful to generate a list of characteristics for what that level is like for you (e.g., "10: my heart is racing, my face feels hot, my shoulders are almost painfully tight").

Finally, develop an operational definition for what anger is like for you at the midpoint level. By defining 5 as the midpoint between the extremes, and then by establishing clear guidelines for how you are experiencing anger at this halfway mark (e.g., "5: I am feeling very angry, but can maintain an outward show of composure"), other ratings, such as 3 or 8, will be readily interpretable as gradations between these established benchmarks.

Triggers

Anger-meter ratings help you understand just how angry you feel in certain situations, but they don't help predict which situations are likely to set you off in the first place. For that, you need to know your triggers.

An anger trigger is any event that signals your brain to activate your body's anger system. Once a trigger has been activated, angry feelings begin automatically. Developing the ability to anticipate and recognize triggers can be liberating, because it moves you from being on "autopilot" to "manual control" of your mood.

FACT

Some emotional triggers, such as the fear of snakes and the fear of embarrassment, appear to be evolutionarily hardwired. These triggers evoke a visceral response even though people may know they are relatively harmless. Humans are less likely to react with fear to dangerous risks that evolution has not prepared them for, such as unhealthy food, smoking, and unsafe sex.

When you are unaware of your triggers, you are vulnerable to being unwittingly dominated by them. In some cases, triggers reveal themselves in situations in which you overreact to circumstances that most people would find upsetting or annoying (e.g., a friend arriving late for dinner). In other cases, your triggers may reveal themselves in situations in which you misinterpret another person's behavior (e.g., a comment from a friend) and respond with anger when it is clearly not warranted. In such cases, it is important to recognize that what set you off is not necessarily anything that would provoke someone else.

Today's Trigger, Yesterday's Pain

As you discover your triggers, you are likely to find that many of the situations that trigger you to "lose your cool" are similar to something that happened weeks, months, or even years ago. When anger or hurt is unresolved, these feelings will resurface whenever a similar situation arises. For example, if you grew up with a highly critical parent, you may have internalized an enduring sensitivity to criticism. Now, say, your spouse confronts you politely about leaving your clothes all over the house. Even though this criticism might be fair, and may have been expressed in a calm and respectful manner, you may still overreact due to your underlying sensitivity to criticism. Criticism has become a trigger for you.

Once you make the required connections between the "then-and-there" and the "here-and-now," you can begin to deactivate those buttons. By first uncovering the triggers that influence you, and then by changing how you respond to these situations, you're able to bring a new, more positive self-understanding to the distressing messages you received when you were younger. At this point, your essential self-image can undergo transformative change.

Three Key Questions

So what exactly pushes your buttons? And just how do you determine what causes you to become provoked? You can answer these questions by looking at specific instances in which you experienced and expressed anger in unhealthy ways. For each incident, ask the following questions:

1. **Event.** What, specifically, was your anger in response to?
2. **Trigger.** What was it about your interpretation or construal of the event that made you angry?
3. **Root cause.** Why did the trigger make you angry in the way that it did? What about the trigger pushes your buttons? Does the trigger relate to earlier experiences or frustrations in your life? How so?

The first question is fairly self-explanatory. You bring to mind, or write down, the relevant details of a particular situation in which you displayed problematic anger.

The second question requires you to dig beneath the surface of an anger-inducing event to discover the core issue or sensitivity that triggered the anger. Perhaps, for example, you became angry at work when your suggestions for a company dinner were not adopted. When you look closely at this reaction, you might recognize that the situation triggered an underlying fear of inadequacy. You interpreted the fact that your suggestions weren't adopted as implying that your ideas were either not very good or somehow devalued by your colleagues. This construal of the situation is a direct reflection of your underlying feelings of inadequacy. You are confusing imagination with reality. For all you know, there may be very different reasons your suggestions were not implemented.

The third question requires you to step back from the situation entirely and ask yourself how this particular trigger might relate to other factors and experiences in your life. For example, imagine that you reacted with anger because you found your girlfriend speaking to an attractive man while waiting to be seated at a restaurant. Imagine that this is an innocent encounter; say, the other person was asking for directions. But also imagine that you have been cheated on a number of times and are therefore sensitized to matters of infidelity. You experience jealousy and secondary anger quite easily. This prior experience of infidelity would be the root cause of your anger at the restaurant, a persistent area of sensitivity that inclines you to overreact to and misperceive these kinds of situations. The result is that, for you, anything that involves your girlfriend interacting with another man can trigger anger.

ALERT

The next time you are triggered, remember that you cannot change the past and can rarely change others. However, you have the power to control how you respond to people and events in the present moment. Think of your triggers as intuitive messages alerting you to certain aspects of yourself that need to be explored. Keep the focus inward.

Triggers, by their nature, are never specific to the particular situation, but rather to a type of situation. In the example just given, for example, you would not say that the trigger was seeing your girlfriend speaking to a man while waiting in line at a restaurant. Your angry reaction was based on a more general sensitivity. Specifically, the trigger in this instance was seeing your girlfriend pay attention to and receive attention from another man. It would not have mattered whether this event took place at a restaurant, a bank, or in some other context.

Discovering Your Triggers

Anger triggers are thematic in nature. Across large numbers of people, there are a fairly limited number of "hot buttons." As a result, it can be helpful to refer to a list of common triggers when working to uncover your own triggers. Common themes that underlie anger triggers include the following:

- Feeling criticized or scolded
- Feeling deceived or misled
- Feeling devalued or disregarded
- Feeling disagreed with
- Feeling disrespected
- Feeling ignored
- Feeling made fun of or humiliated
- Feeling powerless
- Feeling rebuffed, spurned, or rejected
- Feeling slighted
- Feeling taken advantage of
- Feeling treated unfairly or falsely accused
- Feeling unappreciated or unloved
- Feeling weak, inadequate, or incompetent

Anything powerful enough to have triggered you in the past is likely to do so in the future. With this in mind, create a list of all the events you can think of that have triggered problematic anger. These would be situations in which you felt immediately impelled to defend yourself, or to go on the attack, such as by verbally striking back or passive-aggressively disengaging from your provocateur.

If this task seems overwhelming, narrow the scope by focusing on the worst incidents when you lost your cool or by working strictly within a defined period, such as the last three months or six months. Catalog everything you can think of within the parameters you set, and in each instance try to answer the three questions. Be sure to consider as possibilities the bullet list of thematic triggers. These triggers are so common that being able to refer to them should help you do this work more efficiently.

As you engage in this task, you are likely to uncover a pattern—that is, you may find the same underlying trigger causing you to become angry again and again and again. If you're like most people, you will probably also discover that you have more than one trigger that leaves you susceptible to problematic anger. That's okay. The simple act of discovering a trigger goes a long way toward defusing it and provides a foundation for helping you focus your anger management efforts.

The Context of Anger

As you bring increasingly greater awareness to your anger, you will begin to appreciate the role of context. In this regard, context has to do with circumstances *outside* an anger-provoking event that either render you more likely to react with anger, or to experience and express that anger more intensely than you otherwise would.

Context is an important consideration. If you know, for example, that certain circumstances make you more vulnerable to experiencing problematic anger, such as when you are especially busy or tired, you can use this awareness to better understand past reactions, as well as to anticipate situations of "anger vulnerability."

The most important contextual determinant of anger is pre-existing anger or hostility. Anger feeds on itself. Once you are in an already agitated state of mind, even at a low level, a proportionally smaller "push" or "provocation" than usual is required to send you to the top of the anger meter.

The next, most important contextual determinant is psychological stress. When you are in a state of stress, you are increasingly vulnerable to experiencing the full array of negative emotions, with anger at the top of the list. A little bit of stress can be good and can actually improve your performance in certain areas. But beyond a certain threshold, stress begins to impair almost every aspect of your functioning. Any time you are aware of being uncomfortably stressed, you need to guard against problematic anger.

Cues to Anger

Once you have discovered your triggers, a second important step in effective anger management is to learn how to recognize when you are angry. Sounds simple, right? In fact, while every person is unique, people with anger problems are often remarkably unaware of when they actually begin to express anger. Many angry people, for example, see their emotions in black-and-white terms—they are either really mad or really calm. This kind of thinking reflects a basic lack of awareness.

People who see anger in terms of extremes have difficulty recognizing when they are experiencing intermediate states. Fortunately, it is possible to use the symptoms of anger—anger cues, as they are called—to learn to recognize more quickly when you are becoming agitated. Anger cues come in four flavors: physical, behavioral, emotional, and cognitive. These warning signs can be used to alert you that you are becoming angry and to monitor the extent to which your anger is escalating.

Physical Cues

Physical cues reflect how your body responds to and expresses anger. Many of these cues were presented earlier when discussing the physiology of anger. For example, you may feel tightness in your chest and your heart rate may increase. Other common physical anger cues include:

- Dizziness
- Feeling hot in the neck/face
- Headache
- Muscle tension
- Numbness
- Pale or flushed face
- Prickly or tingling sensations
- Rapid heart rate
- Rapid or shallow breathing
- Shaking or trembling
- Stomachache
- Sweating, especially the palms
- Temperature changes (usually an increased sense of "heat")

Physical cues can be a good indication that you are angry, that your anger is getting worse, or that you are approaching a level 10 on the anger meter.

Reflect on some recent instances where you became angry, and try to identify some of the physical cues that you experienced. Alternatively, be mindful of physical sensations the next time you are aware of experiencing anger. Although there are many symptoms that people experience when angered, it is likely that you tend to experience a smaller subset of these symptoms more frequently (e.g., a clenched jaw and feelings of "heat").

Behavioral Cues

These are the characteristic behaviors that you exhibit when you become angry. Behavioral cues may be overt and directed outward, such as when you raise your voice. Or they may be more subtle and self-contained, such as when you grind your teeth or clench or tighten your muscles. Common behavioral cues include the following:

- Acting in an abusive or abrasive manner
- Beginning to yell, scream, or cry
- Clenching fists
- Cupping one fist with the other hand
- Frowning
- Grinding teeth
- Pacing
- Rubbing of the head
- Speaking in a sarcastic tone

These behavioral responses are warning signs that you may be approaching a 10 on the anger meter.

ESSENTIAL

Anger cues can be difficult to identify, especially the ones that occur first and that are the most helpful. Consider asking a friend for assistance—someone who has opportunities to see you becoming angry. What are the first things she notices?

What are some of the behavioral cues that you have experienced when you become angry? Reflect on a recent instance where you became angry, and identify as many behavioral cues as you can. Which cues occur most frequently when you are upset? Which do you become aware of first?

Emotional Cues

Emotional cues refer to feelings, other than anger, that you experience either *concurrently* with or *immediately preceding* your anger. You are most likely to become aware of these cues during situations in which you are experiencing secondary, or defensive, anger. In such cases, the emotional cue actually represents your primary emotional response to the triggering event. Recall that secondary anger develops in response to another, more vulnerable, emotion such as hurt or shame and protects you from feeling vulnerable or weak. For example, you may become angry when you feel abandoned, afraid, discounted, disrespected, guilty, humiliated, impatient, insecure, jealous, or rejected (i.e., the primary emotions). Other common emotional cues include:

- Cravings (e.g., for a drink, a smoke, or other "relaxing" substances)
- Desire to flee or run away
- Fear/anxiety
- Guilt or shame
- Hurt
- Irritation
- Jealousy
- Rejection
- Resentment
- Restlessness
- Sadness
- Stress

It is very tempting to discount these primary feelings, precisely because of the vulnerability they imply. Don't make that mistake. When primary emotions are discounted, unacknowledged, or suppressed, they become trapped—there is no way to release them. This will only worsen your difficulties. Becoming aware of, and working through, the primary emotions that produce secondary anger is an important component of anger management.

Cognitive Cues

Cognitive cues are the thoughts you have that either cause you to become angry, that demonstrate that you already are angry, or that make you even angrier as time goes by. These cues occur during the escalation phase of anger and will often exacerbate angry feelings. Cognitive cues may also occur *before* you are conscious of being angry and may contribute to your having been angered in the first place. Examples of cognitive cues include thoughts such as:

- "That jerk probably bumped into me on purpose. She's trying to make me look like a fool in front of all these other people. I can't let her disrespect me like that."
- "He should know better than to leave the house looking like this. He never listens. He doesn't care about me or anyone else but himself."
- "He says that I'm financially irresponsible? Who is he to judge me? He doesn't even make as much as I do."

For people with anger issues, cognitive cues such as these show how events can be interpreted in certain characteristic ways that are consistent with defensiveness and aggression. Thinking tends to be critical and hostile in tone and content; blame is externalized; worst-case scenarios are embraced.

Cognitive cues can consist not only of evaluative and judgmental thoughts (such as the previous examples), but also of images and fantasies that can increase anger. Revenge fantasies are especially common. These can be seductive, because they allow people to say and do things that they might not even be able to do in real life, or that would have serious negative consequences for them. Unfortunately, these kinds of fantasies and images can also serve to increase your anger, and may even increase the likelihood that you will become angry again in the future.

The Aggression Cycle

The aggression cycle provides a framework for integrating anger management concepts, namely, the anger meter, triggers, and cues. There are five phases: activation, agitation, instigation, extermination, and the aftermath.

Activation

The activation phase corresponds to ratings on the anger meter from 1 through 3. This phase is marked by increasing levels of annoyance. People enter the activation stage when provoked by minor irritations, or at the outset of a more intense bout of anger that quickly rises into the more severe phases. During activation, parallel processes are initiated at the level of body and mind. At the body level, the physiological process of anger begins at this phase. Your body's threat system is initiated; you have entered the initial stage of arousal. At the mind level, the initial surge of anger is first experienced emotionally (you notice that you "feel" angry) while, at the same time, your mind begins to process the situation, looking for threats, facts, implications, and so forth. Your bread-and-butter everyday annoyances will often not escalate beyond this phase, although they can. For people skilled in anger management techniques, anger will rarely rise beyond activation. Anger cues can be difficult to detect at this early phase, especially if you have not yet had time to develop basic awareness.

Agitation

The agitation phase corresponds to levels 4 through 6. As you move into this phase, the situation becomes more volatile. You are still in control of yourself, for the most part, but this control is now being actively challenged by the intensity of the anger you are feeling. Small eruptions might occur, such as raising your voice or deliberately making provocative statements. You are acutely displeased. Your body has begun to tense, your tone of voice is changing, your body language is more aggressive, and your facial expression shows definite signs of anger. The agitation stage is sometimes thought of as the key inflection point that determines whether your anger will remain at the level of annoyance, or rise toward the level of full rage. Objectivity begins to be seriously challenged at this level, and rationalizations may be fabricated to justify an angry outburst.

ALERT

Remember that the farther you move up the anger meter, the more difficult it becomes to manage your anger and respond effectively. By the time you reach the instigation stage at the upper end of escalating anger, it becomes very difficult to slow down. Be vigilant in your awareness of triggers and cues—awareness is your greatest ally.

Instigation

The instigation phase corresponds to ratings 7 through 9. This is the phase of "no more Mr. Nice Guy." Anger cues—physical, behavioral, emotional, and cognitive—are front and center. Almost anyone in the world would be able to recognize that you are angry at this point. People sometimes describe this phase as "dizzying" and "overwhelming," in part because the level of physiological arousal at this stage clouds awareness and memory. Things are moving fast. There is still a modicum of self-control, but it is badly frayed. You are flooded with aggressive impulses, a pronounced desire to lash out. At the same time, your motivation to resolve the situation is weakening. The sheer intensity of anger at this phase interferes with clear thinking and reasoned decision-making. It still remains possible at this stage to reverse course toward a lower, less agitated state, but this requires a decisive response to your anger cues. One way to think of the instigation phase is as the final stopping point before reaching extermination, the most dangerous anger phase.

Extermination

The extermination phase corresponds to an anger-meter rating of 10. It is marked either by an out-of-control discharge of anger, or by some action that leads to negative consequences, such as forcible suppression or aggressive acting out. All bets are off.

At the extermination phase, anger has progressed from an acute emotional state to an aggressive behavior that actively seeks to injure your opponent. This is the "red zone"—a level of outright verbal and physical violence.

If you are not physically assaulting the other party at this phase, then you are seeking to discharge your rage in some other way, such as by venting against an inanimate object, or by speaking the most hurtful words that come to mind. This is the phase where crimes of passion occur. Although it should be emphasized that not every rupture into the extermination phase results in physical violence, this is a clear and present danger that merits close consideration. The intensity of rage that people experience during this phase is acute, and the dangers stemming from loss of self-control are very real. Negative consequences become an inevitability by the time you have reached anger extermination, ranging from damaged relationships to a lengthy stay in prison—or worse.

The Aftermath

The final part of the aggression cycle is the aftermath. It is characterized by negative consequences resulting from the verbal or physical aggression displayed during the extermination phase. These consequences may include going to jail, making restitution, being terminated from a job or discharged from a drug treatment or social service program, losing family and loved ones, or experiencing feelings of guilt, shame, and regret.

Using an Anger Journal

An anger journal is a useful tool for tracking your experiences with anger, identifying triggers and cues, and learning to predict what situations will provoke or challenge you. Being able to anticipate challenging situations is a powerful aid in helping keep your anger under control. You can choose to avoid provoking situations entirely, or, if that is not possible, you can prepare yourself with ways to minimize the danger of losing control prior to facing difficult situations.

There is no "best" way to develop an anger journal. Experiment to find what works best for you. One approach that works well builds on the three questions that were posed earlier during the section on triggers. These questions can be expanded to provide a comprehensive snapshot of an anger episode, as shown here:

- **Baseline (or the pre-anger state of mind).** Write down any noteworthy aspects of your state of mind before the anger-provoking event took place. For example, were you stressed or worried? Were you experiencing other negative emotions, such as sadness, hurt, or embarrassment? Were you short on sleep? Were you very busy?
- **Event(s).** Briefly describe the event or series of events that seemed to cause your anger.
- **Trigger(s).** Describe the specific aspect of the event that caused you to become angry.
- **Root cause.** Describe, to the best of your understanding, why the trigger affected you as strongly as it did.
- **Cues: behavioral, physical, and emotional.** Describe any behavioral, physical, and emotional cues that you experienced.
- **Cognitive cues.** Write down or describe any cognitive cues that you experienced.
- **Anger-meter rating (highest).** Write down the highest anger level you reached during this episode.
- **Response to anger.** Write down how, if at all, you attempted to manage and control your anger once you became aware that it was escalating.
- **Response to person(s).** Not all anger-provoking events involve other people, but most do. Write down how you expressed and addressed your anger with the other person(s) involved.
- **Consequences.** Describe any consequences that you experienced from this situation.

The more accurately you observe your feelings and behaviors and the more detailed your anger journal, the more likely you will be to identify anger triggers and how you react to them. Understanding the ways in which you experience anger can help you plan strategies to cope with your emotions in more productive ways.

After recording this information for a week or so, you should be in a good position to uncover circumstances surrounding an anger-provoking event that make you more likely to react with anger (i.e., the context), to discover recurring triggers, and to identify your most salient anger cues.

ESSENTIAL

> Thoughts, or cognitive cues, are among the most powerful determinants of anger. Using an anger journal will help you identify anger-triggering and anger-exacerbating thoughts that recur repeatedly. Be sure to track your thought patterns in addition to external triggers and other kinds of anger cues. This will help you uncover the common themes in your anger.

The 3R Method: Relax, Reassess, and Respond

Now that you've learned the basics of anger, including triggers, cues, and the aggression cycle, it's time to turn your attention toward learning the techniques and principles that will allow you to use this information to manage anger in your own life. The next three chapters will present the 3R method, which offers an effective and practical model for cooling down situational anger—the kind of anger that is evoked by specific events in your life. Later chapters will present additional principles and techniques that will further help you to control situational anger, to work with long-term, seemingly intractable anger, and to reduce the overall prominence of anger and hostility in your life.

CHAPTER 7

The 3R Method: Step 1. Relax

Anger can boil over with dizzying speed, and it can simmer for years. Once anger has you in its grip, it can be difficult to regain a sense of perspective, control, and objectivity. Anger control planning using the 3R method—relax, reassess, respond—is an effective way to prepare for these challenges. The first step of this method, relaxation, helps you reclaim a calm, clear mind. Using techniques such as breathing relaxation, you can regain the clarity you need to think through the situation and respond.

The 3R Method

The 3R method is a three-step framework for anger control planning and management. The basic steps are the same for everyone: relax, reassess the situation, and respond. At each of these steps, there are a range of techniques and approaches that can be applied, depending on the demands of the specific situation and your experience of what is most effective for you. Once you have had time to fine-tune your plan and master the basic techniques and guidelines, an anger plan based on the 3R method should help you regain control in seconds.

Awareness, Support, and Motivation

The foundation for effective anger control planning using the 3R method (or any approach, for that matter) is awareness. Most important, this means maintaining vigilance toward triggers and cues. If you know that you will be entering a situation in which you are likely to be confronted with an anger trigger, you can prepare to meet this challenge. Further downstream, the sooner you realize that you are becoming angry, the sooner (and more effectively) you can take corrective steps to resolve the situation. If you are monitoring your anger and can see that it is escalating rapidly, this is a clear indication that you need to take immediate action to implement your anger plan.

ESSENTIAL

Social support offers benefits that go well beyond recognizing when you are falling back on old patterns. In fact, one of the greatest benefits of social support isn't in identifying or managing anger, but in preventing it in the first place. Developing a strong, healthy network of supportive relationships provides a sense of belonging, an increased sense of self-worth, and feelings of security.

Your partners, friends, and trusted associates can often recognize when you are getting angry before you can, so it is a good idea to include them in your anger plan, if possible. Agree on a signal that they can give you when they see you start sliding into old aggressive patterns. Once you receive the signal, you will know you need to change your behavior to avoid escalating your anger. You may want to take a time-out or agree to postpone your argument until you can speak about it from a calmer, more rational place.

To get the most out of the 3R method, you need to maintain a high level of motivation. Taking the time to thoughtfully write out an intention statement and to read it at the start of every day will go a long way toward keeping you prepared for challenging situations.

It can also be helpful to develop a list of reasons you want to stay calm and cool in certain situations. These reasons should be informed by the realistic consequences that might result from allowing anger to get out of control. Read over these reasons frequently so that they stay fixed and clear in your mind. In addition, there are many immediate "temptations" that can weaken your resolve, so review them as well. In the short term, anger can tempt you in the following ways:

- By offering you the instant "reward" of feeling morally superior to whomever, or whatever, you're angry at; this "justified" sense of righteousness (or self-righteousness) can actually bolster a somewhat shaky self-image
- By helping you defend against an underlying anxiety, or general sense of vulnerability; the adrenaline rush of anger (however superficially) may help you feel empowered
- By protecting you from experiencing an underlying depression or deep sense of loneliness or alienation
- By restoring a semblance of control when, in your momentary frustration, you may suddenly feel out of control
- By helping you, through intimidating the other person(s), get your way (however, there will be innumerable negative longer-term effects on relationships!)

Practice

Without question, the best way to learn these techniques is by practicing with milder daily irritations. Doing so will prepare you for intense anger-provoking situations. Most people experience incidences of mild irritation or annoyance during the week. You can apply the same basic steps of the 3R method to these low-level irritants, experimenting with different techniques and approaches. This will help build both confidence and skill. You'll see that you do not have to give in to your habitual angry impulses, which will enhance your ability to respond effectively.

Learn to Relax

The first step of the 3R Method is to relax—to calm down and maintain self-control. When you're angry, you are in a compromised state. You are certainly well prepared for a life-and-death struggle, but you are far less prepared for coming to terms with mundane annoyances or resolving an interpersonal rupture. In these situations, the tendency is to "act first and ask questions later." You are reaching conclusions and making decisions under a storm of arousal, buffeted by a powerful surge of adrenaline and other hormones. The best way to combat these forces is to slow down. To deliberately and self-consciously *relax*.

If you are in an immediate life-or-death situation, don't do this. Slowing down won't help you. But for the overwhelming majority of bouts of anger, where you are not in actual physical danger, taking the time to slow down and relax can give you the edge you need to manage your anger. If necessary, take a break. You'll be able to re-address the situation more effectively when your mind is stable. Another potential difference-maker here is knowing how to calm yourself down. Relaxation techniques such as deep breathing give you an added edge, helping you to settle down and problem-solve difficult situations.

FACT

Relaxation directly enhances clear thinking, attention, and concentration. People need breaks to quell stress, lower inhibiting hormone levels, clear distractions, and extend energy reserves. Research suggests that the human body benefits most from a twenty-minute reprieve about every one and a half to two hours. Without this recovery time, people may become more agitated, aggressive, hypersensitive, or depressed.

The relaxation response becomes stronger with practice. This is an important point. People often learn these techniques under quiet, controlled circumstances and quickly experience a satisfying relaxation effect. So far, so good. Then they may do very little with the technique until the next time they are upset, at which point they find that it is only somewhat helpful in helping them return to calm. The more you take the time to practice these techniques, the more quickly and more effectively they will help you during emotionally challenging situations. Consider setting aside time each day to practice relaxation. Anywhere from 5–15 minutes is usually sufficient. This time provides a great opportunity to slow down, connect with yourself, problem solve, and, most importantly, to strengthen your relaxation skills.

Avoid Stereotypical Anger Behaviors

You undoubtedly have vivid images of anger behaviors. The furrowed brow, the clenched teeth, the balled-up fists, the booming voice—these are the faces of anger. What you may not realize is that these behaviors not only *reveal* or *demonstrate* anger, they also *feed into* anger. They make the anger grow stronger. There is even evidence that these behaviors, closely associated as they are with escalating levels of arousal, can become addicting over time.

Giving yourself permission to engage in unchecked anger behaviors not only heightens rage, but is associated with increased anger in the future; you are more likely to become angry again. To stop this cycle in its tracks, start by avoiding stereotypical anger behaviors. Don't posture and provoke; don't yell, insult, or menace. You will experience a strong impulse to do some of these things, but you do not have to yield to that impulse. It's a choice. Adopt the mindset that you will not give yourself permission to engage in these behaviors. Should you find this to be particularly difficult, consider adding this objective to your intention statement. Avoiding anger behaviors will help you to regain calm and to think more clearly.

Take a Time-Out

When dealing with a contentious situation, the most obvious solution is to remove yourself from it. Not quitting or running away, but tactical retreat. A good way to approach this is thinking about probable outcomes. When you've reached a high level of anger at the agitation and instigation phases, there is a point of diminishing returns. Trying to engage with the other party is no longer helping resolve the situation, and there is now a real risk of making the situation worse. When you become aware of multiple anger cues coming on fast and furious, that's a good indication that you might need to take a break, particularly if you can sense your control weakening. Give yourself some space. Once you've cooled down and taken the time to reassess the situation, you will be in a far better position to constructively address your concerns.

Some basic ground rules will make your time-outs more effective. These include:

1. Don't walk away without explanation. Giving the appearance of "blowing them off" is not likely to be received well by the person you are arguing with. Let the other party know that you need a break in order to calm down, and then clearly express that you will want to re-engage with them as soon as possible.
2. Establish a mutually-understood timeframe for continued discussion with the other party.
3. There may be times when a time-out is advisable because it is clear that the other party needs an opportunity to wind down a bit. Don't ever say this to them. Telling the other party that they need time to "relax" or "cool off," however true you might believe that statement to be, is likely to be irritating and provocative from the other person's point of view. Just say that you need a break.
4. Finally, during your time-out be careful who you talk to and what you say about the situation. A third party might offer you great advice, or . . . not so much. It is also possible that gossip will be spread, or that you might inadvertently poison the third party against the person you are in conflict with. Try to minimize these possibilities.

Taking the opportunity to step away from an angering situation will give you space and time to calm down and to evaluate the situation from a more rational, cool-headed perspective.

How Long Should a Time-Out Last?

Keep in mind that taking a time-out will not be appropriate in every situation. There will be times when leaving the situation would be impractical or raise additional concerns. The optimal amount for a time-out depends on the situation. In some cases, a few minutes will be all you need, especially if you are applying strategies such as deep breathing. In other cases, you might need more time. Ultimately, listen to yourself and make the best judgment. Experience helps a great deal. The more you use time-outs as an anger management strategy, the better you will become at deciding when to re-engage.

As an illustration, when a fight breaks out between you and your spouse or partner, agree to take a temporary break from the fight to allow both of you to cool down. Taking a few minutes to step away, calm down, and think critically about the situation can put both of you in a better frame of mind to deal with the issue at hand.

ESSENTIAL

In situations when taking a time-out is impractical, consider taking a "mental time-out." When you feel the first surge of anger, instead of reacting to it, pause. Try counting backward from 10. Or simply delay your reaction. Delaying any kind of reaction, even for a few minutes, can help diffuse anger.

Breathing Techniques

One of the simplest, most effective ways to relax is by implementing a breathing technique. When you've been triggered, the tendency is to breathe shallowly, using only the chest, which can actually increase your sense of agitation. Shallow breathing disrupts the balance of oxygen and carbon dioxide necessary for a relaxed state and helps to perpetuate anger.

Deep (Diaphragmatic) Breathing

For the record, *deep breathing* means the same thing as "diaphragmatic breathing," "belly breathing," and "natural breathing." Deep breathing uses the diaphragm, a dome-shaped muscle located under your ribs and just above the stomach. When you breathe in deeply, you push the diaphragm down, and your stomach moves forward and appears to expand. When you breathe out, the diaphragm moves back to a resting position and your belly moves back in. There is little or no upper-chest movement. To learn deep breathing, follow these basic steps:

1. Sit comfortably, with your knees bent and your shoulders, head, and neck relaxed.
2. Place one hand on your upper chest and the other just below your rib cage. This will allow you to feel your diaphragm move as you breathe.
3. Complete a full exhalation to begin the deep-breathing exercise. If possible, make sure that you are breathing only though your nose.
4. Once you are ready, relax your abdominal muscles and breathe in through your nose, trying as much as possible to "fill your belly" with air. The hand on your upper chest should be still, while the hand just below your rib cage should be rising steadily as you take in more air. Your breath should enter your belly first, then your chest, and finally your upper chest just below your shoulders.
5. Once you've completed the in-breath, begin the out-breath by tightening your stomach muscles, letting them fall inward as you exhale through your nose. As before, the hand on your upper chest must remain as still as possible, while the hand below your rib cage moves back in.

FACT

One of the pioneering researchers on breathing and relaxation was Herbert Benson, a cardiologist and the author of *The Relaxation Response*. During the late 1960s, Benson found that the simple act of changing one's breathing and thought pattern could produce beneficial changes in metabolism, heart rate, and brain activity.

If you are using deep breathing alone to help yourself relax, consider slowly repeating a calm word or phrase, such as *relax* or *take it easy*, to yourself while breathing.

Controlled Breathing

Controlled breathing is a simple and easy-to-learn breathing technique. Many people find that it works well for them, without having to add more complicated elements. The practice of controlled breathing allows your body and mind to settle down into a calm, stable rhythm, dissipating anger's sharp edges. More generally, this is a great technique to use in times of stress, particularly if you feel dizzy or lightheaded. Follow these steps:

1. Get into a comfortable position.
2. Begin deep breathing.
3. Move in a stable pattern of breathing, a sense of rhythm. One pattern that works very well is to inhale for three seconds, hold the breath in for two seconds, and then exhale for three seconds. Silently count to yourself while you do this (e.g., "IN, 1-2-3; HOLD, 1-2; OUT, 1-2-3").
4. Maintain this breathing pattern for at least two minutes or more, as needed. You should notice a relaxation effect within that time.

Seven-Breath Count

The 7-breath count is a breathing relaxation technique that doesn't require changing your breathing pattern. Instead, you count your breaths backward from 7, following these steps:

1. Bring your full attention to your breathing. Don't try to change your breathing in any way.
2. Begin by silently counting each in-breath and each out-breath, counting down from 7 to 1, like this:

In-breath 7, out-breath 7
In-breath 6, out-breath 6 (notice the movement in the body)
In-breath 5, out-breath 5
In-breath 4, out-breath 4

In-breath 3, out-breath 3

In-breath 2, out-breath 2

In-breath 1, out-breath 1

If you lose count, no problem—just start where you think you were. Focus on your breathing, and let the counting be a soft whisper in the background.

Resting in the Gap

This method of breathing relaxation draws its name from its most unique feature: It calls for "resting" during the "gap" between breaths. How slowly should you be breathing? *As slowly as you can without causing discomfort.* It takes practice, but the optimal rate of breathing using this method is about six breaths per minute. Here are the steps:

1. Sit (preferably) or stand in a comfortable position, with no tension in your shoulders or neck, and no slouching. If sitting, keep your back straight and your hands on your knees.
2. Begin diaphragmatic breathing, slowly filling your lungs with air. Be aware of your belly expanding first, and then your chest, and finally your upper chest. Notice how this feels.
3. Exhale slowly through the nose. As you do this, notice where the air in your lungs is going. Breathe deeply across the lung's full range. Feel your ribs expand as your lungs expand. Pay attention to how your ribs return to their original location as you exhale completely.
4. Rest in the gap: Once the exhalation is complete, pause for two seconds before initiating the next breath.
5. Repeat this sequence for five to ten inhale-exhale sequences, or until you feel calm and at peace with yourself. Return immediately to normal breathing if at any time you feel odd, or out of breath.

Start by using a stopwatch to determine your baseline rate of respiration—that is, how many breaths you perform per minute while breathing normally. Respiratory rate is easily calculated using twenty-second intervals; just multiply the number of breaths by three to find your baseline. Once you've practiced slowing down for a few minutes, use the stopwatch again to determine your progress compared to the baseline. Aim for six breaths per minute (or less) to obtain an optimal relaxation effect.

Learning to rest in the gap is a potent way to maximize the calming effect of deep, slow breathing. The "gap" is simply the *space between breaths*. It is the interval that exists between completing the exhalation from one breath and beginning the inhalation for the next breath. Here, you will try to draw this space out. Initially, these pauses will be quite brief, but with practice you will be able to comfortably extend resting in the gap to about two full seconds, which is ideal.

FACT

Breathing relaxation offers a simple way to regain emotional calm, but it is much more effective with practice. For the first week, consider setting aside ten minutes every day to practice breathing relaxation. Practicing will help you perform the technique correctly, but it will also help "train" your relaxation response so that it works more quickly.

Muscle Relaxation Techniques

Muscle relaxation is a tried-and-true approach for calming angry feelings. Tension builds in your muscles when you're upset, stressed, or angry, exacerbating negative feelings. Muscle relaxation can help you to feel more relaxed in general and to maintain control.

The basic principle is the systematic tensing and releasing of different muscles in the body. The progression of tensing and releasing is performed while maintaining body awareness, focusing on the sensations experienced while performing the exercise. This focus enhances the relaxation effect. With practice, it has the added benefit of enabling you to more quickly recognize and respond to the onset of tension, a common physical anger cue. Muscle relaxation can be as simple as deliberately tightening and releasing the muscles in your shoulders for a few seconds, and as elaborate as working through every major muscle group in the body, requiring forty-five minutes or more.

Brief Muscle Relaxation

The point of brief muscle relaxation is to be able to use this technique in almost any real-world situation. Practice is essential. Practice is most effective when you use the same muscle groups each time. That way, when you are trying to calm yourself during a tense situation, you won't have to think about what to do; it will feel automatic and natural.

1. Find a quiet, comfortable location that is free of distractions. You can sit, stand, or lie down, however you prefer.
2. Bring your attention to your breathing. Deliberately allow your breath to deepen and slow.
3. Decide which muscles you want to focus on. Suggestions include some or all of the following:

   - **Legs.** Tighten your calves, hamstrings, quadriceps—all at once.
   - **Stomach.** Tense your abdomen muscles.
   - **Arms.** Clench your fists and all the muscles in your arms simultaneously.
   - **Shoulders.** Shrug your shoulders upwards, toward your ears, and then squeeze the muscles in your shoulders.
   - **Face.** Frown and clench. Close your eyes, screw up the entirety of your facial muscles in a tight squeeze, and clench your jaw tightly.

4. Tightly squeeze each major muscle group for about five seconds. Tense vigorously, but without straining. Notice what this feels like.
5. Now, let go of that tension and relax your muscles. Allow the muscles to go completely limp for five to ten seconds. As before, notice what this feels like. You should have a sense of tension washing away. People sometimes describe a sense of warmth or tingling.
6. Move on to the next muscle group, until you are finished.

As you move through the various steps and muscle groups, check in with your breathing periodically to ensure that you are keeping it a relaxed, regular pace. Once you've finished, allow yourself a few minutes of stillness to allow the sense of relaxation to settle throughout your body. If you notice any areas of residual tension, try to relax those areas as best you can. When you're ready to move on, you may find that your calm is strengthened by concluding the exercise with three slow, deep breaths, or by slowly counting backwards from five. Feel free to experiment.

Progressive Muscle Relaxation

Progressive muscle relaxation (PMR) is a more systematic, detailed implementation of the relaxation technique. During PMR, you carefully apply the process of tensing and releasing in every major muscle group in the body.

A number of studies suggest that PMR can benefit people with health problems. For example, one study found that PMR relieved anxiety and improved quality of life among cancer patients. Another study showed that PMR reduced blood pressure among people with heart disease. One of the primary benefits appears to be a reduction in the levels of the stress hormone, cortisol.

There are two primary limitations on using PMR for anger management: It is best used when lying down (not always practical), and it requires a fair amount of time (up to thirty minutes or more). That said, PMR is a powerful tool for relaxation and should not be dismissed lightly. It has been success- fully used to help people cope with a range of issues (such as anxiety, insom- nia, stress, and hypertension), as well as cooling down the agitation that accompanies anger. Following is a step-by-step guide for performing PMR.

1. Begin by noticing your breathing, noticing your abdomen rise and fall with each breath (pause after each breath). As your breathing becomes more relaxed and restful, take your awareness up to your face. Then start this process with the muscles in your face.

2. Tense the muscles in your face by making a sour face, like you just ate a lemon; hold that face for four seconds and then release the muscles in your face. Repeat the process two times in various muscle groups throughout the body.

3. Notice the tension just washing away. With each tense-and-release cycle, it becomes easier to release and relax each muscle group. Repeat the

process, except inhale through the nose and exhale through the mouth, relaxing even more with each breath.

4. Move your awareness to the shoulder and neck area. Notice the muscles in the shoulder and neck area. Tense the muscles in the neck by pressing the shoulders toward the ears and holding for a count of four seconds, and then release. With your awareness in the neck and shoulders, tense them again and hold for four seconds, and release. Notice the difference between a tense muscle and a relaxed muscle as you go through the process. Remember to inhale through the nose and exhale through the mouth, releasing any residual tension; it becomes easier and easier to release and relax each muscle group. Repeat the process, relaxing even more with each breath you take.

5. Continue working through your muscle groups: hands, arms, upper back, legs, and feet. Remember to breathe deeply throughout the entire process.

FACT

You can also combine controlled deep breathing and muscle relaxation to help ease tension. Begin by deep breathing for a few minutes, and then commence tightening and relaxing your muscles. Give yourself about fifteen minutes to practice this technique.

Become the "Human Lightning Rod"

The idea behind this technique is to "ground" yourself against the flow of anger. Metaphorically, this approach can be likened to the use of a lightning rod. Just as the conductive metal in a lightning rod offers a low-resistance path that safely redirects electricity into the ground, the "human lightning rod" lets you do a very similar thing with your anger, allowing the energy to harmlessly flow away.

How do you become a human lightning rod? Recall that when you are angry, the tendency is to tense your muscles, shifting you toward a ready-for-action state. Tensing in this way intensifies anger and weakens self-control. With the lighting rod technique, you do the opposite. By deliberately relaxing your muscles as the anger runs through you, you can effectively block your anger from escalating. Instead of moving you closer to the extermination phase, the negative charge of anger finds nowhere to take hold, and gradually dissipates. You may notice that the anger holds on for a while, but as you continue to hold your body in a loose, relaxed state, the dissipation will spread. Use the following steps:

1. Stand straight (not rigid), and allow your arms to dangle loosely.
2. Breathe deeply, using your diaphragm.
3. Relax the muscles in your body. If necessary, first tense your body all at once for a few seconds, and then allow the tension to dissipate.
4. Standing with your muscles relaxed, allow the sensations of anger to gradually fade while breathing deeply and slowly.

Focus on your breathing during this process, slowly breathing in and out to reduce the pace of your agitation. On each exhale, imagine that you are directing any negative energy deeper into the ground.

You can also try yoga for muscle tension. Yoga offers many benefits, including stress reduction, improved fitness, and alleviation of chronic conditions. A recent study looked at the effects of practicing twelve minutes of yoga per day for eight weeks. Participants exhibited a significant decrease in inflammation, an established cause for health problems such as heart disease, depression, rheumatoid arthritis, and diabetes.

Calm Your Face

Calm your face, calm your mind. A number of experiments have looked at what happens when people are forced to furrow their brow. In general, these studies have found that people with furrowed brows generate more negative emotion. For example, in one study, golf tees were taped to each eyebrow, and the subjects were asked to touch them together. The subjects viewed and rated a series of pictures; when their golf-teed brows were furrowed, it was found that they experienced more sadness. Another study simply asked participants to "push their eyebrows together" when viewing pictures. Furrowing the brow increased feelings of anger and disgust, and made them less happy, less agreeable, and less interested. The forehead-furrowing muscle is called the corrugator supercilii. It pulls your eyebrows down and together, causing the forehead to wrinkle. You use this muscle to express displeasure, anger, worry, and other negative emotions. In the same way that your brain notices when your "smile" muscles are flexed, and thinks you must be happy about something, it also notices when your corrugator supercilii is flexed and thinks you must be upset.

What happens when your furrowing muscles are relaxed? Some interesting evidence here comes from research on people who have received cosmetic Botox treatment. Short for botulinum toxin, Botox is a neurotoxin that gets rid of wrinkles by paralyzing certain facial muscles. When that muscle happens to be the corrugator supercilii, it becomes very difficult to create a furrowed brow. People who get this treatment report fewer feelings of anxiety, simply because they can't create the facial expressions associated with negative emotions such as anger or fear.

Applying this information to anger management is simple. When you notice yourself becoming frustrated or angry, take a moment to notice your forehead. Relax it a little and notice how you feel. This very simple method is ideal for times when you can't leave an anger-provoking situation and need something quick to help relax.

Use Humor

Humor is a great antidote for anger. It's awfully difficult to feel angry and silly at the same time. By directly reducing the intensity of angry feelings, laughter can quickly blunt the adverse effects of anger on your mental clarity. You can look at the situation with fresh eyes. Research suggests that humor induces the release of protective hormones that combat the effects of stress. A recent study, for example, was designed so that participants were led to expect that they would be shown a funny video. The researchers found that these participants exhibited reduced levels of stress hormones simply as a result of this anticipation. That is the power of humor.

FACT

Humor helps you in many ways. In the short term, humor can relieve the stress response, soothe tension, and even stimulate your organs. In the long term, humor can improve your immune functioning, relieve pain, increase personal satisfaction, and improve overall mood.

One good and fairly commonsense approach to using humor to relax is to remember a humorous event from your life, either something you experienced directly, or something you saw on television, at the theater, or at a comedy club. If you have experiences that you can draw upon (and certainly most people do), make a mental note of some of the more hilarious moments so that you can quickly draw upon them when you need to calm down.

ALERT

There are two cautions in using humor. First, don't try to just "laugh off" your problems; rather, use humor to help yourself face them constructively. Second, don't give in to harsh, sarcastic humor; that's just another form of unhealthy anger expression.

Don't take yourself too seriously. For example, when you're angry, you almost invariably experience a sense of righteousness and perceive any blocking or changing of your plans as an unbearable indignity that you should not have to suffer. Should you find yourself feeling this way, try picturing yourself as a god or goddess, a supreme ruler, who owns the streets and stores and office space, striding alone and having your way in all situations while others defer to you. The more detail you can get into your imaginary scenes, the more chances you have to realize that maybe you are being unreasonable. You'll also realize how unimportant the things you're angry about really are.

Distraction

Distraction is another effective technique through which you can reassert calm in the face of anger. By giving your mind a new target to focus its attention on—one that does not feed into the escalation of anger—you can gradually regain sufficient clarity of mind with which to more effectively respond to the situation. Distraction can be a good supplement to some of the other techniques presented in this chapter, because it can readily be used in heat-of-the-moment situations when it is not practical to use one of the other techniques, or when you need to slow things down in a hurry.

Distraction is exactly what it sounds like: You deliberately move your attention away from troubling anger cues, and focus instead on something that is emotionally neutral or positive, such as the sounds of passing traffic or the quality of light as it enters through a window. Distracting yourself in this way is of course only a temporary measure, but it can help defuse your anger very quickly. Distraction is not the same thing as avoidance, because you do so with the express intent of calming yourself down so that you can more effectively engage with the other party. Some ideas that you can use to distract yourself from troubling anger include the following:

- Notice details in your immediate environment—sights, sounds, smells, and so on. Allow these details to fully engage your attention.
- Count backward from 1,000 in multiples of 7.
- Focus on your breathing.
- Count things that you can see that begin with a particular letter.
- Visualize yourself in a safe, beautiful, peaceful location (e.g., an alpine meadow). If there is a specific place or memory that has a strong positive emotional resonance for you, visualize that.
- Listen to your favorite music. Try to pick out all the different instruments and sounds that you can hear.
- Engage in vigorous exercise. As the saying goes, "When anger strikes, move a mountain." Run up a hill, swim laps, find a punching bag, do anything physically exerting to help get that tension out of your body. However, it is important how you approach this activity, particularly if

it is something with aggressive connotations, such as punching a bag. Do this not with the intent of "taking your anger out" on something, as that can actually exacerbate an anger problem. Instead, as you exert yourself, imagine that the energy you are expending is drawing the anger out of you.

CHAPTER 8

The 3R Method:
Step 2. Reassess

The second step in the 3R method is to reassess the situation. This is when you turn your attention back to the situation at hand, with an eye toward processing the situation objectively, determining whether you need to take some kind of action, and then deciding what that action should be. Now that you have attained a reasonable level of self-control using relaxation methods, you will be in a much better position to really think about what is happening.

Accept Responsibility

When reassessing an anger-provoking event *as it is happening*, you must accept responsibility for your emotions and behaviors within the narrow boundaries of that particular situation. Once you've regained a sense of calm as part of that first step of relaxing, connecting with this sense of responsibility is a critical next step in terms of effectively handling the situation.

ALERT

People will often find that the stages overlap. A very common point of overlap is reassessing the situation (step 2) while taking a time-out (step 1). As you begin to apply your anger plan to real-life situations, allow yourself the flexibility to modify your approach to meet the unique demands of each situation.

The concept of personal responsibility is sometimes frustrating, especially when you are convinced that you are "right." You may, in fact, be 100 percent right, but that is actually irrelevant. Accept responsibility anyway. It will help you succeed.

It is always easier to blame someone else. When you accept responsibility, you let go of this kind of blaming. While this may be difficult, it is also incredibly empowering. When you take responsibility for your own feelings, you begin to take back your life. You're putting yourself back in the driver's seat. When you blame someone else for your anger, you're stuck. You'll be angry forever unless the other person changes. But when you take responsibility, you are owning your experience.

It is important to be clear about exactly what it is you are accepting responsibility for. You are not accepting responsibility for the other person's choices and feelings. Neither are you necessarily admitting fault regarding the issue at hand. Accepting responsibility does not mean that you "surrender," nor does it mean that you stop advocating on behalf of yourself, your beliefs, or the things that are important to you. What it does mean is that you accept responsibility for your feelings and behaviors. The other person may have cheated and lied to you. You may not like that very much. However, the fact that you don't like it says as much about you as it does about the other person. You can own that, and you can own, completely, responsibility for your behavior in responding to that person.

FACT

Keep in mind that other people's actions can never "make" you feel a certain way. Emotions provide information. Negative emotions, such as anger, provide specific kinds of information; they are souped-up warning indicators.

Generally speaking, your emotions result from whether your needs are being met.

During an interpersonal flare-up, anger results from focusing your attention on what another person "should" or "shouldn't" do and then judging them as "wrong" or "bad." However, as your attention shifts to identifying which of your needs isn't being satisfied in a situation, your feelings will shift as well. When you discover that you didn't receive treatment that met your need for respect, you might feel hurt, or scared, or disappointed—but without thinking in terms of the way others "should" behave and then passing judgment, you won't feel angry. It's your need that wasn't being met. See that—and own it.

When your feelings have served their purpose—when your attention is fully focused on your needs and values—then anger melts away. This transformation is not the same as repression, and it's not the same as "calming down." The emotions you feel when you are in touch with your needs may be intense and painful, but they will be different emotions than anger.

Practice Empathy

A helpful way to neutralize anger is to recognize your anger in others. Recognition, in this sense, means acknowledging aspects of yourself that are apparent in those you are angry with. Being able to recognize that your "adversary" is struggling with difficult emotions that you have also dealt with can be a bridge toward greater empathy. At a very basic level, you are not as different from other people as you imagine. Your emotions are a map of the human condition; the frustrations you experience in life are not dissimilar to frustrations experienced by others. This commonality can be used as a guide for understanding other people and learning to respond to them in a congruent manner.

Be wary of confusing empathy with sympathy; they are not the same. To sympathize with someone is to have compassion, such as feeling bad because someone was hurt. *Empathy* means to understand and connect personally with someone's experience, either because you have experienced it yourself or because you are able to put yourself in the other person's shoes.

When someone lashes out at you, for example, take a step back and see if you can recall being angry about a similar event. Identifying a shared experience can help you understand where that person is coming from. In situations where you see yourself as the aggrieved party, try to view the situation from the other person's perspective. There will be times, without question, when it is clear that the other person had malign intent. More often than not, however, even when the other person is in the wrong, the reality will be that he didn't intend to upset you.

In some cases, you will be able to recognize that the other person's thought process is compromised by the strong emotions that he was experiencing. In such cases, your best course of action will likely be to acknowledge each side's position and then respectfully ask to postpone further discussion until the emotions have cooled down. If you are following the 3R method, you will likely have cooled down considerably by this point, but the other person may need more time. Again, use your best judgment.

Use Compassion

Compassion is an anger management tool that doesn't get nearly enough attention. Practicing compassion doesn't mean you need to like the person you are angry at, to feel sorry for him, or even to nurture him. Instead, you first need to develop compassion for the human experience, in all of its flawed glory. Every person is on his or her own journey, and some are farther along than others. Some are more enlightened, kinder, more self-aware, more disciplined, more thoughtful. Others simply aren't.

You can hope that people are learning from their mistakes, but that may not be the case. Have you ever just seen a miserable person and felt sorry for her spouse? Or can you imagine being that person? You have to put up with her for a time, but she has to live inside herself. You might choose to exclude such a person from your life, and that may be a perfectly sensible decision. But you don't need to marinate in anger toward her. Decide what behaviors you are, and are not, willing to tolerate in others, set your boundaries accordingly, and let go. Let others be on their journey.

For example, if you are angry with someone because you feel as though he is taking advantage of you, rather than being mad at him, you might even feel gratitude for providing the catalyst for your growth. Difficult people and situations are your teachers. Your mistakes are your best teachers.

Having compassion for a person with whom you are angry can be very helpful. Imagine you are driving behind someone who is driving slowly on a two-lane road, leaving a long line of cars trailing along. "What an inconsiderate jerk!" you might think, teeth clenched in annoyance. But when you pass this person, you see that she is elderly, has a disability, or is in some kind of obvious distress. You will probably feel differently about that driver. The more deeply you can understand why something is happening, the easier it becomes to let go of resentment and anger.

ESSENTIAL

Angry people can be very hard on themselves. The more you can find compassion and understanding for your own foibles, the easier it will be to practice with others.

Of course, connecting with a sense of compassion is most difficult when you have good evidence that the other party is deliberately provoking you, or is being maliciously disrespectful. If you find yourself struggling here, try something like this: "Her arrogance is likely to catch up with her sooner or later, and it won't be pretty." You can have compassion for the difficulties in her life, and whatever obstacles might be created by those difficulties, knowing that they are not yours. Alternatively, you can pause to consider the circumstances that would lead someone to act in this manner.

Remember happy, well-adjusted people do not upset others simply for the sake of causing harm or to amuse themselves. Happy people are quite friendly, while unhappy people are often the most difficult people to get along with. If you encounter someone who is behaving aversively, you can pretty much bank on the fact that you are dealing with someone who is troubled or unhappy, who may very well have had a very difficult life, and who is, at minimum, not exactly enjoying the best of days. Understanding this can help you generate compassion under even the most trying conditions. At the very least, it can go a long way toward enabling you to detach from the other person's actions so that they don't feel quite so personal. From that vantage, it is quite a bit easier to come to terms with the situation for what it is, and ultimately to move on without any lingering rancor.

Reality Testing

Angry people make snap decisions. They then focus on their feelings and immediate reactions to the exclusion of anything else, heightening their feelings of anger. This is the classic pitfall of not being able to see the forest for the trees. Avoid this trap. You are in a much better position to manage your anger if you can take a step back from your knee-jerk thoughts and feelings. Reality testing helps you do this.

To apply reality testing effectively, you have to give up the assumption that your first impressions of a situation are always accurate. More often than you may realize, you base your reactions on partial truths, half-truths, qualified truths, and outright distortions. You see only one side—yours. In reality testing, you don't have to completely reject these initial assumptions, but you do need to step far enough away from them so that you can survey the bigger picture. Even when your initial interpretations are spot on, there's a good chance you have overlooked considerations that are relevant to the matter at hand.

Remind yourself that your first impulse to be angry might turn out to be as misguided as your ancestors' belief in a flat Earth. You need to stop and gather more complete evidence before passing judgment and setting upon a course of action. This is the essence of reality testing.

FACT

> Sigmund Freud originally defined reality testing as the individual's ability to distinguish between what is occurring in his mind and what is occurring in the outside world. When angry, people are far more likely to misperceive the intentions of others.

Look Clearly at What Happened

Have you ever asked someone what she is angry about? More than likely, she told you all about the terrible things that someone else said or did. Here is an example of a business professional reacting to a colleague: "He doesn't take anything seriously! He wrecked the sales pitch! His lack of professionalism was inexcusable." These statements appear to be informative but actually say little about what happened.

In contrast, to look clearly at the situation, you must adopt the cool objectivity of a detective. "Just the facts, please." This emphasis produces very different kinds of information, even when referring to the same incident. For example, the professional in the earlier example might have said instead: "He walked in ten minutes after the meeting started. He visibly struggled to answer the client's questions, even though he had been asked to prepare for this. He also brought the wrong slides for his part of the presentation." This is an objective description of what happened.

When you are angered, look clearly at what you are reacting to. Ask yourself, "What would a video camera have recorded?" Doing so will allow you to separate facts from interpretations. When you can objectively describe what happened, you are more likely to be clear about your own needs. You will also be in a much better position to appreciate other perspectives and concerns. Other people will be less likely to respond defensively, because they can more easily agree with what you've said.

Examine Your Angry Thoughts

How you view a situation is one of the most powerful determinants of your emotional reaction to it. The ability of thinking to shape emotional reactions cannot be underestimated.

If someone cuts you off on the freeway and you imagine that they are in some sort of emergency, you may respond by feeling concern or compassion. But if you believe they cut you off out of sheer rudeness and disrespect, you will be more likely to respond with anger and aggression. The situations are identical; the difference here is in your interpretation. For people struggling with anger issues, the pronounced tendency is to interpret events in a negative manner, thus "seeing" hostile intentions in others that might not actually be there at all. This feeds directly into the aggression cycle. How biased are your perceptions?

The first thoughts that come into your mind when you are angry are likely to be impressionistic, judgmental, and overly harsh. When you react to these incomplete impressions, you are in danger of making a bad situation worse. Carefully reflect on your initial thoughts and assumptions in light of your "just the facts" description of what actually happened. Are your assumptions reasonable? Are you reading something into the other person's intentions or motivations? Have you overreacted in some way? Do you have all the information you need to make a firm judgment?

FACT

Angry people make a number of characteristic logical errors. One of the most common is black-and-white thinking; there is no middle ground—everything is either good or bad. "I'm right and you are wrong." "You always let me down." Such thoughts are invariably untrue, but they directly contribute to the escalation of anger.

Learn to recognize the types of situations that trigger you, and the types of characteristic angry thoughts that tend to occur when you are faced with those triggers. Retrain yourself to think logically about provocative situations that would otherwise be guided by your automatic (and sometimes ill-informed) emotional reactions. For now, here are some basic, helpful ways to think differently during a bout of anger:

1. Identify any triggers that may have been activated.
2. Take control of the way you talk to yourself. Instead of allowing negative self-talk to dominate your thoughts, work to generate positive, rational responses. Thus, if a self-pitying "everyone is busy besides me" pops into your head, you might respond by saying to yourself, "I wish I was busier than I am, but I'm going to use this extra time productively. I'm going to make it count."
3. Keep a sense of perspective. Things will not always go your way, but that's an inevitable part of life—it's not always someone's "fault." However bad things might seem, the world is not out to get you.
4. Be realistic. If your expectations are unreasonable, you are almost guaranteed to experience frustration.
5. One of the most important guidelines: choose your battles thoughtfully. You cannot always get what you want. Not everything is worth fighting for. Step back from the situation and think about what will really be important next week, next month, or next year.
6. Stop believing that life must be fair. It's a cliché, but that does not make it any less true. Life is not fair. Feeling that it should be sets you up for resentment and rage.
7. Be flexible in your thinking. Suppose the irritating person can't be stopped or avoided, such as a cantankerous boss. You can try to attribute the irritating behavior to new, more acceptable causes. For example, you might assume that your boss is under great pressure or is acting out her own issues (i.e., it's not personal). Be prepared to give the other person the benefit of the doubt. Or, assuming you have been angered by a situational irritant, such as realizing that you left your cell phone at home, remind yourself that becoming upset only makes the situation worse. It's bad enough that you have to turn around to get your phone. Having to do so while angry only makes the situation that much more unpleasant.

Key Questions to Ask Yourself

In the context of evaluating your thoughts about an anger-provoking situation, there are four key questions to ask yourself:

1. Is the situation or event that triggered my anger important? That is, is the thing that triggered my rage something that threatens my well-being?
2. Is my anger appropriate, given the facts of what happened? Faced with the same circumstances, would the average person get angry?
3. Is the situation modifiable? Is there something I can do to change it for the better?
4. Is it worth it to try to modify the situation? That is, is it worth my time and effort?

You will often answer no to at least one of these questions. In that case, this is a good indication that you would be better off letting go. If you find that you are still struggling to release any residual anger, use one of your relaxation techniques to further dissipate this energy while reminding yourself that what happened is not really all that important.

If you answer yes to each of these questions, then you need to think carefully about how best to act. Before doing anything, spend some time brainstorming possible responses. This simple approach can go a long way toward restoring your tranquility. When you answer the four questions and either distract yourself or take constructive action, you no longer feel quite as helpless about the situation. You're taking control. This can be a very powerful way to reduce the anger you feel.

Focus on Opposite Emotions

Think of how fire is extinguished by water, an "opposite" element. The idea of focusing on opposite emotions is similar: You work to extinguish the fires of rage by introducing an opposite emotion. When you experience an impulse to behave angrily, the idea is simple: Focus instead on opening yourself up to opposite emotions such as peace, joy, and love.

To do this effectively, you must be specific. Focusing on the opposite emotion in a very general way, such as, "I'm going to connect with the experience of love," sounds nice, but it is too abstract to be helpful. Instead, think of a poignant experience from your life when you actually experienced that emotion: the day you married your spouse, the birth of your child, the support your friends gave you when you were in the hospital. In other words, use your memories. Even if you are skeptical that you can actually "feel" an opposite emotion in the midst of rage, try to remember the experience of that opposite emotion as vividly as possible.

People often feel like they have little to no control over their emotions. However, with opposite emotions, you are deliberately choosing to open yourself up to a certain kind of emotional experience—one that is at odds with the here and now. Shifting toward a different emotion is not a simple technique that you can expect to do at the drop of a hat, but with practice you will get better at, shifting with greater and greater ease. Do not confuse the technique of focusing on opposite emotions with the suppressive and repressive emotional-regulation strategies used by people with an avoidant anger style. Your emotions are a genuine, honest expression of how you feel at any moment; do not deny the legitimacy of these feelings. Instead, acknowledge whatever angry feelings you are experiencing, face them honestly, and then step back so that you can open yourself up to experiencing more positive feelings that can help you to put your anger in its proper context.

Use Anger As Impetus to Change

If you are angry about something in the world, in your work or relationships, or in your lifestyle, consider using your anger as an impetus to change. The anger is telling you *something*. In these kinds of situations, the anger can be likened to a giant neon arrow pointing you toward the fact that there is a real problem that requires your attention. Address this problem. Doing so—in fact, even the act of *deciding* that you will do so—goes a long way toward cooling the anger and instilling a sense of personal control. The energy that anger provides can ignite the furnace of positive action, as well as negative action. Anger is a very powerful motivator. Being able to redirect your agitation in this way, where it serves as a catalyst for constructive action, is one of the hallmarks of healthy anger.

ESSENTIAL

To make good use of anger, shift the focus of your anger from external circumstances to what it is you desire to change within yourself. Then, once you commit to making the change, be careful to release your anger by shifting your focus away from what is missing in your life (evoking anger) to what you want to positively create (inspiring passion).

CHAPTER 9

The 3R Method:
Step 3. Respond

The respond step is when the rubber hits the road. This is when (gulp) you re-engage with the other party for the sake of talking through, troubleshooting, and otherwise resolving the conflict. It is the culmination of all the work done in the previous two steps.

It is possible to structure the respond step in a rigid manner, but there are such a wide variety of situations that can be encountered when responding to an anger-provoking event that the best way to approach this effort is in terms of general principles that can be broadly adaptable. By combining various strategies such as talking it out, taking action, engaging with the other party, listening actively to what she has to say, and expressing yourself in an assertive, respectful manner, you should, with practice, be able to resolve the majority of interpersonal conflicts.

Talking It Out Helps

After you've had an opportunity to relax and reassess the situation, you might still be unsure how best to proceed. In these cases, sometimes the best response is to consult a trusted friend, colleague, or family member, or someone who was there to witness the events unfold. What do they think happened? How do they think the problem was caused? What suggestions could they offer? You might be surprised.

If you believe that a particular person has wronged you, for example, and other people see the situation in the same way, you have good reason to feel more justified in feeling angry than if other people see the situation very differently. Often, it's something of a mixed bag: Other people will validate aspects of your position while calling attention to other relevant matters you might not have considered. Their input can help you appreciate more of the complexity of the situation.

Hearing honest feedback from others can be a great way to understand and change your emotional responses. Indeed, sometimes the people around you will be better at recognizing your characteristic emotional responses than you are, provided you're willing to ask them. Just be careful not to go overboard. Rehashing your anger with more than a couple of people can actually reinforce your angry feelings, making them more intense rather than less.

Take Action

In step 2, reassessing an angry situation, anger was discussed as an impetus for making positive change. *Taking action* is the behavioral expression of this impetus; it's when you actually begin to implement the changes you've decided upon. Perhaps you've recognized that you have some very powerful anger triggers, based on earlier experiences, that need to be resolved. Perhaps you've realized that you're in a bad relationship that has led you to compromise your values and sense of self-respect. Perhaps you've realized that your struggles with anger reflect an underlying dissatisfaction with your career progress. So, what are you going to *do* about it? You may have generated some idea when you were reassigning your anger. Thinking and planning is great, but it only gets you so far. Now is the time to take action. More than likely, your guardian angel isn't going to swoop in and make this change for you. So you have to take control. Even one small step in the direction of meaningful growth and change can be incredibly empowering. It is only by taking these steps that you begin to create a sense of positive momentum in your life.

Engaging with the Other Party

If you choose to respond by engaging (or re-engaging) with the other party, what is the best way to initiate this conversation? There are no hard-and-fast rules, but there are a few basic things to remember. First, as much as possible, be sure you can maintain a reasonable level of calm and self-control during the interaction. Second, politely express to the other person that you would like to talk about what happened and then *ask* if they would be willing to do so. Be especially mindful of your approach. Adopt a calm demeanor, a measured tone of voice, and avoid any gestures, facial expressions, or body language that might be perceived as aggressive, provocative, condescending, or arrogant.

Third, do not assume that the other person will be ready to talk to you just because you now feel ready to talk. Don't play guessing games; *ask* the other person if he would be willing to talk to you, and be prepared if he says no. This is a valid and acceptable response in most cases. Should the other person decline your invitation (or worse, should he do so rudely), this is not a reason to get upset or act out. *No* can mean many things, but, more than likely, it can be interpreted to mean that the other person is not yet at a place emotionally where he can discuss the situation with you in a constructive manner. If the other person feels that way, there's an awfully good chance that he's right. Pressuring him further under these conditions will only produce resentment (in him) and frustration (in you). He may even feel disrespected, which would represent a worsening of the situation, rather than movement in the direction of resolution (which is ostensibly what you want).

You might politely phrase the request a second time—e.g., "Look, I know you're really upset with me, but I've had some time to think about what happened and I really think we can resolve this mess if we just talk about it"—but after that, it's important to acquiesce to the other person's wishes. Conversation is like a dance, and you all know "it takes two to tango." If the other person doesn't feel ready to hit the dance floor with you, give him time. Let him know that you respect his choice, but also emphasize the fact that you would very much like to discuss the situation later on when he feels ready. At that point, you can agree to speak at a later time, or let him know that you will check in later to see if his feelings have changed.

Active Listening

Once you've made your initial approach and the other person has agreed to speak to you, invite him to express (or re-express) his position. Do this *before* articulating your needs, concerns, and perspectives.

Giving the other person the floor, and then really *listening* to what he has to say can be quite challenging. It runs against the grain of your sense of being in the right. However, it is a very important step, one that helps you better understand the other person's point of view, and helps you communicate and problem-solve more effectively. For now, it is important simply to recognize that listening to what the other party has to say is an essential part of resolving almost any significant interpersonal conflict.

Speak Assertively

Assertiveness was earlier presented in terms of the assertive anger style, in which people are able to express and stand up for their feelings while showing respect and concern for their "opponent." This is precisely the right kind of approach and attitude to adopt. For one reason, it demonstrates a healthy respect both for yourself and for whomever you happen to be speaking to. Another good reason to adopt this communication style is more practical: It's a good idea to speak assertively, because assertive communication is by far the most *effective* approach for achieving real, meaningful, and satisfactory results. Assertive communication is a large and important topic area in terms of anger management.

Guard Against Escalation

When you are angry, the temptation to engage in overkill, or to hurt the other person, can be very strong. Be wary of this. Words and actions can be hard to take back. There are at least two significant problems with excessive retaliation. First, it invites the other person to attack back just as hard. Second, it increases the likelihood that you will think of the other person more negatively in the future, as you now have a vested interest in convincing yourself that she "deserved" the punishment you meted out. Violence breeds violence. The net result is an increased level of hostility, and a fading hope of peaceful resolution. In contrast, evidence suggests that moderate retaliatory behaviors that are proportionately modulated to the other person's behavior is associated with more satisfaction and less regret. Instead of trying to "trump" or "outdo" the other person's provocations, work to moderate your responses. Even better, if you can see that she is trapped in a hostile mindset, allow her to have the last word until she's cooled down. You'll probably have a much better outcome simply by waiting.

Avoid Coercive Behaviors

Coercive anger processes were first introduced in terms of family dynamics, but such processes can emerge in any human relationship. Coercive processes are a particular manifestation of a much larger truth: You train people how to behave toward you (whether you realize it or not).

Coercive processes occur when each party in a relationship reinforces maladaptive behaviors in the other. This dynamic is most likely to emerge in a relationship where one party is more aggressive (the "aggressor") and the other is more passive (the "victim"). If the aggressor gets what he wants by making demands, threatening, yelling, being nasty, and so on, his hostile behavior is being positively reinforced by the other person. By giving into demands that were expressed in an aggressive way, the victim unwittingly rewards this aggressive behavior, which encourages continued aggressive behavior in the future.

Reinforcement runs the other way as well. Being on the receiving end of aggressive demands is unpleasant. By giving in to those demands, the victim finds that the unpleasant aggressive behavior is withdrawn by the other party, which has the effect of encouraging the act of giving in (it is more likely to occur in the future). In this way, dominant-submissive or abusive relationships can be maintained for long periods.

Be mindful of this kind of trap. When speaking to the other party, refuse to engage in or tolerate intimidating behaviors. It can be tempting to use aggressive behaviors to get your way, especially when you've had success with this tactic. But doing so will only increase the probability that you will become angry again in the future. Remind yourself that while behaving aggressively might feel really good in the moment, the long-term costs just aren't worth it. The greatest proof of strength in the midst of an angry encounter isn't lashing out at the other person, but being able to control yourself.

Nor should you yield to angry or disrespectful demands from the other person. Doing so will encourage him to behave this way again in the future. If the other person is acting intimidating, disrespectful, or bullying, this behavior needs to be confronted in a calm but firm manner. Explain that you would like to continue discussing the issue at hand, but that intimidation and abuse are not acceptable—this kind of behavior is hurtful, and it is a major impediment to real communication. If the behavior persists, consider postponing further conversation until the other person has calmed down. It is important to establish clear boundaries regarding how you expect to be treated. When you fail to confront mistreatment, you become an accomplice to your own abuse.

Reward Yourself

Write rewards for yourself into your anger contract each time you successfully do the things you said you'd do. The reward you choose should be simple and reasonably healthy—something you won't mind going without if you have a setback in working your program, but nevertheless something you want, are willing to work for, and can feel good about enjoying when you succeed. For example, you might reward yourself with a small portion of your favorite food, or a small donation to your favorite charity. Small, frequent rewards are more useful than infrequent, larger rewards.

Handling Setbacks

In the real world, behavior change is rarely a linear process of one positive improvement after the next. Hiccups, setbacks, and relapses are an expected part of the process. As you work on overcoming your anger problem, it is likely you will experience times when you revert to earlier anger habits. You may become inappropriately angry, belligerent, or passive-aggressive.

When this happens, the most important thing you can do is keep going; refuse to give up or be discouraged. Do not let a lapse turn into an excuse for quitting your anger plan, or for forgetting what you have learned. Instead, treat a setback as a learning experience. Examine your lapse carefully so that you can learn how it occurred. Then use this information so that you can do better next time.

For instance, if you encountered an anger trigger, and your strategies for handling that trigger didn't work, make a note of that. Think about what you could do differently next time so that a similar lapse won't occur again. If some new thing has succeeded in triggering your anger, it is time to add that new thing to your list of triggers and to include it into your anger plan. Planning in advance how you can anticipate and avoid these kinds of problems will go a long way toward preventing them in the future.

CHAPTER 10

Communication and Assertiveness

Communication skills are very important. For people struggling with issues related to unhealthy anger, good communication skills can make a decisive difference. Effective listening and assertive communication enable a person to express himself or herself better, to resolve difficult interpersonal issues, and to dissipate anger before it becomes a problem.

Anger and Communication

Angry people are poor communicators. Very often, their attempts at sharing their thoughts, making requests, and problem-solving hurt themselves and those around them. They frequently attribute their anger problems to the fact that they "just don't communicate very well." The reasons for such a problem are rarely this simple, but there is little doubt that a poor communication style can result from and contribute to ongoing anger management issues.

The most common type of poor communication takes the form of the aggressive anger style, in which the person becomes explosive and lashes out. Angry people tend to say whatever comes to mind; they may even argue that being "brutally honest" is the best way to live. They are not interested in being "polite" or "kind," which are characteristics they associate with weakness. They don't particularly care how their communication affects other people. Despite these tendencies, they still often react with surprise, indignation, and emotional pain when others pull away, which is usually the end result of this type of behavior. It is ultimately a self-defeating pattern.

Passive-Aggressive and Avoidant Expression

Angry people may also express themselves in a passive-aggressive manner. They may hurt others by responding in sarcastic or indirect ways. They are able to communicate their angry feelings, but they have difficulty facing these feelings directly and will often deny their existence ("Me? Upset? I'm not upset!"). Their reluctance to publicly acknowledge and directly address their angry feelings creates many relationship problems. Tensions build and build, and there is never any resolution.

Some anger problems are manifested in a complete absence of communication or of acknowledging underlying feelings. People with an avoidant anger style tend to "clam up," saying nothing at all. Even when their needs are being directly violated, they will often avoid responding. Instead, they "bottle up" their feelings and tell themselves that everything is okay. As a result, they carry around the constant resentment and frustration that comes from "stuffing" negative emotions, with a very real risk of developing other kinds of psychological problems such as clinical depression.

After more than twenty years of research, Dr. John Gottman of the University of Washington, a foremost expert on couples studies, concluded that the single, best predictor of divorce is when one or both partners show contempt in the relationship.

Active Listening

The foundation for effective communication is listening. You have a pretty good idea what your thoughts, feelings, and preferences are at any given moment, but if you're having a conversation and are genuinely interested in exchanging ideas, the only way to gauge where the other person stands, or to reach some kind of agreement, is by understanding his or her thoughts and feelings as well. Unless you have the unique ability to read minds, the way to develop that understanding is through listening and observation.

The reality, however, is that most of us are bad listeners. It's even worse when you're angry, which is one of those times when good listening skills could help the most. Active listening implies more than just hearing the words being spoken. It implies that you are actively trying to understand what the other person is experiencing and where she is coming from.

This kind of engaged or active listening can be hard. When you're angry, or even just emotionally invested in a certain point of view, you tend to feel as if what you want is sacred, whereas the other person's desires are irrelevant. Your wants loom large as other people's concerns shrink to relative insignificance. You listen halfheartedly at best. As the person prattles on, you are in your own head, "half-listening, half-thinking," and feverishly planning your next retort or verbal zinger.

Resist the temptation to do this. *Really* listen to the other person. Listen to understand her perspective, not to tell her what's wrong with her viewpoint. Adopt a mindset of curiosity and interest. Ask clarifying questions. Show interest. After all, no matter how strongly you may be convinced of the other party's "wrongness," and no matter how muddled or distorted you believe the other person's perspective to be, it is always worthwhile to understand how she thinks about the situation. The more you grasp the other person's understanding and concerns, the better position you will be in to respond appropriately and to express your own viewpoint in a manner that she can relate to as well.

ESSENTIAL

When people communicate, especially when they're angry, the tendency is to focus on what *they* wish to express. However, experts agree that actively listening to what the other party is trying to express—through words, tone of voice, and body language—is the most essential first step in effective problem-solving and communication.

Moreover, even if you are convinced that you've fully grasped the other person's position, this kind of listening can still be beneficial from the perspective of demonstrating basic respect, civility, and good will. Showing this behavior to the other person is like holding out an olive branch. It can have the effect of disarming your opponent to the point where she will be more receptive to what you have to say. Further, if you truly do listen well enough to understand the other person's perspective, you will have a much greater chance of getting what you want. Ask any skilled salesperson. The more a salesperson understands her customer's concerns, the more she will be able to present her "pitch" in a persuasive and compelling manner.

Empathy Responding

Empathy means understanding what another person is experiencing; it is one of the more important skills you will ever acquire. *Empathy responding*, as the phrase implies, is a component of empathy, which means responding to what someone said in a way that demonstrates your understanding, interest, and concern. You connect with other people empathically first by listening to what they have to say, then by using empathy responding to offer clarifying statements and questions, and finally by using your own experiences as a vehicle to relate to what the other person is communicating. In fact, empathy responding is a key component of active listening. It is listening with such focus and intensity that you connect directly with the other person's thoughts, feelings. You are sharing in their experience.

Empathy responding can be useful in a number of ways. One obvious benefit is clarity. If your response shows a misunderstanding of the other person's position, this gives her an opportunity to clarify herself. Another benefit is de-escalation. Empathy responding demonstrates respect and consideration, interest and openness. These qualities help to defuse anger. They support increased closeness and trust, inviting the other person to open up and to explore deeper issues. Further, by helping you better understand the other person, empathy responding helps reduce your level of anger. There is real truth to the notion that "to understand is to forgive."

Reflective Responses

Reflective empathy responses, or *reflections*, capture the gist of what the other person is expressing. Reflections restate or paraphrase the speaker's feelings and words. Reflecting does not involve asking questions, introducing a new topic, or leading the conversation in another direction.

Reflections allow the speaker to "hear" his own thoughts and focus on what he says and feels. They show the speaker that you are trying to perceive the world as he sees it and that you are doing your best to understand his messages. Reflections help defuse angry feelings, build a sense of connection between speaker and listener, and encourage the speaker to continue expressing himself in an open and constructive manner.

Reflections can be a mirroring or rephrasing of the speaker's words:

- **Speaker:** "I am stunned right now that she would have done this again!"
- **Listener:** "You didn't see this one coming."

- **Speaker:** "I expected you back from your trip yesterday morning. I made plans for us. I was really looking forward to going out together. I can't believe you did not let me know you'd been delayed."
- **Listener:** "I'm so sorry, I can see that you're disappointed that I didn't get back yesterday. You missed me."

An important type of reflecting is *emotional reflecting*—mirroring back the speaker's emotions as she makes her statements. Tuning into the speaker's emotions is an important communication skill that many people lack. If you, as the listener, miss the feeling content that is being expressed to you, you will have missed a major part of the speaker's communication. Here is an example of reflected emotion:

- **Speaker:** "She trashed my apartment last night! Stuff was everywhere!"
- **Listener:** "You're ticked off!"

In many cases, you will have the choice of reflecting either the speaker's words or emotions. Both types of reflection are important and should be used interchangeably. The key advantage is that emotional reflection allows the listener to connect with a deeper level of the speaker's experience. Here's another example:

- **Speaker** (eyes downcast, sad facial expression): "I guess she found someone else. It had to happen eventually, right? Just didn't expect it to happen so fast."
- **Listener (reflecting words):** "She's moved on already."
- **Listener (reflecting feelings):** "You're hurt that she's moved on so quickly."

Reflection, Validation, and Understanding

Just as a mirror reflects an image, the listener verbally reflects the speaker's words and feelings in a way that lets the speaker know that the message sent was the message received. This *validates* the speaker's experience, which is an effective way to defuse angry feelings, build (or re-establish) rapport, and increase closeness. To be clear, validation is about acceptance and understanding. It is not about agreement. For example, you might disagree completely with a friend's assertion that you are very critical. At the same time, you can recognize that his perception (right or wrong) is a genuine experience, with real feelings attached to it. Reflecting this back to your friend demonstrates your attentiveness and concern; it is a fundamental display of respect. This technique softens the other person's position, helping him open up more, and creating a space where he will be better able to listen to your perspective and consider alternative points of view.

ALERT

As well as reflecting the speaker's verbal messages, it is important to recognize the other person's emotions. Accurately gauging someone's emotional state allows you to better understand and respond, particularly during a heated exchange. Use reflection to help build greater understanding not only of what is being said, but also of the content, feeling, and meaning of messages.

Reflecting is difficult to learn but well worth the time and effort. It pays off big-time in developing solid connections between partners, but it also works well in other situations. Often when couples learn this skill, one or both will report back that reflecting was effective in a situation at work, with one of their children, or with a friend. In addition to fostering trust and openness, reflection is a great way to check your understanding by giving the speaker an opportunity to clarify his or her meaning. For example:

- **Speaker:** "I've had it up to here with you being late all the time. I've told you before, and you agreed with me, and yet you keep doing it. Enough already. This is unacceptable. You knew that was an important business dinner, and you completely embarrassed me!"
- **Listener:** "You're mad because you were embarrassed."
- **Speaker:** "Yes, I am. I didn't appreciate that at all. But mainly I'm pissed because it keeps happening. It'd be completely different if this was an isolated incident."
- **Listener:** "The fact that it keeps happening makes it feel worse."
- **Speaker:** "Yes. Exactly."

Reflection can also help the speaker understand herself better:

- **Speaker:** "I wish I could be full of energy again and wake up in the morning longing to jump out of bed."
- **Listener:** "You mean you want to be more physically fit?"

- **Speaker:** "Yes. Well no, in a way. I want that, sure. But now that I think about it, I think it's more about motivation. I just want to have the motivation to do things."

Finally, there is the concept of *summative reflections*. This reflective response is designed to recap the major themes of the conversation and comes after an extended period of conversation. During the course of a conversation, bits of useless information can accrue. The summation helps the speaker sort through the litter and construct a more complete and compact conceptualization of the issue being discussed.

Assertiveness

Angry people tend to have distinct communication postures, which can be summarized in terms of the four anger styles and their core themes:

- The aggressive anger style says, "I count, but you don't count."
- The avoidant anger style says, "I don't count."
- The passive-aggressive anger style says, "I count. You don't count, but I'm not going to tell you about it."
- The assertive anger style says, "I count and you do, too."

Angry people tend to use the aggressive and passive-aggressive postures a great deal. Aggressive communicators are more likely to start an argument than they are to achieve the results they want; however, being avoidant in interactions is also a mistake, because it communicates weakness and tends to invite further aggression.

The assertive anger style is by far the most useful and balanced style; it is the only posture that communicates respect for all parties. Insist on being treated fairly; you have every right to stand up for your rights and interests. Assertive communication allows you to stand up for yourself without violating the rights of others. In other words, you can tactfully, justly, and firmly express your preferences, needs, opinions, and feelings. Assertiveness is also a highly pragmatic style of communication, since it is the most likely way to ensure that everyone's needs are met. Learning how to become assertive rather than aggressive, passive-aggressive, or avoidant is an important step in discovering how to communicate appropriately with others.

How to Practice Assertiveness

People who are habitually aggressive tend to misunderstand what it means to be assertive. Specifically, they confuse assertiveness with aggression and think they are acting assertively. Although both aggressive and assertive postures can involve fierce and persuasive communication, they are fundamentally different. Aggressive communication tends to go on the offense by attacking and berating the other person, whereas assertive communication uses anger and ferocity only in defense.

FACT

Developing assertive communication skills will benefit many areas of your life. Assertive people tend to have fewer interpersonal conflicts, which translates into much less stress. They get their needs met (which also means less frustration over unmet needs), and they help others get their needs met as well.

Assertive people stand up for themselves and their rights, and they manage to do it without becoming aggressive; they do not attack the person they are communicating with unnecessarily. Assertiveness is "anger in self-defense"; aggressiveness is "anger because I feel like it."

The good thing about assertiveness is that it reinforces itself. Demonstrating assertiveness by voicing your complaints effectively will generalize to other areas of your life and allow you to feel more assertive in those domains as well.

Here are a few quick pointers to get you started:

1. **Think things through beforehand.** Think about what you want to achieve and make sure to express that to the person who can give you what you want. Often, this will be obvious; you address the person you are angry with (or who is angry with you, in turn). In some situations, though, you will need to think this through a bit more. For example, if you're

dissatisfied with the service in a restaurant, you will often get better results by speaking to the manager, not the cashier or the wait staff.

2. **Get in touch with your emotions.** In particular, ask yourself, "What is my primary emotional response to this situation?" Even though you might feel incredibly angry, there is a very good chance that anger is not the primary emotional response you are having. Anger is often defensive, functioning as a secondary emotion, especially when the underlying primary emotions have a vulnerable quality, such as hurt, fear, or disappointment. Look beneath or alongside the anger—is anything else there?

3. **Be calm and respectful.** Express yourself as calmly as possible, without anger or attitude. The more calmly you can express your position, the better the other person will be able to listen and respond to the substance of your concerns. Be brief but specific, and give relevant details.

4. **Take responsibility.** If you can identify any of your behaviors that contributed to the situation, even if indirectly or to a small degree, take the initiative in accepting responsibility. Doing so is a powerful demonstration of good faith. It shows the other person that you are sincerely interested in resolving the issue constructively, rather than simply attacking. This, in turn, increases the other person's motivation to hear you out in full.

5. **Be concrete and objective.** Describe the troublesome situation as you see it. Be specific about time and actions. Don't make general accusations such as "you're always hostile . . . upset . . . busy." People often don't know how to respond to very general statements and are more likely to feel defensive. Be objective; don't suggest the other person is a total jerk. Focus on his or her behavior, not on apparent motives.

6. **Be clear about what you want.** Many people neglect to state what the other person can do to make them feel better about the situation. Instead, they often focus on what they *don't* want. It's much easier for others to respond to your complaint when they know what you want.

7. **Use "I" statements.** The logic of using "I" statements is to express yourself in terms of your own subjective experience, rather than making hard assertions about objective reality. Thus, instead of telling your spouse, "You never have time for me!" you might say instead, "*I feel* like you never have time for me." Rather than saying things are this way or that way, you instead express your perspective in terms of how you feel. This might

seem almost trivial, but the difference in how these approaches impact other people can be huge. The first statement is sweeping in scope, and is likely to produce a defensive or angry response. The second statement is heavily qualified, speaking only in terms of your subjective experience; the other party is much more likely to respond constructively.

8. **Use straight talk.** When angered, people often avoid expressing primary emotions that have a vulnerable quality, such as hurt. Instead, they express anger as a secondary, defensive emotion in order not to feel vulnerable. For example, instead of telling your spouse that you felt hurt and embarrassed (the primary emotions) when he teased you in front of his friends, you might instead exhibit anger. These kinds of responses escalate anger and evoke defensiveness in the other person.

They also obscure core issues (you felt hurt). In contrast, speak from the heart, offering genuine emotional transparency. Be willing to share real, primary feelings. Emotionally transparent requests that share the true reasons for the request are far more likely to motivate the listener to act than accusatory requests.

How to Assertively Respond to Criticism

There are various ways of reacting when you are criticized. You may become angry and indignant, seeking to punish the other person. This is an aggressive response, communicating a message of "I count, you don't." You may respond very little, even seeming to accept the criticism, only to retaliate later by avoiding the other person, gossiping about him, or engaging in covert activities intended to harm or annoy. This is an "I count and you don't, but I'm not going to tell you" style. You may feel intimidated, frightened, or guilty, readily accepting blame even when it is undeserved. This kind of reaction is consistent with a "You count, I don't" perspective.

As an alternative to these kinds of reactions, you have the option of adopting an assertive approach that embodies an equitable "we both count equally" perspective:

1. Take ownership. If the criticism is true, acknowledge that. Excuses, evasions, and reactive counterattacks make you look weak, and they only

complicate the situation further. It is okay to explain yourself, but start by accepting personal responsibility wherever that is appropriate.

2. Look for common ground. Even if you find little in the criticism that you find credible, try to find something, however small, that you can agree with. Gestures like this are very meaningful, because they communicate to the other person that you aren't just out to oppose her, but are instead making a genuine effort to look at your possible mistakes.

3. Make good use of active listening and empathy responding.

Angry interpersonal interactions are rarely one-sided; each person has a point of view, with unique feelings, concerns, and desires that they want to express. It is important for both sides to be able to take as well as they give— to be able to respond to criticism by looking in the mirror instead of balling up a fist. Responding constructively to criticism is difficult for most people. Be the one to set the tone.

ALERT

Assertiveness is a powerful asset, but there will be times when disagreements cannot be resolved. If that is the case, your best option might be to move on politely, saying, "That's certainly something to think about going forward, and I appreciate the feedback." This presents you as someone genuinely trying to do the best job possible and places the focus on future interactions.

The Complaint Sandwich

The complaint sandwich is a clever, effective technique, developed by psychologist Guy Winch, author of *The Squeaky Wheel*, for voicing complaints and requests in an assertive manner. The primary strength of this approach is that it is designed to circumvent defensiveness and anger in the other person.

The complaint sandwich starts with an "ear-opener"—a statement that is complimentary, conciliatory, or in some way "positive." The ear-opener is intended to help the listener become more sympathetic and open to what you have to say. This is followed by "the meat," which is your actual request or complaint to the other person. Finally, there is the "digestive," or words designed to increase the listener's motivation to help you.

For example: "You are one of my best friends in the whole world—we've been through a lot together, and you've always stood by me. Yesterday, when you criticized me in front of the entire dinner party, I was caught off-guard and felt embarrassed. In the future, could you please address those kinds of issues with me in private? That would mean a lot. You have great insights, and I very much value your honest feedback."

Practicing your assertiveness by complaining effectively is easier than you might think. You'll feel better about yourself by taking this kind of approach. You'll also increase trust and closeness in the other person. With assertiveness, it is always a "win-win" mindset.

CHAPTER 11

Why People Remain Trapped in Anger

Sometimes anger can be very difficult to relinquish. You may find that even the most fervent application of relaxation and reassessment strategies is only somewhat helpful when it comes to cooling intense anger symptoms. Or you may find that anger control strategies are helpful in coping with the *symptoms* of anger—that is, cooling down once anger has been provoked—but less beneficial in *preventing* you the anger in the first place. And that can be a problem. When you find that your anger habit is especially hard to break, you can bet that there is a good reason.

Unresolved Past Issues

The number-one reason people have difficulty letting go of anger is unresolved past issues. Because old emotional wounds are often buried far beneath the surface, you may only be dimly aware of their existence, if at all. But make no mistake, emotional baggage is a deadly poison that can slowly eat away at you and your relationships, from the inside out.

Your unique history impacts your psychological functioning, sense of identity, and interpersonal relationships. This is true for everyone. When you have painful, unresolved issues from childhood—ranging from abuse and neglect to milder, but still profound, wounds that can stem from aversive parental relationships, family dysfunction, and bullying—you are at an increased risk for developing deeply entrenched anger triggers.

Some of these issues may appear to be more serious than others. The reality is, however, that almost any unresolved emotional issue can grow and fester, manifesting in unhealthy, reactive, and uncontrolled bouts of anger that are disproportionate to their triggering events.

Many people have avoided facing painful issues directly, believing that they will eventually disappear. Time does not heal all wounds. More than 100 years of psychological research has demonstrated that emotional healing does not take place unless action is taken to facilitate that process. If you find that anger is running your life despite the careful application of anger control techniques, past emotional baggage is the first area to explore.

How Past Issues Lead to Anger

Unresolved past issues create sensitivities. For example, imagine that you have had a deeply painful experience in which you were rejected by someone you loved. If the hurt from this rejection has never been resolved, you will likely become sensitized to interpersonal rejection in your present and future relationships. This likelihood will increase if you have had multiple experiences of rejection or betrayal, which is not uncommon.

Being sensitized to something like rejection has a number of implications. For one thing, you are likely to become vigilant toward signs of being rejected again. This only makes sense: Once you've touched the fire, you're more attentive to its dangers. As often happens in the world of the mind, this vigilance is likely to generalize to some extent. Thus, for example, you will be on the lookout not only for direct signals indicating that a rejection might occur, but for indirect signals as well. In the extreme, almost any experience you have with another person in which you feel slighted, ignored, or misunderstood can be interpreted as a warning that you are about to be seriously hurt.

In addition, there is now an increased likelihood of *misperceiving* interpersonal events. Because of your underlying sensitivity, innocent behaviors from a friend or loved one, such as not responding quickly to a missed phone call, have an increased potential to be misunderstood as implying something more sinister—that you are being deliberately slighted in some way.

Vigilance toward interpersonal threats, combined with a tendency to misperceive social information, can increase the frequency with which interpersonal sensitivities are evoked. But that's not the whole story. These factors also directly impact the *intensity* of your emotional responses. For example, if a friend or romantic partner has to cancel an engagement, you are left a deep emotional wound that would appear quite excessive to most people.

The Emergence of Vicious Cycles

Anger is seductive. It puts a tight lid on painful emotions and, in the process, blocks awareness. You only see the anger. This can occur with or without conscious direction. Many people have done this all their lives, so much so that their capacity to recognize and experience primary emotions is impaired. The long-term effect of hiding feelings behind anger is to lose touch with these feelings altogether. Feelings, pleasant and unpleasant, provide information; they are vital signals that let you know what needs to be changed in your life. When anger takes over, this information is watered down, corrupted, or simply lost. The result is that, over time, you become disconnected from yourself and from those around you. You become more thin-skinned and less self-aware, which impedes your ability to learn from painful experiences.

When anger becomes your "go-to" coping mechanism, a vicious cycle emerges. First, you use anger to defend against painful feelings that are elicited in specific situations. The process is straightforward. Over time, however, these primary unresolved emotions accumulate like a heavy psychological weight, diminishing your ability to experience pleasure while heightening feelings of depression and anxiety. Now the situation is more complicated; you have to ramp up your anger to higher and higher levels in order to "protect" yourself from the festered emotions left over from earlier experiences when you used anger to defend against vulnerable feelings. At the same time, you continue to use anger to cope with new triggers that emerge in day-to-day life, which further traps you in an unending process of irritability and rage. You may begin to wonder why you are so angry all the time. Indeed, the most insidious aspect of using anger to cope with emotional pain is that these behaviors are powerfully self-reinforcing and habit-forming. It becomes a way of life.

Anger, Shame, and Fear

Shame and fear may not be obvious bedfellows with anger, but they spend a lot of time together. Shame and fear are experienced as vulnerabilities. Any time there is a sense of threat or danger, there is a door through which anger can pass.

FACT

People are sometimes confused about the difference between guilt and shame. The classic distinction is that guilt is feeling bad about something that you have done, whereas shame is feeling bad about who you are. Shame has a strong social component as well. It is strongly influenced by your sense of how you appear to others.

Part of the confusion is that shame and fear are signals, not actual threats. A lion is a threat. A burglar is a threat. Fear is an emotion. When you respond to these signals reactively, as if you were in some sort of immediate danger, you might be missing the deeper, more important implications. An emergency siren might be startling and abrasive, but it calls your attention to something important. It can save your life. Similarly, emotions like shame, fear, and anxiety can be difficult to bear, but they also provide the motivation to make important life changes. What are these feelings really telling you? How can they guide you to improve your life? When you cover

over shame and fear with a protective veneer of anger, you obscure important underlying issues. These important signals are stripped of their capacity to motivate connection, understanding, exploration, and resolution. You've adopted a bunker mentality, and only see the world through that one tiny window.

Anger and the Wounded Self

Chronically angry people suffer from significant self-image deficits. This is not a coincidence.

You have seen that unresolved emotional issues are a major cause of anger problems. More often than not, this relationship is mediated through a deep wounding of your sense of self-worth. People with stubborn anger problems can be quite successful in their careers and in a very broad range of endeavors, but they are less successful in their relationships, where anger triggers are plentiful.

Ironically, the most intimate relationships are the most likely to arouse intense, unhealthy anger: relationships with your spouse, children, and closest friends. Because you are the most emotionally invested in these relationships, you are also the most emotionally vulnerable. This vulnerability can directly precipitate inappropriate, defensive anger.

ALERT

Feelings of inadequacy are a common driver of anger problems. Anger can be an effective way to mask insecurities, but there are costs. People who rely on anger to hide their vulnerability become dependent on that surge of energy to feel strong and capable. They have to make themselves angry again and again, becoming increasingly isolated.

When the underlying issues of unresolved pain have not been adequately addressed, the associated sense of personal inadequacy is highly resistant to corrective information. This can give rise to a phenomenon that, for many, is often perplexing and strange: highly accomplished, capable, and attractive individuals who are fundamentally insecure regarding their own self-worth and competency. They may even secretly view themselves as "frauds." How can this be? It is because the psychic wound that gives rise to such beliefs has never healed; it festers in the shadows, tainting every experience. Underlying scripts such as "I'm not good enough" and "No one can be trusted" persist unabated.

Chronic anger is used to "cover up" the pain of deep hurt. These experiences include feeling devalued, unappreciated, misunderstood, accused, guilty, unlovable, inadequate, flawed, rejected, powerless, and ignored. Anger, by its very nature, has the ability to combat such hurtful and unpleasant feelings. It takes on a life of its own as the frontline method for coping with unpleasant feelings.

The psychological concept of self-soothing is helpful here. Everyone needs to find ways of comforting or reassuring themselves when their self-esteem is endangered—whether through criticism, dismissal, or any other outside stimulus that feels invalidating and so revives old self-doubts. If you're healthy psychologically, then you have the internal resources to self-validate: to admit to yourself possible inadequacies without experiencing intolerable shame. But if, deep down, you still feel bad about who you are, your deficient sense of self simply won't be able to withstand such external threats.

The Seductiveness of Anger: Power and Control

Anger is quite effective in managing feelings of powerlessness. Not only does anger help numb painful feelings, it also produces a surge of energy—the adrenaline rush that so many people experience during acute bouts of anger.

This can be incredibly seductive, anger as the ultimate "quick fix." Anger efficiently transforms feelings of defeat and powerlessness into a visceral sense of power. Someone calls you "inconsiderate," and you feel angry. Someone cuts in front of you on the freeway, and you feel angry. Someone attacks your friend, and you feel angry. Someone tells you that you will not get the pay increase you think you deserve, and you feel angry. What causes you to feel anger? What do all of these situations have in common?

A simple answer refers to one of anger's most basic functions: a defiant assertion of power in the face of a perceived threat. But the threat here is to the ego, to your wishes, or to your values. You are frustrated about not getting what you want or expect.

If anger can make you feel powerful, if it is the quick fix that is able to address your deepest doubts about yourself, is it any wonder that it can end up controlling you? In a sense, anger is every bit as much of a drug as alcohol or cocaine, which are widely used forms of "self-medication" for troubled people. Few people actually think about their anger as a coping mechanism. Rather than leaving them feeling weak or out of control, anger produces an intoxicating sense of invulnerability.

Chronic Anger Is an Illusion of Power

Chronic anger creates a false reality, an illusion of empowerment, that deceives a person into believing he is stronger and safer when he chooses to get angry or to allow rage to take over. This illusion is frequently on display in team sports. For many athletes, getting really angry—about a penalty, a cheap shot, or a teammate's mistake, for example—sparks a surreal feeling of strength, a sense of "unstoppability." These athletes feel as if such bouts of rage improve their performance. They are seduced. In reality, as any keen sports observer can attest to, uncontrolled anger gets the best of players by causing them to start fights, sustain major penalties, and get expelled from the game.

When you experience bouts of anger, you may begin to think that here is a secret, naturally occurring source of total empowerment. Perhaps you wonder if you could control the force of that anger and harness its power to protect yourself or those you love. But the power that comes from anger is dangerous.

Anger is a beast. Negativity begets greater negativity, anger begets anger, and hatred begets hatred. The snowball effect of your anger is manifested in rage, fury, and blinding hatred; it clouds your natural sense of good judgment and overcomes patience and prudence.

Targeting Anger

Using anger as a source of power is like throwing a dart at a target to feel the power of making contact with focused intent. The targets are people and situations around you—your closest friends, family, coworkers, or pets. By raising your voice, you are trying to make the targeted person hear you and then fix or solve the problem. People who use anger as a source of power alienate their friends and family because they are unfamiliar with other ways of working with anger.

Imagine, for example, that you have yelled at your child for spilling milk. In fact, your anger has nothing to do with the milk on the floor. Not *really*. It points to something inside of you that is not being addressed, something that is sapping your internal harmony. Perhaps you're unhappy because you are in a fight with your spouse. Perhaps you are stressed about your job. In over-reactive spilled-milk situations, the true target is moving and vague, because it's an unrecognized part of yourself that wants resolution. If you are the one reacting with anger and who feels threatened, ask yourself, "What is underneath the anger?" and "What is its source?"

ALERT

Don't control your anger—control yourself. "Control" of the wounded self acting in anger is about masking insecurities and avoiding pain. To "control" the mature adult acting in anger, you must make committed choices that are directed toward the fulfillment of your core values.

What Is Power?

If anger is an illusion of power, then what is true power? Power can take many forms such as having confidence, strength of mind, or the ability to lift 300 pounds of steel with one hand. Those are aspects of power, but true power is the connection with your core. It is being able to stand in the face of chaos while also maintaining a calm presence. True power is saying yes to situations and relationships that push your boundaries, help you grow, and lift you toward joy and fulfillment, and saying no to situations and relationships that dull your experience and no longer support your life path.

It's tricky business to walk the edge, knowing that something or someone no longer serves your life. The edge holds grief, and anger is grief's vehicle. Anger is a way to show you that you need to shift something in your life, such as your job, your relationships, your family, your friends, or your community. If the anger is not addressed, it attacks other people when milk is spilled on the floor. Anger gives you the opportunity to transform your life rather than be a vehicle of pain. Transformation occurs by naming the pain, expressing it with others, releasing the anger associated with the pain in a healthy way, and resolving the pain with acceptance.

It takes courage to step off this vehicle of pain and step into the power of self. It takes strength to walk the path of self-discovery, because then you have made the commitment to look deeply at your wounds, pain, and emotions, at how you are in the world. This is the path of true personal power. All it takes is one moment when rage drives you "too far" and you irreversibly change or destroy someone's life. The lure of anger is false empowerment. True strength diffuses your rage, and it comes from peace of mind.

Anger Addiction

Can anger be addictive? Addiction is normally associated with drugs, alcohol, and sex, but is it possible to be addicted to anger? The weight of available evidence—not to mention the experience of thousands of people and clinicians—suggests that anger addiction is very real. In fact, as any anger junkie can tell you, rage can be exhilarating.

The prototypical anger junkie, or "rageaholic," seeks reasons to get offended. This is someone with an aggressive anger style who always seems to be in the middle of a crisis. From minor irritation to full-blown rage, anger junkies are prone to frequent, dramatic conflicts with people in their lives, exploding in rage and causing drama over the pettiest concern. They rely on anger for a range of coping functions, but over time they become attached to the experience of anger itself. Common drivers of anger addiction include the use of anger for energy or motivation, for pain relief, for confidence and power, and to reduce anxiety and fear.

The Endogenous Chemical High

Anger addiction can be linked to specific endogenous biochemical compounds released by the central nervous system. *Endogenous* simply means that these compounds are produced by the body, as opposed to an *exogenous* substance such as morphine or cocaine, which is synthetic.

The process begins in the limbic system, the area of the brain that regulates emotion and memory. As anger escalates, the limbic system triggers the release of chemicals that facilitate the fight-or-flight response. These endogenous compounds—most notably, the hormone epinephrine (more commonly known as adrenaline) and the neurotransmitter norepinephrine—are experienced much like an amphetamine and an analgesic. They give a surge of energy while numbing pain. This combination is seductive and plays an important role in anger addiction.

FACT

Anger can feel good. The rush of adrenaline and dopamine feels good. Releasing stored-up tension feels good, too. Anger allows these things to happen in a very dramatic way. When a person gets angry and expresses it aggressively, she is also temporarily "rewarded" with an illusory boost in power and status.

The limbic system causes the secretion of dopamine, the neurotransmitter associated with pleasure and reward. Dopamine (where we get the word *dope*) is the chemical stepping-stone to addiction. It is the endogenous pleasure chemical unleashed by the brain in response to—and in anticipation of—fun stimulants such as a vodka martini, a cigarette, sex, food, or a shopping spree.

Since the release of dopamine after becoming angry is pleasurable, the person learns to repeat the behavior that caused this to happen. Once stimulated, the reward center of the brain actively wires itself with mental associations of cause and effect. The result? The brain remembers what thing or activity produced this pleasurable effect so the next time it can summon its resources to achieve a similar gratifying outcome. Thus, the person is more likely to become angry again. In this way, anger can take on a life of its own; the process feeds on itself. When these inherent rewards are combined with an intrinsic motivation to use anger as a coping strategy, as discussed earlier, the danger of developing an addictive relationship with anger is greatly increased.

The Crash

The "high" associated with the release of epinephrine, norepinephrine, and dopamine is obtained at some cost. Inevitably, a crash follows.

Epinephrine is an especially powerful chemical, which is sometimes injected directly into the stilled hearts of coronary victims to get them to beat again. As with any amphetamine, once the surge of anger burns out, there is a drop in mood. That surge of energy has to come from somewhere, and, in a sense, it is "borrowed" from the future. Thus, the experience of anger is always followed, to some degree, by depression. Not necessarily sadness, but rather a combination of lethargy and joylessness (what psychologists refer to as *anhedonia*, a diminished capacity to experience pleasure).

Think about it: The last time you got really angry, didn't you feel down afterward? The angrier you got, the more depressed you were once the anger wore off. And that is merely the physiological response; it does not take into account whether you did something while angry that you're ashamed of, such as hurting someone you love.

This difficulty is broadened considerably when the effect of dopamine is taken into account. The problem with chronic dopamine release is that, with time, the brain's receptors become desensitized and bring little pleasure. A small amount of dopamine can only help you feel temporarily "normal" again. As with drugs, an anger junkie will crave a larger release of dopamine to feel the same high—and the only way to achieve this is to up the rage and act out more, either verbally or violently. This is how anger addiction is born.

The Hijacked Brain

When addiction occurs, the underlying neural circuitry that facilitates anger in the brain is strengthened and reinforced with repeated activation. Over time, the impulses can become so strong, and the behavior of acting them out so "wired in" (through repetition), that this behavior seems totally natural. So much so, in fact, that anything contrary to that state creates internal tension. Worse, the ability of the brain's executive control center to regulate this process through reasoning and judgment becomes diminished over time. This relative strengthening of the anger response, combined with a weakening of executive control, gives rise to the "hijacked brain."

This is the reason anger addiction can be just as serious as any addiction to drugs, alcohol, or gambling.

Dealing with Anger Addiction

Anger addiction repeats the pattern over and over . . . except that with time it usually gets worse. These patterns are hard to stop, and the results are devastating to everyone involved. But you don't have to live like this. Fortunately, you have a lot of choices for how to deal with anger addiction and rage addiction:

1. Understand and take care of your own unmet needs. First, learn about the basic emotional needs people have as children. There's a wounded child inside every anger addict, even though she may not know it. A very effective way for you to meet your own unmet emotional needs is by nurturing your inner child. As you get better at taking care of yourself and feeling better all around, you will find your love relationships becoming much more comfortable.

2. Figure out what your patterns are in your relationships. Get some help from books, counseling, or anger programs to help you identify those patterns.

3. Learn how to provide relief from the anger that causes your blowups. This is a very powerful way of dealing with anger and breaking the anger addiction cycle. Getting plenty of exercise, eating a healthy diet, relaxing, and meditating help a lot with taking care of yourself emotionally. In addition, a good night's sleep is absolutely necessary for good anger control.

4. Learn how to get your anger and rage out in healthy ways. This will break the anger and rage addiction cycle every time.

5. Find out how healthy anger can work for you instead of against you, fueling powerful, positive action that makes your life and relationships better.

CHAPTER 12

Working Through Intractable Anger

Intractable anger is just what it sounds like: anger that is very hard to release, even after sustained efforts. By its very nature, intractable anger is rooted in the past. "Anger work" is an anger management approach that can be effective with this kind of hard-to-let-go-of anger. The basic premise is to let go of emotionally painful events by focusing on them and expressing anger about the pain. By focusing on the trauma over and over, the pain will gradually go away and will never affect you again. Anger work allows you to release anger through venting and focused emotional expression, therefore surrendering the emotional baggage from old wounds so that you are calmer, engaged, and satisfied.

Who Needs Anger Work?

Sometimes people find anger very difficult to let go of, even using the techniques mentioned in this book. This difficulty typically occurs in situations when the anger is based on deep hurt and disappointment. In some cases, this difficulty is complicated further by the impossibility or impracticality of directly addressing anger issues with the object of your anger.

There are three categories of people who can benefit from anger work. The first category is comprised of people who are already consciously angry and need to find some constructive way of resolving their feelings. The second category consists of those who don't feel angry, but who struggle with interpersonal or intrapersonal difficulties and have never fully processed the traumatic events that shaped them and set them up for the problems they face today. The third category includes those individuals who have successfully dealt with all the issues from their past, but are interested in healthy ways of handling aggravating situations that come up in their current, daily lives.

On Venting and Catharsis

Venting or discharging emotions involves vigorously expressing the emotion—fear, sadness, anger, dependency—so completely that you feel "drained." This process markedly reduces the strength of the emotion or eliminates it altogether.

FACT

Catharsis is a Greek word that means "purification" or "cleansing." It was used to describe the effect of tragic plays and other art forms in providing an emotional release for the audience. Philosophers such as Aristotle believed that through the arousal of pity and fear evoked by viewing a tragedy, for example, audience members experienced a purgation of these emotions that restored emotional balance.

The use of venting as a means for releasing pent-up emotions is not new. The ancient Greek idea of catharsis overlaps significantly with the idea of emotional venting. In the modern era, this approach is associated with the work of Sigmund Freud, whose ideas formed the basis for the hydraulic model of anger. This model posits that frustrations lead to anger and that anger, in turn, builds inside a person. The pressure continues to increase until it is vented or released. If the anger is not vented, the buildup will cause the individual to explode in an aggressive rage or to experience a range of other problems.

A Note of Caution

Many professionals doubt the effectiveness of venting as a way to "clean out" toxic emotions such as anger. A number of research studies suggest venting anger is ineffective for anger management and can even exacerbate anger problems. In one 2002 study, researchers found that people who vented their anger by hitting a punching bag were likely to behave aggressively after doing so, significantly more so than if they had done nothing at all. Findings such as this have given rise to the "catharsis myth," which, in its strong form, states that efforts to release anger through venting has the paradoxical effect of teaching people to be more, rather than less, angry. This perspective acknowledges that venting can "feel good" in the short term, but emphasizes that this payoff is obtained at great cost: an increased likelihood of anger and aggressiveness in the future.

Other research suggests a more complicated picture. A recent study conducted at the University of Illinois Urbana-Champaign, for example, found that people who vented their anger experienced sharp decreases in anger, with no apparent downside. Although some forms of venting are maladaptive (such as abuse, physical violence, and verbal attacks), there is evidence that adaptive (nonviolent) forms not only create a calming effect, but also empower participants with the tools necessary to regulate anger emotions in the future.

To achieve the desired outcome, the mindset in which venting is approached is every bit as important as the manner in which it is carried out. As psychologist Rollo May observed, the blind venting of emotions is "an egregious mistake . . . mainly the illusion that merely experiencing or acting out is all that is necessary for cure. Experiencing is absolutely essential; but if it occurs without the changing of the patient's concepts, symbols, and myths, the 'experiencing' is truncated and has a masturbatory rather than a fully procreative character." With this in mind, do not engage in venting without following the guidelines laid out in this chapter.

ESSENTIAL

When dealing with trauma, such as from a heinous crime or accident, there is a risk of being traumatized again through the use of venting techniques. If you suspect that you have been traumatized in some way, do not do anger work without first consulting a professional. There are alternative approaches specifically tailored to healing from trauma.

Keys to Successful Anger Work

There are three essential keys to making venting work productive.

1. Do not vent or "act out" your anger on yourself.
2. Do not act out your anger on others (this includes animals).
3. Do not act out your anger with hostile intent.

Part of the definition of anger work is that it does *not* involve directing your anger at others or yourself. Even "imaginary" acting out, such as physically exerting yourself in some way while focusing hostile feelings toward the object of your anger, is counterproductive. If you engage in venting with a hostile or aggressive mindset, you're not doing anger work—you're just getting mad.

Even when you're not in the midst of a venting session, always observe these three guidelines to the best of your ability. If you do, you will find that your anger work sessions are productive. You will see definite progress because you will be working through your existing issues and will avoid creating new issues. Not following these principles will greatly inhibit your progress.

Perhaps an analogy will help. Think of all the negative experiences you need to heal from (such as abuses, losses, and failures) as a pond that you have to empty in order to plant a garden. For some people, it's more like a puddle or a lake, depending on the amount and severity of the emotional wounds. When you vent appropriately, it is like bailing water out of that pond. However, every time you act out your anger on yourself or others, or engage in covert hostile activity, you are adding water to the pond. You may enjoy a sense of short-term relief, but the anger problems will likely return. Rather than taking steps toward your goal of achieving increased harmony, you may be taking a step back. It is critical that you follow the three guidelines.

QUESTION

Is it really possible to act out your anger without hostility?
Yes. Your anger work might look aggressive, but the mindset with which you are doing it is important. Do not fantasize about retaliation as you express your anger. Instead, maintain a focused intention on cleansing away any hostile feelings you may have.

How to Do Anger Work: Five Steps

The following steps for anger work will help you take control of your anger. Follow each step closely, and keep the three guidelines in mind while working.

Step 1. Connect with Your Feelings

For venting to be successful, it must be directly connected to and rooted in the true source of your anger. If your anger is focused on a particular person or group of people, you may experience it as animosity directed toward this person or group. An effective way to step back from this is to focus on the person's behavior—what actually *happened* to provoke your negative feelings—rather than on the person. The goal is not to develop feelings of aggression toward someone who may have wronged you, but to connect with the wrong itself and the way it impacted you. As you review the situation, the final part of this step is to connect directly with the emotion that you wish to release.

If you are inclined to avoid feelings, such as occurs with people who have an avoidant or passive-aggressive anger style, this is a particularly important step. If you are not feeling immediately connected with the anger that you are trying to vent, your results may be disappointing. If necessary, consider finding a quiet, private place where you can talk to yourself about your feelings. Talk out loud. When you notice a feeling, stay with it and let it grow to its full strength. Often people shut off feelings so they won't get stronger. You want to do the opposite: Allow your feelings to grow or even exaggerate them. Think back to the event or events that are associated with your anger, and let the feelings that you originally experienced wash over you anew. Pay attention to any physical sensations. The more you connect with your anger, the more you will notice physical sensations such as muscle tension and shallow breathing. Invite these sensations to take center stage.

Step 2. Focus Your Intention on Letting Go

Research shows that blind venting, especially venting carried out in a spirit of hostility, can increase anger problems. Don't make this mistake. Venting should not be confused with aggression. Once you've connected with your angry and hurt feelings, and *before* you attempt any actual venting, develop a focused intention to *express and release this anger*. Remember the goal of venting is not to get angry, but rather to let go of the anger that is already inside you.

Step 3. Vent or Express Your Anger

You may find yourself in one of two conditions: overwhelmed with intense emotions and needing to get them under control, or boiling with "bottled-up" emotions and needing to express these feelings. Venting works well with both conditions. There are many ways to vent, and some of the more common techniques are discussed in the next section. Feel free to experiment with different methods.

Regardless of the approach that you adopt, maintain the focus on letting go that you developed in step 2. As you exert yourself, say again and again, "I am releasing this anger." The idea is to drain out or use up the anger (or other emotion), so that in the end you are calm and more able to cope. Vent until you are exhausted, completely drained of anger and sadness. Don't stop until you feel that the negative emotions have been drained away, as much as possible.

Step 4. Return to Calm

Many people end their venting work after step 3, but this is a mistake. The process is left incomplete. After step 3, you will likely be feeling quite spent. You may notice residual sensations of physiological arousal have begun to fade. Once you have drained the feeling of anger, and any associated emotions such as sadness or shame, you need to consolidate this work by intentionally returning to a state of calm. Engage in slow, deep breathing. Sit or stand with good posture (shoulders back, spine slightly arched), close your eyes, and just breathe, deeply and slowly. Allow yourself at least five minutes for this step. As you breathe, notice any physical sensations that you might have, and observe these sensations dissipating as your body returns to a state of calm.

If necessary, and particularly if you notice acute muscle tension anywhere in your body, engage in applied muscle relaxation, first tensing the muscle group in question, and then releasing that tension. Notice how this feels. Continue to focus on your breathing. Allow yourself to become more and more relaxed, more and more peaceful. Take your time as you do this.

Step 5. Salving

Just as you might apply a medicinal salve to soothe and heal a cut or bruise, this final step in the venting process calls for you to apply an emotional salve to the psychological wound at the heart of your anger. As you settle into a pattern of relaxed breathing, try to connect with the feeling of love and compassion—for yourself, for the person who angered you, for anyone, really. Allow that feeling to wrap around you like a warm blanket.

Anger Work Methods

There are many, many options for venting anger—far too many to list in this book. As long as you follow the basic five steps outlined in the previous section, improvise and experiment with them as you wish. What's most important is that you find an approach that works best for *you*. There is no right or wrong way to do this, just be sure that your venting doesn't hurt anyone.

Anger Work Through Exercise

A favorite form of anger work is exercise. Your exercise of choice could range from an intense form of professional athletic training to a nice walk in the park for half an hour each day. Information about exercise is ubiquitous; read books or magazines, talk to professional trainers or people you know who work out regularly, try dance CDs. Any form of exercise can be used as an effective way to express anger.

Many studies have demonstrated that exercise, especially a program that includes aerobics, can prevent or reduce feelings of depression. Now there is new information about the impact that exercise can have on feelings of anger. In one recent study, researchers found that participants were significantly better at managing angry feelings on days when they engaged in thirty minutes of aerobic activity.

If you have not been exercising regularly, start slowly. Talk to your medical doctor and possibly find a personal trainer to help you get started. If you work your way up gradually, you will be more likely to stick with it. The great thing about using exercise to do your anger work is that there are so many positive side effects such as stress reduction, mood regulation, and physical fitness.

Intensity is not as important as commitment and regularity. Whatever you choose to do, just stay with it. Keep in mind that exercise alone is not enough to heal you from your emotional wounds; many people who exercise are still unhappy or depressed. You must do some form of anger work while exercising. What is important is that you feel the anger.

Anger Work Through Hitting Things

Hitting things is one of the most popular ways people complete anger work. You can grab a plastic bat and start pounding away on a bed, couch, toy, or an object that represents the person with whom you are angry. Some people prefer to use their hands instead of a bat. Some people use gloves and a punching bag. All these methods are fine, as long as you are not hurting yourself and are adhering to the basic five steps discussed earlier.

ALERT

Be careful not to use an object that either you or someone else will miss if it is destroyed.

Remember, the point of this work is to focus on your feelings about some issue or event that still causes you to feel angry, hurt, or sad. It is not necessary to focus on a specific event. Simply allow your feelings to flow into your actions, and start hitting with the intent of releasing those feelings.

Anger Work Through Scream Release

Another popular way to do anger work is through scream release. The technique is rather simple: Just yell. Letting go of your deep inner anger in this way can be very satisfying. Just be careful, or you may lose your voice.

Many people are, of course, afraid that other people may hear them. If you are concerned about this, here are a few things you can do to lessen the worry:

- Find a pillow or two and scream into them. Add more cushions if you think that others can still hear you. The noise may sound loud to you, but you can tape-record it or ask a close friend to listen to ensure that it's not loud enough to disturb anyone else.
- Scream while driving alone in your car, if you have one. If you are driving at a normal speed with the windows up, no one will hear you. However, you must also concentrate on driving to ensure that you don't lose control of the car.
- Go to a concert or sporting event where screaming is part of the ambiance. Everyone else will think you're just a devoted fan!
- Go into the wilderness where you are alone and let your angry voice ring through the hills or on the beach.
- Scream underwater. No one will hear you.

Anger Work When You're Not Alone

How can you express your anger when these methods aren't appropriate? For example, if you are in a classroom or at work, or in a car with your spouse when you are angry with him, you do not have the privacy you need to do the typical forms of anger work. You do not want to draw attention to yourself, or frighten the person you are with, but you need to get these feelings out because you can feel the pressure rising. You don't want to blow up at the person, or get another one of those wretched tension headaches. In addition to setting good boundaries and being as assertive as you can without becoming aggressive, here are some suggestions that you might find helpful.

Try the hand-squeezing technique to let your anger out. Simply roll one or both hands into a fist and squeeze. If you hide your hands, no one will notice. Or press down on the floor with your feet or tighten the muscles in some other part of the body. These are forms of isometric exercise that you can do when you are with people.

If the situation is especially aggravating, you are going to need to address it again during your private anger work time, or using other methods presented in this book. However, these techniques should help you make it through the conversation or situation, and you can deal with the rest later.

ALERT

Many people clench their jaws or contract the muscles in their neck and shoulders in an unconscious reaction to stress. This reaction frequently leads to headaches, sore muscles, and jaw and joint conditions such as TMJ (temporomandibular joint disorders). Instead of *reacting* to stress in these harmful ways, why not proactively *respond* to it? Teach your mind and body to work together to bring about greater health for yourself as a whole being.

Artistic Anger Work

Art can be an excellent means of self-expression and a very helpful tool in therapy as well. However, both research and clinical experience suggest that the usual creation of art for art's sake is not enough to heal you from the effects of chronic anger.

FACT

> When you feel angry but haven't yet learned how to show it, expressing anger through art can be a freeing, creative, and healthy outlet. It's a great alternative when you can't allow yourself to verbalize your anger or don't know how to do so. Art can be a first step in learning to express what you might otherwise experience as a "dangerous" emotion.

As with the other forms of anger work presented in this chapter, follow the five steps when using art to facilitate healing from emotional wounds. Children, and many adults as well, love to do artistic anger work. They may create a descriptive image with their angry feelings, or they may create and then destroy their art. Allow your anger to flow as you create. One survivor of sexual abuse may create abstract paintings dominated by deep red tones. Another may create a jumble of body parts expressing the confusion and disconnectedness that he feels.

Some other modes of artistic expression include expressive dance, creative movement, and creative visualization. You could create a dance that tells a story. You do not need to have special training. It is your story, and as a whole being—body, mind, and spirit—you can express your experience with yourself as the only audience.

Creative movement is different than expressive dance. It can be one, simple, repetitive movement or a series of movements that have symbolic meaning to you. Creative visualization is another helpful tool. For example, you can imagine a cleansing fire burning away all the evil in a person and leaving behind only what is good and worthy of remaining. Use your imagination and visualize symbolic scenes that will help you heal.

Here's something fun that you can do with creative visualization. Visualize yourself rising above your current problems. Pretend that you are hiking on the path of life and your particular problems are vines trying to grow around your ankles and keep you from climbing to higher ground. Visualize yourself overcoming that challenge by stomping on them, hacking them up, or simply climbing over them—whatever works for you. Feel the thrill of overcoming those obstacles. This is just one example; the possibilities for creative visualization are as limitless as your imagination.

Journaling

Some people find that daily journaling ensures that they get their anger out. It is very similar to the scream-release technique in which you "tell" the offending person exactly what you think and feel about her or her actions. The only difference is that your words are written instead of spoken. If you like, you can later read your entry aloud with a close supportive friend or therapist.

How Long Does the Anger Work Continue?

You may understandably want to know how long you will need to do anger work to heal from the abuse and pain of your past. The best answer, although not an entirely satisfactory one, is that you must keep doing anger work about your past until you can tell that you are fully healed. The actual number of days, months, or years it takes to arrive at this place varies from person to person depending on how severe the emotional wound is and how consistent you are about working on it.

You will know that you have reached this point when you can look at the event that has wounded you and no longer feel intense anger or sadness. The memory is clear, but no longer has the power to evoke strong emotions. Recalling the event feels almost like watching a play or movie. It is tragic, and yet you walk away feeling only slightly moved. This is how you will eventually feel about your past.

When you have finished processing the memories of your past and they no longer have power over you, you will still need to work at maintaining your health. This will mean dealing with the aggravating situations of every-day life and not letting them fester.

CHAPTER 13

Compassion and Forgiveness

People are often uncertain of how to apply concepts such as forgiveness, tolerance, compassion, and acceptance in their daily lives. In addition, they are often highly resistant to these ideas. Compassion and forgiveness rank among the most powerful methods for dissipating anger, even the kinds of intractable anger that are resistant to other methods.

Quench Your Anger with Compassion

Compassion requires a sympathetic awareness of another person's distress coupled with a desire to prevent or alleviate that suffering. It is hard to feel angry and compassionate at the same time. When you cultivate compassion, you soften the reactivity of aggression and hostility that stem from anger. Compassion facilitates healing and resolution and makes it easier to forgive.

Compassion is also reasonable. It's a rational response to a world of uncertainty, difficulty, and confusion. Human beings need compassion because life is hard. Everyone is susceptible to disease and injury, and everyone will die eventually.

Because death can happen to anyone, at any time, there is a sense that we are all in this together. No one escapes. The more you can work with the people around you, the more bearable you can make the journey. The Buddhist tradition has a simple way of expressing this: "Just like me, you want to be happy; just like me, you want to be free of suffering." That recognition of common fear and yearning is the basis for compassion.

ALERT

The evidence suggests that the brain can be trained for compassion. When researchers at Emory University in Georgia evaluated the effects of compassion training, they found that stress hormones in the blood had been lowered overall among study participants, and this benefit was strongest for those who spent the most time doing compassion exercises.

Compassion can certainly be difficult when you are angry or are in a fearful or agitated state. The hardest forms of compassion to feel are for people you don't love—or when your connection with that sense of love seems far away, as it so often does when you are angry. It's also harder to be compassionate toward people who seem dissimilar.

In addition, life experiences can diminish your ability to give and receive compassion. People are often caught in psychological loops that prevent them from accepting compassion from others or from themselves. Pain blocks compassion. Anger blocks compassion. Confusion blocks compassion. And yet, if you can just stretch past these blockages to connect with your compassionate heart, these powerful negative emotions can be transcended.

But you can break those loops by becoming aware of how your brain works—by becoming aware of your own awareness. You can begin to cultivate compassion deliberately by learning to nurture compassionate attention, compassionate thinking, compassionate feeling, and compassionate behavior. You can learn to be open to suffering in others as well as in yourself—and then you can act to alleviate that suffering.

The Trouble with the Human Brain

Your brain was created through genetics; it was not created by you, but for you, and it is capable of both wonderful and terrible things. In fact, the way your brain has evolved means it can give you a lot of trouble—and that is because you really have *two* brains.

You have an old brain, which has an abundance of motives and desires that evolved long ago and that you share with other animals. Just like your dog, you are naturally motivated to avoid things that could harm you, and you can be territorial, possessive, and concerned with status. You are also motivated to form friendships, reproduce, and care for offspring. In addition, just like your dog, you can experience the emotions of anxiety, fear, anger, lust, and joy.

However, you are also very different from other animals. About 2 million years ago one of your primate ancestors started to evolve humanlike intelligence, so you are now capable of imagining, reasoning, and using symbols and language. This "new" brain is fabulous when used wisely, but much depends on how it interacts with the old brain.

For example, imagine a zebra spots a lion and runs away. The older, animal brain is good at detecting and responding to threats. If the zebra escapes, it will settle down, go back to the herd, and start happily eating again. But if the same thing happens to a human, the new brain won't allow the same scenario to occur. The human will start thinking, "What would've happened if I were attacked by a lion?" Then, in the middle of the night, the human will wake up thinking, "What about tomorrow? And how do I protect the children?"

The threat is over, but the new brain can't let it go. The new brain ruminates and runs simulation after simulation. Now, of course, this can be very useful for working out how to avoid lions in the first place. But it can also be a trap known as *emotional memory*. Here is another example, this time closer to modern times. Suppose that you like holidays. When you think about holidays, you are excited. But then on one holiday, you are beaten and robbed, and you end up in the hospital. What will happen the following year when you think about holidays? Well, that traumatic memory will surface, and so holidays will no longer be pleasant for you.

Evidence suggests that it is possible, through meditation, to control brain functions that are typically believed to be outside conscious control. Experienced meditators have produced dramatic physiological changes in the meditative state, including lowered pulse and respiratory rates, decreased oxygen consumption and blood lactate levels, and alterations in the brain's electrical activity. These changes have been termed the *relaxation response*.

The same mechanism is at work with the child who is loved in the morning by the same parent who beats him when she gets drunk at night. The attachment system—the parts of the brain that facilitate loving connection with parents—fuses with the fear system. So as that child grows up and begins to feel connection with other people, he is opening up the attachment system; unfortunately, in his emotional memory, attachment is also toxic. He now has a mental health problem.

Many people with mental health problems are in loops they can't escape. They ruminate about things that frighten them; they concentrate on being no good or inferior. They focus on all their negative aspects. This is not their fault; all people have a natural, old-brain threat bias. The brain is like Velcro for negative- and threat-based issues, but like Teflon for positive ones.

Fixing the Trouble

Fortunately, human beings are built with the skills to reconcile the old brain with the new. Attention is like a spotlight; whatever it shines on becomes brighter in the mind. This knowledge can help build compassion.

ALERT

Try this exercise. Imagine the excitement you feel when you are packing for vacation or when you buy a lottery ticket. Focus on that excitement for a minute or two and notice what happens in your body. Then switch your attention (on purpose) to an argument or one of your core worries at the moment. Notice what happens in your body. Did you feel very differently, according to where your attention was focused?

Attention also puts events outside the spotlight, into darkness. Let's say you are shopping for the holidays and you enter ten shops; in nine of them, the assistants are very helpful, but in one shop the salesperson is very rude. Who do you think about when you go home? "Where do they find these people?" you say to yourself. "Should I write to the store manager and get her fired? She was so rude." You're in a loop now and you're in the anger system. You've forgotten all the shop assistants who were nice to you. They're in darkness because the spotlight is on the rude one.

Of course, once you notice what the mind is up to—and why—then you can begin to take control of your attention and use it purposefully. What about if you, on purpose, decide that you're going to recall the other nine people? Just spend time remembering how kind one was, or another's smile, or how one tried so hard to find you the item you wanted. Taking that step of breaking out of the anger loop requires intention—and that intention is a key to cultivating compassion.

Compassion is rooted deeper in brain systems having to do with intentionality and motivation. If you orient yourself to compassion, then you're going to change the whole orientation of your mind. The key is to understand that you can select, on purpose, one of your basic motivational systems—for caring—and you can cultivate it and help it grow and mature, through practice. You also need to understand that doing this will change your brain and give you much more control over your thoughts and your life.

Therapy that focuses on developing compassion trains people to remember, remember, remember, to notice, notice, notice kindness—and then to build upon those remembrances. Your mind is like a garden; it will evolve naturally. But if left uncultivated, a garden is influenced by the weather and whatever seeds are in the wind. Some things will grow and others will shrivel—and in the end you may not like the result.

You can learn to cultivate compassion within you, and that process will heal and reorganize your mind so that you can become the person you want to be—in other words, you can have the garden-mind you want. This process requires courage. If you're an agoraphobic, compassionate behavior isn't sitting at home eating chocolates, because that's easy. Compassion means confronting your anxieties.

You are hardwired to connect. Recent research has linked the experience of compassion and empathy with "smart cells" in the brain called *mirror neurons*. These specialized cells fire when you experience an emotion and when you see others experiencing an emotion, such as happiness, fear, or sadness. Mirror neurons allow you to understand others' actions, intentions, and feelings.

There are two types of courage: physical and emotional. There are many examples of physical courage. Emotional courage is the ability to move into areas of deep suffering and pain. Compassion can help you explore these areas, but you must be prepared to confront your pain and to alleviate it.

Forgiveness

A concept that is closely related to compassion is forgiveness. When someone you care about hurts you, you can hold on to the anger, resentment, and thoughts of revenge, or you can embrace forgiveness and move forward. Compassion makes it easier to forgive, forgiveness makes it easier to experience compassion. These actions are mutually supportive.

Most people have been hurt by the actions or words of another. These wounds can leave lasting feelings of anger, bitterness, or even vengeance, but if you don't practice forgiveness, you might be the one who pays most dearly. The hurtful act might always remain a part of your life, but forgiveness can lessen its grip on you and help you focus on positive parts of your life. Forgiveness can even lead to feelings of understanding, empathy, and compassion for the one who hurt you. By embracing forgiveness, you can also embrace peace, hope, gratitude, and joy.

What Is Involved in Forgiveness?

Part of what makes forgiveness difficult is that it means letting go of your anger. That is not easy to do. Complicating things further is the sense many people have that to forgive their offender is to somehow make what happened "okay," to be permissive toward wrongdoing, or to be complicit in one's own mistreatment. At the same time, you might feel motivated to forgive if you recognize that doing so will help to free you from the burden of resentment and anger, and will help you to move forward in your life. Unpacking all these concerns can be confusing, to say the least. Consider the following, which should help to clarify what forgiveness is *not*:

- Forgiveness does not mean that you approve of or agree with the offense, nor does it mean that you now regard the offense as somehow less serious than you did before.
- Forgiveness does not mean you are forgetting about what has made you angry. In fact, your forgiveness is predicated, in part, on the fact that you have not forgotten. It is never reasonable to expect to forget being hurt.
- Forgiveness does not imply that you would condone a repeat offense. It does not mean that you have changed your position about what happened in any way.
- Forgiveness does not mean that you believe the offender had no responsibility for what happened. If you didn't believe the other party had some degree of responsibility, the forgiveness would have no meaning.

Forgiveness is letting go. It means letting go of anger, resentment, and bitterness. It also means allowing yourself to wish the other person well. You are not denying the other person's responsibility for hurting you, and you are not minimizing or justifying the wrong. You can forgive the person without excusing the act.

You are deciding to no longer hate the person who wronged you; you are releasing your venom, your hatred. Forgiveness is your attempt to heal yourself, to find some peace. Research supports a positive relationship between forgiveness and self-acceptance: The more you accept others, the more you like yourself, and the reverse.

QUESTION

Is there scientific research demonstrating that forgiveness is beneficial?
Yes! One recent study, for example, found that those who were trying to, or had, forgiven the perpetrators of a crime reported improved coping, less involuntary engagement, and more meaning finding than those who were unsure about forgiveness and those who did not believe the perpetrators should be forgiven.

Forgiving Someone

The essential part of forgiveness is not captured in anything you might say or do to another person, but in a change that takes place within yourself. First and foremost, forgiveness benefits the person who is forgiving. It offers release from the turmoil of resentment, a salve for body, heart, and mind. In fact, you do not have to interact with your offender in any way in order to forgive him. Research suggests that forgiveness can take place in a meaningful and satisfying way without the parties involved being directly engaged with each other.

There are a number of factors that influence the ease with which you can forgive someone. These include your unique personality and beliefs, the nature of your relationship with the other person, your understanding of what precipitated the offender's behavior, your assessment of the offender's remorse, and the magnitude of the hurt that was done.

While forgiveness is ultimately a private act that does not require any positive gesture from the offender, forgiveness is often easier and more satisfying when both parties are meaningfully engaged. If you think about it, this makes a lot of sense. When the offender offers his hand in an open manner, it is easier to let go of the desire for retribution, reaching back instead with compassionate understanding.

Forgiveness is more than words or gestures. It's more than the ritual proclamation of "I'm sorry" and "I forgive you." It is not uncommon for people to verbally express forgiveness while still holding on to angry feelings. This is an example of cheap forgiveness. It can be likened to the metaphor of "sweeping things under the rug," where the cleansing is wholly cosmetic. It offers little in the way of depth or substance. Instead, a forgiving gesture is offered for the sake of quickly smoothing things over and avoiding the difficulties inherent in serious attempts at engagement, communication, and reconciliation. If you have not let go of bitter thoughts and feelings toward the offender, then your forgiveness is still incomplete. Because of this, many experts prefer to think of forgiveness as process that extends through time, rather than as a simple act that is performed once and quickly completed.

Preparing to Forgive

Forgiveness is not something that has to be rushed into. It is a significant and demanding act that can only be performed when you are ready to let go. You may feel that you have unfinished business—issues, concerns, and ideas that must be explored. You may need time to think it through, to allow your anger to settle down, or to process the situation with someone you trust. Certainly, if you are still hot with anger, you almost certainly aren't ready to forgive. For most people, forgiveness helps to release the vestiges of anger, but it also requires that the anger has already cooled to some extent. When you feel ready to actively work to rid yourself of such feelings, you may be ready to approach forgiveness.

In preparing to forgive someone, it is very helpful to try to understand where he was coming from. To consider, in a thoughtful and open way, the thoughts, emotions, concerns, blind spots, insecurities, and stressors that might have influenced the other person. Not because any of these things necessarily excuse or justify the behavior, but because consideration of these things serves to humanize the other person and to make his actions more comprehensible. Consider the immediate context in which the offense occurred (e.g., perhaps the other person had been under severe stress when the incident occurred). Consider the broader context as well—whatever background information you know that is relevant to understanding the other person. This includes factors such as religious and cultural influences, psychological problems, and painful childhood experiences. Use this information to understand what took place. What concerns were influencing him at the time? How was he seeing things?

Clearly, another relevant consideration here is the other person's behavior toward you in the aftermath of his offense. Is he showing remorse? Is he reaching out to you in an effort to repair the harm? Is he committed to ensuring that something similar doesn't happen again? None of these questions requires an affirmative response in order for you to forgive, but, at the same time, it is much easier to forgive someone who appears to be genuinely apologetic about what he has done.

Within yourself, it can be helpful to approach forgiveness by exploring why you might be encouraging your resentment and pain. Are you giving free rein to thoughts of resentment and self-pity? Are you using what happened for some kind of secondary gain, such as receiving attention and recognition from others? As you prepare to forgive, it is important to try to minimize these behaviors: It is hard to let go of anger by releasing it with one hand while holding tightly with the other. Both hands must let go. Take the time to think about your own mistakes and flaws. Have you ever hurt someone before? Have you ever failed to live up to your own expectations? The recognition of your own fallibility will make it easier to accept that fallibility in others. When you are able to do that, you are practically knocking on the door of forgiveness.

If after all of the above you are still "on the fence" with respect to forgiving, take the time to consider costs and benefits. What is forgiveness likely to cost you? What do you stand to lose? It is helpful to answer these questions for yourself, with consideration of your own unique situation, values, and concerns. At a general level, though, it can be said that the primary costs associated with forgiveness are, first, having to let go of your sense of indignation, and second, the investment of time and personal resources that is required to forgive. Not an easy thing when you've been hurt. On the other hand, consideration here will highlight some pretty compelling benefits. Many obvious ones have already been presented: feeling less angry and agitated; feeling free from what happened; feeling more peaceful and engaged in your day-to-day life. If you can stop carrying the burden of resentment and blame, if you can release this poison, it is to your benefit. It is not a decision to be made lightly, but what a relief to be able to surrender the burden of anger and pain.

Techniques for Facilitating Forgiveness

Most people will experience variable levels of difficulty when trying to forgive someone, depending on the situation. Because forgiveness can be a real struggle, it is helpful to use a systematic approach. The following six-step process, adapted from the research of Wade and Worthington (2005), incorporates an approach that has been proved effective in scientific studies:

1. **Define forgiveness.** Make sure that you clearly understand the differences between forgiveness, forgetting, and condoning the perpetrator's behavior.
2. **"Tell your story."** This can be done internally (in your thoughts), through journaling, with a friend or therapist, or in other ways. Take the time to process what happened, from the perspective of how you experience the situation as it was unfolding. Describe your thoughts and feelings. Give full attention to the hurt, the confusion, the anger, and the unfairness you might have experienced.
3. **Practice compassion and understanding.** Consider how the offender experienced the situation: her thoughts, feelings, motivations, and concerns. Then step back and consider these factors in light of the bigger picture of what you know about her and about her unique history.
4. **Remember times when you hurt someone.** Doing so will allow you to connect with the offender through a recognition of your shared humanity and imperfection. The recognition of "common ground" directly facilitates compassion, understanding, and letting go.
5. **List the anticipated advantages of forgiveness.** Consider, as well, the disadvantages associated with not forgiving.

6. **Reduce or eliminate thoughts and fantasies that generate anger.** These thoughts make forgiveness difficult. They keep you boiling with fresh hurt and anger. Instead of simply eliminating these thoughts, consider replacing them with inspirational remembrances of people who have forgiven others.

CHAPTER 14

Going Deeper:
The Role of Thinking

Sometimes anger is the result of a miscommunication or misinterpretation of information. The appraisal theory tries to determine how many of the emotional difficulties people experience, including unhealthy and chronic anger, are the result of thoughts, beliefs, and interpretations. Anger is often a result of thinking that you have been unfairly treated or disrespected, or that others have fallen short of or broken your rules, standards, or expectations.

The Hidden Cause of Anger: A Case Study

Joseph is society's vision of a man who has his act together. He is an educated, successful family man who is dedicated to his wife, Deb, and to their children. He is not the kind of guy you would expect to have an anger problem. And yet, increasingly over the course of his marriage, he struggled with angry outbursts that seemed to occur with little warning.

The breaking point came during a family vacation. Joseph had just driven the family to their hotel for the night, and everyone seemed to be in a good mood. But then, as they were preparing to vacate their car, Deb took a few moments to quickly tidy up some trash. Joseph viciously snapped at her, "It's fine—don't worry about it!" These words were uttered with such anger and loudness that the entire family went quiet. With prompting, the kids followed him into the hotel while Deb stayed behind in the car. She sat there for about half an hour.

Joseph later apologized, and the trip moved forward as planned. But the incident cast a pall over next day. The problem was that this had happened before. Too many times. And almost always with the anger directed toward Deb. Joseph was puzzled and disturbed by this, because he loved his wife and admired her greatly. He had vowed in the past not let it happen again, but it did. He was losing confidence in himself. He felt ashamed and disheartened. He discussed the matter with Deb, and they agreed to explore psychotherapy.

What the therapy revealed, in time, was the underlying issue here had less to do with Joseph's relationship with Deb, and more to do with himself and his past history. Joseph had been raised in a loving family, but it was also a family marked by criticism and high expectations. One effect of this was that Joseph had internalized a strong tendency toward self-criticism and self-judgment. He was constantly comparing himself to others, and usually found himself lacking. Despite his outward success, he did not feel confident in who he was. These insecurities were triggered, accidently, by his wife Deb. He felt diminished by her competence, her spontaneity, and her skill with handling the children. In his mind, she was always better than him, and at times he imagined that she was deliberately trying to "show him up." This was what happened with the incident during their vacation. He interpreted her cleaning up the trash in the car as a rebuke of him. While he attributed this rebuke to Deb, it really came from within himself. Being able to recognize this represented a significant breakthrough.

"Not Good Enough"

Thoughts and beliefs have a powerful influence over emotions. In Joseph's case, he associated feeling hurt with the trigger of his wife, Deb—in particular, with the idea of her being better than him. To protect himself, Joseph used anger to push her away. This only created more tension for him. It was clear to Joseph that Deb couldn't be the ultimate cause of his anger. She hadn't done anything that he could really object to.

We operate on beliefs and assumptions. These beliefs and assumptions are accrued over time, in the context of life experiences. If you are like most people, you often aren't aware of how your beliefs influence your emotions. You may not even recognize that the beliefs are there. Too often, people accept their first thoughts or assumptions without reflecting more deeply.

ALERT

Anger that arises from insecurity is particularly efficient at destroying intimate relationships. Learning to recognize what's going on beneath your anger can empower you to deal with maladaptive thoughts and beliefs that are at the root of insecurity.

For Joseph, the unconscious comparisons and self-judgments driven by these hidden beliefs caused his anger.

Same Situation, Different Emotions

Imagine your supervisor is criticizing you for your deficient response to a critical situation, which had severely negative consequences for other people. What emotions would this situation evoke? Both appraisal theory and cognitive behavioral therapy assume that this essentially depends on how you interpret the situation. You might respond with anger if you believe that the allegations are unjustified. You might respond with shame if you think that this failure revealed your true incompetence. Or you might respond with, or at least maintain, positive emotions if you believe you had done an excellent job and expect to be vindicated.

The idea that people respond with different emotions to the same situation depending on how they interpret, or appraise, the situation is one of the core assumptions of cognitive appraisal theories. In this view, it is the appraisal of a situation, not the situation per se, that determines the quality and the intensity of an emotional response. Specifically, appraisal theories of emotion assume that the emotions elicited by an event are determined by how the event is interpreted through a number of appraisal dimensions, including the importance of the event, its expectedness, the responsible agent, and the degree to which it is possible to control the event.

Appraisal Theory

The important connection between thought and emotion is not a particularly novel idea. It dates back to the ancient Greek philosophers.

In the mid-twentieth century, psychologists Magda Arnold and Richard Lazarus began to apply this idea to basic research on emotion and stress. In early experimental research, Lazarus and his colleagues showed violent film excerpts to participants, who were first read passages designed to increase either emotional distance or the perception of threat. The participants viewed the same film clips, but those in the perceived-threat group had been led, beforehand, to "expect the worst." The results were striking. The emotional-distance group displayed reduced emotional reactions; the film excerpts did not impact them as strongly. The perceived-threat group, however, showed a heightened response. They had by far the strongest emotional and physiological reactions.

The implications of this study are very important, since the participants all viewed and reacted to the same films. The only difference between the groups was in how they were directed to think about these films. That difference—how they *thought* about the films, what they *expected* to happen—was everything. Experimental findings such as this helped lay the foundation for appraisal theory, which offers a comprehensive account of how thoughts, beliefs, and expectations powerfully shape emotional experience. The word *appraisal* in this context simply refers to your evaluation of a given situation and of yourself in relation to that situation (think of the earlier example of Joseph *negatively apprais-ing* himself in relation to his wife).

FACT

Magda Arnold was not only a pioneering psychologist, she was also among the first women to break through the gender wall that had traditionally kept women out of academics and research. Her research helped lay the foundation for modern appraisal theory, and she also made important contributions in the field of personality measurement and psychological testing.

Based on such evidence, Lazarus developed a general concept: Stress is determined by thinking (appraisal), not by situations. To express this more carefully, appraisal theory basically says that the impact that any given situation has on your emotional state is controlled by how you think about (appraise) that situation. Appraisal is thus a universal process whereby people evaluate the significance of events and react emotionally on the basis of that evaluation.

Appraisal theory emphasizes the balance between psychological resources and environmental demands. When there is a perceived imbalance between situational demands and personal resources, the individual experiences stress. Conversely, if there is a misperceived balance between demands and resources (i.e., if a person sees himself as capable of meeting a particular challenge, but he is actually not capable), then the individual will not experience stress—at least not until the imbalance comes to light!

In the theory Lazarus put forward, cognitive appraisal can be subdivided into three more specific forms of appraisal:

- **Primary appraisal.** An environmental situation is regarded as being positive, stressful, or irrelevant to well-being.
- **Secondary appraisal.** An account is taken of the resources that the individual has available to cope with the situation.

- **Re-appraisal.** The stimulus situation and the coping strategies are monitored, with the primary and secondary appraisals being modified if necessary.

Appraisal theory has been enormously influential. It has forever changed how social scientists think about stress, emotion, behavior change, and human development. It also left an indelible impact on the field of clinical psychology by placing cognition front and center in terms of treatment interventions targeting various psychological problems.

Research Findings

There is a vast (and growing) body of scientific research regarding appraisal theory. While a review of this research would go beyond the scope of this book, it is helpful to highlight certain findings to illustrate the breadth of the relationship between cognition and emotion.

Studies show that appraisal plays an important role in children's emotional reactions. For example, research has found that the emotional impact of parental fighting on children is largely controlled by the children's appraisal of the situation. In one study, the researchers tested coping strategies and measured child adjustment based on the children's self-reported emotional and behavioral adjustment. They found that a child's negative appraisals of parental fighting—such as self-blaming, or imagining that her parents might divorce—were associated with greater feelings of depression and reduced feelings of self-worth. This study and others like it demonstrate the relevance of cognitive appraisal processes for children's ability to cope with emotionally challenging circumstances.

In another study of emotional coping targeting adults, researchers found significant relationships between appraisal, coping, and emotional discomfort. The individual's primary appraisal of a situation was the main contributor of predicting how that person would respond emotionally. Other research has substantiated the importance of appraisal by looking at what happens when people's evaluation of a situation is actively manipulated. In one study, participants were presented with narrative vignettes and were told to identify with a central character who performs poorly in the story. For the first group of participants, the central character put the blame on unhelpful assistants—that is, her appraisal of the situation was that it was someone else's fault. For the second group, the central character argued that he had made too many mistakes, putting the blame on himself. These appraisal manipulations had the predicted effects on the participants' emotional reactions. Anger was more common when there was other-accountability (blaming someone else) rather than self-accountability, whereas guilt was more common when there was self-accountability rather than other-accountability. The participants' emotional response to the story was decisively impacted by the way they *interpreted* the main character's behavior.

Confirming evidence about the central role of cognitive appraisals in emotions comes from research on emotion regulation. Research in this area shows that voluntary changes in the appraisals of a situation—in other words, deliberately thinking about a situation in a different way—can powerfully influence the intensity of an emotional reaction. These results show that changing the way people think about a situation can be sufficient, by itself, to change the intensity of reactive emotions such as sadness, fear, and anger. By comparison, other emotion-regulation strategies, such as teaching people to actively inhibit their emotion reactions, are significantly less efficient at changing the intensity of emotions.

Anger Appraisals

Research on anger has identified the following four kinds of appraisals that are systematically related to anger.

1. **Goal-blocking.** The appraisal of goal-blocking or goal-obstacle—also referred to as *frustration*—is generally accepted as an important determinant of anger and aggression. When people believe that their desires are being impeded, they are more likely to become angry.

2. **Other-accountability.** The appraisal of other-accountability refers to believing that somebody else is the cause of an undesirable event. This appraisal is essentially the same as the goal-blocking appraisal, with the major difference that in this case someone else is actively blamed. The other-accountability appraisal is considered by some theorists to be the core component of anger.

3. **Unfairness.** The relation between anger and the appraisal of unfairness has been documented in a number of studies. Perceived unfairness is

closely related to the appraisal of illegitimacy, which is also considered a determinant of anger.

4. **Threat to self-esteem.** The experience of anger and the display of aggressive behavior have been related to the appraisal of threatened self-esteem; the expression of anger is then seen as an effort to maintain self-esteem. Thus, when something happens that makes you feel bad about yourself, or that you feel tarnishes your public image, you are more likely to become angry. This was precisely what happened to Joseph at the beginning of this chapter.

The frustration-aggression hypothesis was originally formulated by John Dollard in 1939. According to this model, frustration is a feeling of tension that occurs when efforts to reach a goal are blocked. Frustration produces feelings of anger, which in turn can generate feelings of aggression. This theory has been utilized to explain much of the violence that occurs in modern society.

Of these four different types of appraisals, the appraisal of frustration (goal-blocking) appears to be the most powerful. One recent study looked at these issues comprehensively, and showed that the appraisal of frustration was a necessary component of anger, whereas other kinds of appraisals, such as other-accountability and unfairness, produced anger in some participants but not in others. Thus, anger was necessarily experienced in conjunction with appraised frustration, but not necessarily in conjunction with other appraisals. Findings such as this are consistent with the frustration-aggression hypothesis, which argues that anger and aggression can arise from frustration even when goal-blocking is not viewed as illegitimate or intentional. Based on such findings, many theorists now believe that aversive, frustrating circumstances constitute the core elicitor of anger, with other appraisals not being necessary for this emotion to occur.

Perception and Anger

One of the most important ways that beliefs have been shown to influence emotion is through the relationship between beliefs and perception. Simply stated, your beliefs exert a powerful influence on how you see the world. If you expect to find goodness in people, you will be more likely to perceive goodness in people. If you expect to find "badness" in people, you will be more likely to perceive that as well. These kinds of dynamics play out in all sorts of ways.

A commonplace example of biased perception is paranoia. Paranoid people, by definition, expect the worst from others. They expect to be maligned, taken advantage of, cheated, and mocked. As a result, they have a pronounced tendency to perceive slights and provocations where none actually exist. In essence, they project their expectations onto real-life situations and then respond to those situations on the basis of their biased perceptions. Angry people do this all the time. In the example of Joseph and Deb, because Joseph's self-esteem was threatened by Deb's conscientious behavior, he interpreted this behavior in a very negative way, thinking that she was only being organized and patient in order to "show him up." This negative interpretation only added to his anger.

Tendencies to perceive events in certain fixed ways are referred to as *cognitive biases*. The most important cognitive biases are as follows:

- **Attentional bias.** The tendency to look for and selectively attend to negative or threatening information. People with chronic anger issues are more likely to seek out negative information that will lead to anger. They expect bad things to happen and are constantly on the lookout for reasons to get angry. They often are not aware that they are doing this.
- **Interpretive bias.** This is the "glass half-empty" bias—the tendency to interpret ambiguous and mixed "good-bad" situations in a highly negative manner. People with chronic anger problems tend to interpret situations in the worst way possible, which leads to more anger.

- **Memory bias.** The tendency to remember negative or unpleasant information over and above positive or neutral information. This is actually a common bias, but it is far more pronounced among people with anger problems. They tend to focus very strongly on the most negative characteristics of past events.

How powerful are your perceptions in shaping your emotional reactions? Probably more powerful than you realize. Experimental research has shown that even brief interventions in which people are trained to pay more attention to positive or negative information, or to interpret events in a positive or negative manner, can have a decisive impact on their emotional reactions.

Appraisal, Perception, and Psychotherapy: The Cognitive Revolution

You may not have heard of it, but during the 1960s there was a quiet revolution—the so-called cognitive revolution in clinical psychology. At that time, behaviorism was the dominant school of thought and had been for decades. Behaviorism maintained that the study of internal psychological events, such as thoughts, was not useful in terms of understanding and ameliorating behavioral and emotional problems. Instead, behaviorists focused on how experiences were shaped by various forms of conditioning, such as in the study of "Pavlov's dog."

In a now-famous study, Russian physiologist Ivan Pavlov found that by pairing food with the ringing of a bell, a dog would eventually learn to salivate at the sound of the bell, even if no food was present. This process, called *classical conditioning*, has been shown to give rise to a range of emotional problems such as phobias.

Starting in the 1950s, new evidence began to shift the tide against behaviorism to focus, instead, on topics such as attention, memory, and appraisal processes. It wasn't that behaviorism was wrong, but rather that it was incomplete. This shifting tide gave rise to a family of psychological techniques that are now broadly referred to as *cognitive behavioral therapy* (CBT). As you might expect from what has already been presented in this chapter, the emphasis here is on helping people resolve their psychological difficulties by addressing their thoughts/beliefs/appraisals (i.e., their cognitions) alongside their manifest behaviors and choices.

The idea that people respond with different emotions to the same situation, depending on how they interpret, or appraise, that situation, is a core, defining assumption of all forms of CBT. The goal of this therapy is to learn that, although you cannot control every aspect of the world around you, you can control how you interpret and deal with situations. That, alone, can make a profound difference. This is the truly insightful implication of the "same situation, different emotions" phenomenon. Simply teaching people to examine their beliefs and assumptions, and to think in a more rational and adaptive manner, can positively transform their mood and overall sense of well-being.

Cognitive behavioral therapy has been studied extensively in clinical research. It has proved to be effective with a broad range of difficulties, including anxiety, depression, bipolar disorder, attention deficit hyperactivity disorder (ADHD), hypochondriasis, stuttering, and anger. A recent analysis pooled the results from fifty studies that looked at the effectiveness of CBT-based treatment interventions for chronic and out-of-control anger. The results were strong, with the average participant experiencing improvement in excess of 76 percent of control group members. A specific application of CBT, Albert Ellis's ABCD method, is presented in the next chapter.

Making Thinking Work for You

CHAPTER 15

Changing Distorted Thinking

Your thoughts affect you greatly, creating emotions like anger, fear, and love based on interpretations of your experience. This is an enormously powerful concept, because it directly points to how you can more effectively take control of your emotional life by owning your thoughts. Psychologist Albert Ellis's ABCD model points to a number of ways that irrational thinking can create emotional problems, and offers a structured approach for learning to make your thoughts work for you, rather than against you.

Making Thinking Work for You

Your thoughts influence your feelings. This is the core idea underlying appraisal theory. If you think people won't like you, you feel disappointed and withdraw socially. If you think nothing will work out well for you, you feel sad or passive and won't try. If you think you must have help to do something, you may feel inadequate and be dependent. If you think someone is blocking you from achieving a goal, you may feel angry.

The insights of appraisal theory sparked a revolution in the field of clinical psychology—a "cognitive revolution" that placed thinking front and center. In research that extended over many years, powerful bidirectional relationships were established between thought and emotion (thoughts change emotions, but emotions can also change thoughts) and between thought and behavior (thoughts change behavior, but behavior can also change thoughts). Psychologists were quick to realize that these ideas could be leveraged to help people live more satisfying lives, and CBT was born.

Challenging Irrational Ideas

Almost all forms of CBT were designed to be used by a trained psychotherapist working directly with a client. However, one particular form, *rational emotive therapy* (RET), is particularly well suited for individuals working on their own. This form of therapy is often referred to as the *ABC* or *ABCD model.*

FACT

"What's old is new"—Cognitive behavioral therapy owes an enormous debt to the ancient Greek and Roman philosophy of Stoicism. The Stoic beliefs that you are disturbed not by things that happen but by what you think of them and that you can discipline yourself to control what you think and how you feel are among CBT's central tenets.

As a form of cognitive behavioral therapy, RET incorporates much of the theoretical underpinnings from appraisal theory. It is built on the central idea that how you emotionally respond at any moment depends on your interpretations of events—your views, your beliefs, your thoughts. The things you think and say to yourself, not what actually happens to you, cause your positive or negative emotions. As Ellis, the originator of RET, would say, "Humans largely disturb themselves . . . your own unreasonable, irrational ideas make you severely anxious, depressed, self-hating, enraged, and self-pitying about virtually anything—yes, virtually anything." This is a very old idea.

If irrational ideas cause most of your intense, long-lasting, unwanted emotional reactions, there is a (seemingly) simple solution: Change your thinking. That is exactly what RET tries to do. RET goes beyond appraisal theory in that it has an explicit focus on helping people to improve their situation. Thus, it affords empirically validated techniques and interventions that can help people to change their thoughts and beliefs, resulting in enhanced emotional functioning and improved quality of life.

In traditional RET, a therapist works with you to identify unreasonable thoughts and beliefs that are creating difficulties. From there, these thoughts and beliefs immediately are systematically confronted and analyzed such that the individual begins to think differently and, as a result, feels and behaves differently. This approach involves persuasion, arguments, logic, and education—essentially insisting that the individual learns to be more rational and scientific. If you don't have a therapist, you can incorporate many of these same principles on your own.

The ABCD Model

Rational emotive therapy is all about the ABCDs. This simple acronym describes an effective, easy-to-remember framework for recognizing and changing irrational ideas. Here are the basics:

- *A is for activating.* These are the red-flag events that trigger your anger. They could be almost anything, such as someone spills a drink or your spouse forgets to pay a bill.
- *B is for belief.* Here, *belief* is a catchall term for how you think about or appraise the activating event.

- *C* **is for consequence.** This refers to emotional consequences in particular. These are the feelings you experience as a result of how you interpreted the event.
- *D* **is for dispute.** This is when you examine your beliefs and expectations (*B*) regarding the activating event (*A*). Are they unrealistic or irrational? Is there a more constructive and emotionally agreeable way of looking at things?

In keeping with the basic tenets of cognitive behavioral therapy, the ABCD model states that it isn't so much the event (*A*) that creates an angry response as what you believe and tell yourself (*B*) about that event. According to Ellis and other cognitive behavior theorists, as people become angry, they engage in "self-talk"—a kind of internal dialogue. Imagine, for example, that you've been waiting ten minutes for the subway. As the train gets nearer, a group of people push their way to the front of the platform. You may start to get angry. Certainly, many people would. You might say to yourself, "Unbelievable! How can people be so rude! They brushed past me like I didn't even exist. This is unacceptable, people should be more considerate. This is yet another example of how society is going into the tank!" Many people would consider this an understandable reaction, if somewhat overwrought. Even so, it is riddled with irrational statements that are sure to escalate anger, such as "Unbelievable!" "This is unacceptable," and "society is going into the tank!"

ESSENTIAL

Ellis argued that you can decrease the number of irrational beliefs by developing three insights: (1) You mainly upset yourself by holding on to inflexible ideas. (2) No matter when and how you start upsetting yourself, you continue to feel upset because you cling to these ideas. (3) The only way to get better is to work hard at changing your beliefs. This requires practice.

The central premise of the ABCD model, and one that is well supported by clinical research, is that events like this do not have to make you angry. Rather, the way you think about what happened is everything. If you thought the people were pushing you aside because of some sort of medical emergency, you would not be as upset. If you thought they were young students excited to be on the way to some event, you might reminisce on your own student days, and feel more tolerant toward them. And if you thought to yourself that these were simply rude, uncaring people, you might conclude that their behavior is not really personal (it says more about them than about you) and is not worth being upset about. On the other hand, if your thinking is dominated by *should's* and *must's*—e.g., people should be considerate toward each other, and it is terrible when they are not—then buckle up your seatbelt. Anger is right around the corner.

Ellis's approach consists of identifying the thoughts and beliefs that are associated with negative emotions such as anger and anxiety, and then disputing them with more adaptive perspectives. It applies sound critical-thinking skills to experiences and emotional reactions. In the example of the subway, is it really "unbelievable" that people would cut in line? Hardly. People have been doing things like this throughout history. Is it "unacceptable" that this would happen? Only if you decide that it is. That's a choice. Should people be "more courteous"? In an ideal world, absolutely. Public interactions would be so much more enjoyable and easygoing. But should you expect people to be courteous and then get angry when they're not? Not if you value your own peace of mind and internal harmony.

From the rational perspective of the ABCD model, the insistence that people should behave in a particular manner (whatever that might be) doesn't fit with reality. People can and do behave in all sorts of ways. Many people endeavor to be courteous, thoughtful, or kind. Some could care less. And sometimes, good people have bad days. You can bet that at any given moment, on any given day, people are engaging in behaviors that you would object to if you were on the "receiving end"—wrong place, wrong time. So, are you going to be angry all the time? That's an option. But if you're taking an ABCD approach, the point is to step back from knee-jerk anger thinking, evaluate the rationality of your response, and consider alternative, less reactive points of view that might make more sense in the bigger picture of your life.

After all, life is short. Perhaps you'd be better off focusing your energy on the things you can control and influence, and on what you can do to create a rich, meaningful life. This is the kind of critical thinking that combats unhealthy anger. This is what the *D* in Ellis's ABCD model is all about.

You may get angry over issues of control and power. "I must always be in control. I must control every situation." It sounds silly when it's stated this way (which tells you something, if you think about it), but many people operate their lives based on these kinds of beliefs—often without having fully admitted it to themselves. It is not possible to control every situation. Taking this approach to life will only cause frustration. Try and avoid these feelings. You might tell yourself, "I have no power over things I cannot control." This is a rational perspective that is powerfully conducive to peace of mind.

The reality is that the world will inevitably present you with circumstances that you find challenging and aversive. You can try to change or control the world, but that's impossible. You will only frustrate yourself further. Focus on changing and controlling how you are affected by events outside your control. You can tell yourself that you will not allow rude, inconsiderate people to control you. "Control me how?" you might ask. By pulling your emotional strings. When you get upset over someone behaving badly, you are allowing that person to dictate your emotional experience. You are yielding power to them. But here's an alternative mindset: "I refuse to allow my emotional harmony to be usurped by random people I encounter in the world." That's another kind of self-talk, one that operates in opposition to knee-jerk reactivity. Rather than being pushed around by circumstance, you are making a conscious choice to own your emotional reactions.

What Is Rational Thinking?

First, you must face the truth of your anger; that's rational. Second, if you view reality for what it is, you will recognize that "whatever happens is lawful, not awful." Everything has a cause. The connections (called laws) between causes and effects are inevitable, the nature of things. So, when something happens that you don't like, accept that the event had its necessary and sufficient causes, and take reasonable steps to avoid it happening in the future.

Third, Ellis urges everyone to constantly use scientific methods of objective observation and experimentation—that is, to use the systematic manipulation of variables to see what happens. For example, if you think no one would accept a date with you, Ellis would tell you to ask out five appropriate, interesting people. If your belief (that no one will go out with you) proved to be correct with those five people, then Ellis would direct you to start manipulating the variable. Thus, how can your appearance or approach be improved, or how can you pick more receptive "dates" to approach? Then observe the outcome.

FACT

All people are capable of thinking rationally, but people tend to cloud this ability because of emotions or prejudices.

In summary, accept what is happening and what has happened as lawful, as the natural outcome of complex laws, and not as awful events that you or someone should have prevented. Although you can't change the past, you can learn to use these "laws of psychology" to help yourself and others. What you can't change in the future, you can accept.

To understand any strong, troublesome emotion, you need to see the first three parts of your experience clearly: the *A*, *B*, and *C*. However, it is difficult for people to recognize that some of their thoughts (*B*) may be irrational, unreasonable, or unhelpful. Therefore, it is important to examine common irrational thoughts that contribute to emotional problems such as chronic anger. With this information, it is easier to distinguish problematic thoughts at the *B*-step and, ultimately, to dispute these thoughts at the *D*-step.

Irrational Ways of Thinking That Keep You Angry

What kinds of ideas are irrational and are likely to make you angry, anxious, and upset? Ellis originally described ten common irrational ideas, such as "Everyone should love and approve of me," "I must be competent; it would be awful to fail," "When bad things happen, I am unavoidably very unhappy and should be," "It is terrible when things don't go the way I want."

There are hundreds of these ideas that have the power to transform life's ordinary disappointments into catastrophes. Your mind transforms preferences that are quite reasonable into absolutely unreasonable *shoulds*, *musts*, and demands, which are very upsetting.

Say, your friend disagrees with you. Imagine, further, that you hold the belief that "people must like me and give me approval in order for me to feel good." If you hold this belief, you are likely to get angry when you face rejection. You are talking yourself into a state of emotional upset, all the while externalizing the cause of your feelings onto your friend. Ellis called this mental process *awfulizing* or *catastrophizing*.

Here are eleven types of distorted trigger thoughts that can prompt you to overreact. If you're able to change these irrational thoughts, the distressing emotions deriving from them should change as well. Even better, the things that formerly provoked you will no longer do so once you've managed to bring a new understanding to them.

- **Shoulds.** The mistake here is to believe that your *shoulds* are somehow universal—that what is intelligent, reasonable, or moral for you ought to be for others as well. In reality, *shoulds* represent imposing your values, beliefs, and preferences on someone with different values, beliefs, and preferences. Others, for their part, are unlikely to be persuaded that they're wrong or bad simply because they haven't lived up to your self-interested standards. Consequently, in your revised self-talk, you might say, "People don't do what I think they should; they do what makes sense to them," or "It is completely unrealistic to expect people to act the way I'd like them to act."
- **Entitlement fallacy.** This trigger is grounded in the belief that if you really want something, it's only right that you should have it. Such thinking leads you to get angry whenever others (as is frequently the case) take exception to your "righteous" expectations and demands. Such demands may not feel at all reasonable to them. If somehow this fallacy has become part of your mental programming, you might say to yourself, "Though I may have the right to want something, others have the right to say no," or "My desiring something doesn't mean that others are obliged to provide it for me."

ESSENTIAL

Ellis identified three *musts* that cause additional problems: (1) "I must do well and win the approval of others or I am no good." (2) "Other people must treat me in exactly the way I want them to treat me." (3) "I must get what I want, when I want it; and I must not get what I don't want."

- **Fallacy of fairness.** The falsehood is that there exists a single standard of fairness and—surprise!—it's yours. The fact is, however, that fairness is a completely subjective concept, based on individual wants, needs, principles, expectations, and values. In short, your definition of what is fair is self-serving (as is everyone else's). So if you've gotten angry because you thought you were being treated unjustly, here are some things you might say to yourself before your next encounter with someone whose notions of fairness may conflict with your own. "My notions on what is fair don't have any more authority than anyone else's," or "Their needs (or values) are just as legitimate and meaningful to them as mine are to me."

- **Fallacy of change.** This idea relates to the unwarranted belief that you can change another's behavior if you work at it hard enough. People change only when it's rewarding for them to do so and when they're capable of it. So to keep from getting angry with others who seem unwilling to cooperate with your (we'll suppose) well-meaning directives, think of saying to yourself, "People only change when they're ready to; no sense trying to pressure them," or "The support (help, recognition, understanding, etc.) that I'm getting is all they're capable of giving me right now."

- **Conditional assumptions.** For example, you assume that because the other person disappointed you, she must not care about you. Once you arrive at such an unverified conclusion, you'll start to feel upset; you are already primed to react negatively to her. In such instances, here is a more rational, "corrective" thought: "I need to realize that my disappointment with her doesn't necessarily mean she doesn't care about me."

- **Assumed intent.** Otherwise known as mind-reading, the fallacy is in assuming that if another person's behavior caused you distress, he must have intended to make you feel this way. Attributing negative motives to his behavior—because, after all, it did hurt or disturb you—is really (if you think about it) what's pushing your buttons. That is, similar to the other irrational assumptions and beliefs already described, it is your subjective (and frequently biased) interpretation of others—rather than their behavior per se—that finally makes you lose your cool (or makes your "blood boil"). So what you need to start doing in your head is formulating "preconfrontation" thoughts: "I won't assume anything; I need to check this out," or "I'm not going to speculate about why he did that."

- **Polarized thinking (or "black-and-white" thinking).** In polarized thinking, there is no middle ground. You are either perfect or a failure. You place people or situations in "either/or" categories, without allowing for the complexity of most people and situations. If your performance falls short of perfect, you see yourself as a total failure. You are similarly polarized in judging others, which leads to frequent experiences of frustration and anger. The key to overcoming this type of thinking is to remind yourself, again and again, that most of life is shades of gray. Read a biography of someone universally honored for their contributions to society—Mahatma Gandhi or Martin Luther King Jr., for example—and see how even the best of us are flawed and imperfect.

- **Jumping to conclusions.** The irrational thinking here is in drawing a firm conclusion (and often *acting* on that conclusion) based on incomplete information and outright misunderstanding. People do it all the time. Rather than letting the evidence bring them to a logical conclusion, they set their sights on a conclusion (often negative) and then look for evidence to support it, ignoring anything to the contrary. The kid who decides that everyone in his new class hates him, and "knows" that they're only acting nice to him to avoid punishment, is jumping to conclusions. Conclusion-jumpers often fall prey to the related fallacies of mind-reading (believing that they know the true intentions of others without talking to them) and fortunetelling (predicting how things will turn out and believing these predictions to be true). To combat this bias, ask yourself how you know the things that you think you know. Are you making assumptions, or does the evidence leave no alternative but to derive the conclusion you have made? (Here's a hint: The latter rarely happens.)

- **Magnifying (or "catastrophizing").** Magnifying is a great way to get yourself worked up in a hurry. All you have to do is exaggerate the significance of someone's words or actions, or of an event that just occurred, in such a way that it seems much worse than it actually is. Tell yourself that it is "awful," "horrible," "unacceptable," "terrible," or "inexcusable," and you are almost guaranteed to feel an unpleasant and unnecessary emotion such as anger, fear, or hurt. If you have even an inkling that you might be magnifying a situation, talk to a few people whose opinion you respect and see what they think. If you can recognize that you do have a tendency to catastrophize, consider rehearsing such messages as "This is unpleasant, but it's not that awful," or "I'm not going to get ahead of myself—this thing probably isn't anywhere as bad as I'm assuming."

- **Disqualifying the positive.** This is a cognitive bias in which you effectively neuter, or disqualify, the significance of positive experiences. You reject positive experiences by insisting they "don't count," or you may even construe the experience in a negative light. In this way, you can maintain a negative belief that is contradicted by your everyday experiences. For example, when a subordinate at work offers you a compliment, you tell yourself, "She is just trying to get ahead by kissing up to me." A related cognitive distortion, called *minimizing*, is (as you might expect from the name) the exact opposite of magnifying: Instead of exaggerating the significance of something negative, you inappropriately shrink the magnitude of significant positive events. As with magnification, getting a second opinion can help you develop greater clarity. If disqualifying the positive and minimizing is something you tend to do, a great way to counteract this tendency is to take time each day to focus on the positive aspects of your life and of the people who are important to you. Taking the time to thoughtfully consider this perspective will help you see things more constructively as you move forward.

- **Personalization.** In this distortion, you incorrectly assume that everything others do or say is some kind of direct, personal reaction to you. You may also actively compare yourself to others, trying to determine who is smarter, richer, better looking, and so on. People who personalize tend to blame themselves or others for things over which they have no control, creating stress where it need not be. They also tend to blame themselves for the actions of others, or blame others for their own feelings. To reduce these tendencies, commit to looking at the evidence and considering alternate possibilities. When you find evidence that disconfirms your assumptions, really think through the situation: "How could I be so convinced of something that turned out to be wrong?" Doing so will sharpen your awareness, allowing you to catch yourself more and more quickly when your personalization bias rears its proverbial head.

The ABCD Model in Action

Frank was injured in a motor vehicle accident when a drunk driver crashed into his parked car. He suffered a number of painful injuries that required several months to rehabilitate. As he recovered, he couldn't get the accident out of his mind. The bitterness festered like an open wound. Even as his injuries healed, he felt worse both physically and emotionally.

Frank never pulled any punches in expressing how he felt about what had happened to him. He remained very angry. He also admitted to feelings of depression. He was furious with the person who hurt him. Frank's response was predictable. In his suffering, he lashed out at the person whom he saw as the cause of his troubles. However, while he was sinking into deeper levels of negativity, his psychological condition worsened.

A therapist working with Frank needed to understand what the accident meant to him and to show empathy. Without question, what had happened was unfair and reprehensible. The other driver's blood alcohol level was over twice the legal limit, and Frank could easily have been killed. Here is a segment from a session with Frank in which the ABCD model was applied to his situation:

Psychologist: The *A* in this situation is clearly the accident. Let's go back to that.

Frank: I'm parked, sitting in my car. Some drunk swerves right into me. It happened in a second, and it pretty much ruined my life. I had three cracked vertebrae, a broken arm. I missed out on a huge job opportunity. I missed my daughter's high school graduation. There was so much pain. It shouldn't have happened. I'm angry, I'm depressed, and I'm tired.

Psychologist: I hear you, it's a big deal. That drunk driver caused you a lot of pain, and a lot of hassle. Not to mention everything your loved ones had to go through. You've gone through something that few people can truly understand. It was wrong. I would only add that these events, taken together, are trouble enough as it is.

Frank: You can say that. But I'm not sure if I'm completely following you.

Psychologist: After all you've been through, who needs more troubles, like anger, depression, and increased pain?

Frank: No one. Not me, for sure. But I didn't ask for this. He did this to me.

Psychologist: Fair enough. The guy put you through a hellish ordeal, no doubt about it. But if you step back and look at the bigger picture, might you might be inadvertently giving yourself a double pain?

Frank: How so? I'm not seeing it.

Psychologist: Go back to the ABCD model, the discussion we had earlier. The accident is your *A*. It was a difficult and painful experience that took you months to recover from. If we apply the model here, the implication is that what you believe, *B*, about the drunk driver produces the emotional conse-quence that you experienced at point *C*: anger, depression, lethargy, all that. The point is you can't change *A*, but you can change *B*. What you tell your-self at point *B* adds a layer of misery to an already bad situation. Blaming and condemning the other driver is a prescription for extra misery—not for him, but for you, and by extension, for those who love you.

Frank: I guess I'm struggling with this. How can I think about this any other way? And how does thinking make it worse?

Psychologist: There are two levels to this, and you're getting nailed on each one. In terms of how you're feeling emotionally, you focus a lot of atten-tion on how you were wronged and on how much resentment you have toward the driver who hit you. Thinking this way feeds and nurtures your anger, adds to your depression, and even leads you to be irritable with your wife and children. In terms of actual physical pain, how you think about what you're experiencing can actually intensify the pain. We know that pain is influenced by thoughts and emotions; up to forty percent of the pain experience can be emotionally driven. Negative emotions such as depressed mood and anger can lead to increased pain—this "surplus pain," that is, pain that doesn't have to be there. By tempering your thinking, you can reduce surplus stresses that exacerbate your pain.

Frank: So when that jerk hit me, the depression and anger that he gave me actually increased the physical pain as well?

Psychologist: Yes and no. Remember that it's always B that causes C, not A that causes C. This is a fundamental confusion that many, many people make. You gave the anger to yourself. Neither you nor I nor anyone else can change what happened. The accident was very real. You suffered terrible injuries. The other driver was grossly irresponsible, and he never even showed remorse. This is the reality. We can't change any of it. But there is much that you can do in the present to help yourself develop a more healthy and realistic perspective about the event. Doing so will spare yourself from the double whammy effect. You don't have to suffer surplus pain.

A Gradual Awakening

The application of the ABCD model illuminates how some of Frank's deep-seated, fundamental beliefs led to unnecessary anger, depression, and pain. Frank asked for some reasonable things: fairness, justice, and freedom from severe injury and pain. However, his problems stemmed from the fact that he demanded these reasonable things. He insisted that he could not be happy otherwise. When he didn't get them—when the *impossibility* of getting them became all too apparent—he found himself trapped in an unending loop of frustration.

Frank didn't buy into the ABCD theory right away, but he was willing to try it. In a short time, a number of dysfunctional beliefs that contributed to his anger were identified. The *shoulds* and *musts* that he imposed on himself and others kept recurring. The accident "shouldn't" have happened, he "shouldn't" be in pain, and he "shouldn't" have to work to free himself from anger because the accident was the other person's fault. In time, Frank came to see that his *shoulds* and *musts* didn't pass the reality test (because people and life are not totally fair according to his definition) or the utility test (because his negative thinking just made him feel worse, not better).

Ultimately, Frank felt empowered. If he was smart enough to talk himself into anger and depression, perhaps he could talk himself out of thinking in a self-destructive fashion. As he worked to develop new, realistic, and functional beliefs, Frank's anger abated. His depression lifted. He prepared himself to make the best of the rest of his life.

Frank's journey can serve as a model for you as well. It takes courage, commitment, and tenacity to take ownership over your own well-being, instead of blaming and externalizing and engaging in "poor me" thinking. It is not easy to look yourself in the mirror, to question your most basic beliefs and assumptions, and then to work toward developing an alternative perspective. But it is very possible. And it works.

CHAPTER 16

Putting Anger to Good Use

Not all anger is "bad." When used wisely, anger can benefit you in many ways: by providing information that can be very useful, by calling your attention to problems and injustices, by alerting other people to your mindset, and by helping you improve your relationships. Anger is also a source of energy and motivation that can be used constructively in numerous helpful ways.

Not All Anger Is "Bad"

People tend to think of anger as a wild, negative emotion. There are all sorts of good, sensible, civilized reasons to avoid getting angry. Not only does anger often make you feel bad, it makes you do stupid things without noticing the risks. It can be flat-out self-destructive. As a result, people often do their best to suppress, redirect, and mask their anger. Anger is considered "negative," a problem, something to be eliminated or solved.

What people so often fail to see is that every problem is really an opportunity in disguise—an opportunity to learn, to grow, to mature, and to make significant changes for the good. In a recent study, 28 percent of respondents said that their anger was inappropriate, because anger is generally harmful or useless. Without question, many long-term outcomes of anger are negative. However, the effects of anger on your health aren't negative in the cut-and-dried way that's often advertised. It's partly a matter of parsing what we mean when we say "anger," because there are many different shades.

FACT

The Greek philosopher Aristotle recognized the positive potential of anger more than 2,000 years ago, but he also recognized the difficulties: "Anyone can become angry. That is easy. But to be angry with the right person, to the right degree, at the right time, for the right purpose and in the right way . . . that is not easy." (from *Nicomachean Ethics*)

Chronic, hostile anger, in particular, has been associated with a range of serious physical, psychological, and interpersonal problems. This is the "type A" profile that was famously associated with an increased risk of heart disease. Studies have also shown that one of the unhealthiest parts of anger comes not from feeling it, but from suppressing it—that is, pretending you're not angry and avoiding expressing the emotion. Repressing anger may lead to psychosomatic symptoms—like headaches, for example—or to depression. There are times when it makes sense to set your anger aside temporarily (e.g., you may not want to lose your job by exploding at your boss), but when anger is generally repressed or avoided, problems are sure to follow.

The more complicated picture that emerges is this: Chronic, hostile, aggressive, suppressed anger can be harmful, but controlled anger, under the right circumstances, can be a pretty helpful emotion.

Healthy Anger Has Tremendous Potential for Good

Part of the wonder of human emotions is that things aren't always as they seem: Happy isn't always good, and angry isn't always bad (although it may feel that way). An unhappy person is more likely to spot mistakes, and an angry person is highly motivated to act. Even scary and dangerous emotions have their upsides, as long as they are used for the correct purpose.

You may not like yourself when you're angry, and you certainly don't enjoy being around angry people. Yet, Aristotle was essentially correct. Like all emotions, anger can be used to good effect. Anger can reduce violence, benefit relationships, promote optimism, and be a motivating force. Anger can be good for you, because it's designed to protect you, your relationships, and your way of seeing the world. In the battle between right and wrong, the bodily effects of anger are meant to tell you that something's wrong.

Here are the key features of constructive anger:

- It is justified and proportionate to the wrongdoing.
- It is expressed as the first step in trying to *solve a problem*, rather than just venting bad feelings or seeking to hurt someone.

The expression of anger can feel good. Doesn't it feel good to "get it off your chest"? Anger may be needed to survive dangerous situations. If you were being attacked, or a loved one was being hurt, you might become angry and decide to either flee the aggressor or fight. Anger can stimulate productive action. Have you ever gotten fed up with something and decided to make changes? Anger is part of the normal grieving process. Loved ones might be understandably upset they are left behind. Perhaps they are angry with the deceased for doing things that led to an early death. The family members of people who have committed suicide are often angry at their relative's choice.

Remember, the most basic purpose of anger is to alert you to danger and, in doing so, to produce the fight-or-flight response. In other words, anger is meant to protect you from harm. The physical effects that you experience when you are angry are there to tell you that something is wrong. Anger can motivate you to make positive changes in your life or to advocate for others. Moral anger can be used to fight for justice and fairness in the world. Expressed anger can lead toward reconciliation in a relationship. Talking about what you feel is wrong in the relationship may lead to positive solutions.

Anger Is Information

First and foremost, anger gives you information:

- About people and situations
- That it's time to deal with a problem
- That something is wrong, frustrating, threatening, or annoying

The purpose of anger is to alert you to problems, not to undermine relationships and well-being. It's rather like the light on your car's dashboard that warns you when the oil pressure is too low. When you see that little warning light flash, you realize something is wrong. Similarly, when you feel anger, you realize that something is wrong with your current situation. Anger is designed to help you. How you express or respond to your anger may or may not be helpful, but that's a separate issue, and one over which you can exert considerable control if you are willing to work at it. When something needs to dramatically change, anger not only lets you know, it also gives you the power to do something about it. For example, if the pediatrician won't listen to your concerns about your child's health, getting angry may help her take you more seriously and get the problem diagnosed and solved.

Anger Alerts You to Problems in Your Life

Perhaps more than any other indicator, anger can be used to know, in modern life, when something is wrong on an individual, interpersonal, or societal scale. There are numerous occasions when the anger resounding within you is a warning signal that what someone is asking or demanding of you is unreasonable, that he's not respecting your basic needs, rights, or limits. Your anger may tell you that you are not addressing an important emotional issue in your life, or that too much of your self—your beliefs, values, desires, or ambition—is being compromised in a relationship. Your anger may be a signal that you are doing more and giving more than you can comfortably manage. Or your anger may be warning you that others are doing too much for you, at the expense of your own competence and growth. Just as physical pain tells you to take your hand off the hot stove, the pain of your anger preserves the integrity of your self.

ESSENTIAL

In one study, a sample of adults were asked about how recent outbursts of anger had affected them. Over half said that getting angry had led to a positive outcome, and a third said that anger provided helpful insight into their own faults. If you are able to notice when you get angry and why, then you can learn what to do to improve your life.

Without experiencing such initial anger as a vital cue that another person is attempting to exploit, take advantage of, or transgress your boundaries, you're likely to fall victim to her again and again (for example, working endless overtime for free, or being subjected to unwanted sexual advances). To get the most out of your anger, you need to be in a position to constructively manage your angry feelings. Another important area to review is that of anger triggers. If you can identify distinct triggers, take the time to look at them and reflect: What do they tell you about unmet needs, old frustrations, or unresolved hurts? You will use this information to address the underlying core issues. In other cases, where your anger is more situational than thematic in nature, follow a similar process: Ask yourself what the anger is telling you (besides the fact that you are angry!). Then, ask yourself how you can constructively use this information to make positive changes in your life and in your relationships.

Anger Alerts You to Injustice

Think of anger as your personal sheriff, riding into town when injustice occurs. The sheriff sends out police bulletins: "Hey, that's not right. That's not how we do business around here." Everyone gets angry at some point, so you can count on that sheriff making another appearance.

If the anger sheriff shows up for the right reasons and deals with the situation in the right way, then getting angry can be good for you. If the sheriff sits down with the perpetrator and has a productive conversation about how to solve the problem, then anger is doing its job. On the other hand, if you've got a reckless vigilante who shoots first and asks questions later, or a cowardly police academy dropout who runs the other way, then anger is not very productive. As with chocolate cake, anger has to be served in moderation.

One of the important ways that anger can be a force for good is when it encourages you to act against injustice. It can be a life guide of sorts, helping steer you away from the situations and people who are problematic for you. When you see the rights of others trampled or someone being hurt, you become angry. Martin Luther King Jr. was motivated by outrage over racial prejudice to start a civil rights movement in the United States. Similar moral anger led the American Founding Fathers to stand up to the abuses of the British crown, to the creation of child-welfare laws, and to numerous initiatives to help the poor and needy. When the energy that accompanies anger is channeled in a constructive way, it can be beneficial on both a personal and societal level.

The power that anger has to motivate people to stand up to injustice is closely related to the alerting function discussed earlier (this was also discussed in the first chapter of this book). Anger calls attention to problems, and it also provides the energy and the motivation to take action. To harness anger constructively, that second step is critical. Guidelines for harnessing anger to take decisive action are discussed later in this chapter, but first let's review other ways in which anger can used beneficially.

Anger Alerts Others

The value of anger as a signaling or alerting emotion is fairly well established. What is often overlooked, however, is the value of expressed anger in terms of alerting others to your state of mind. There are times when thoughtfully expressed, controlled anger enables you to communicate negative sentiments more forcefully, and optimizes the chance that you'll be heard. For example, with a child whose rambunctious impulses have momentarily gotten the better of her, her parents may need to raise their voice simply to get the child's attention. Or it may be helpful to display a bit of anger with a colleague or employee to get his attention and communicate your level of seriousness. Anger is used this way all the time. If done correctly (and sparingly), it can be helpful.

Anger tells others it is important to listen to you—that you feel agitated, and that it is wise to be alert to your words and actions. Healthy, controlled expressions of anger may also lead to compliance by others. Strongly asserting that you were first in line at the cashier may lead to better service. In the short term, others may be more likely to comply with your requests when you are angry. "Don't go in the street without holding Mommy's hand!" said angrily to a small child could save his life. As in almost any area involving anger, self-control is the key. If you can manage the anger you are feeling, and express yourself forcefully but respectfully, that will be enough in some situations to get others to moderate their behavior.

FACT

Controlled anger has been shown to help people at certain negotiations. In a 2005 study at Stanford University, researchers asked participants to role-play a negotiation. Those who were told they had poor alternatives to making a deal were much more likely to concede to people expressing controlled anger than they were to concede to people who were not angry.

Anger can be a legitimate way to get what you want. In one study of negotiation, participants made larger concessions and fewer demands of an angry person than of one who was happy. So there's some evidence that anger can be used as a negotiation strategy, but it's more complicated than that. You can't just let loose your rage and expect to win everything you want. Anger is likely to work best when it's justified, if you appear powerful, and when the other side's options are limited. In the right circumstances, then, it's possible to get mad *and* to get even.

Anger Can Help *Improve* Your Relationships

Anger is a natural reaction to being wronged, and it's a way of communicating that feeling to others. When identified and used effectively, this kind of anger can help relationships grow.

When you're angry, you tend toward confrontation. Sometimes people feel anxious about this, but it isn't always a bad thing. Although confrontation can be physical and spiteful, it can also be constructive. It depends on how you go about it. Self-control, assertiveness, and emotional honesty are the keys to confrontation. A recent study, for example, found that confronting a romantic partner with assertive anger was quite useful in helping people set boundaries and self-define and clarify needs within the context of the relationship.

Expressing your anger assertively allows you to state your needs, to indicate to important others when boundaries have been crossed, or to signal that you felt betrayed, insulted, or treated unfairly. Anger can motivate you to leave or change a bad situation. Anger helps express tension and communicates negative feelings. Of course, anger is notorious for causing problems in relationships, but that is mismanaged anger. If used constructively, anger can actually help resolve conflict in relationships. In fact, research has shown that hiding anger in intimate relationships can be detrimental. When you hide your anger, your partner doesn't know he's done something wrong. And so he keeps doing it—and you keep getting angry. This cycle does not benefit your relationship. The expression of anger, if justifiable and aimed at finding a solution rather than just venting, can actually strengthen relationships.

To use anger constructively in your relationships, follow these basic guidelines:

1. **Know what the anger is telling you.** For example, if you are angry because your boyfriend teased you in front of his friends, then you almost certainly felt hurt and embarrassed, in addition to feeling angry. For anger to help you in a relationship, you need to be able to recognize and communicate the core issues that gave rise to the anger in the first place.

2. **Be willing to express vulnerability.** This might not always be appropriate—for example, at work—but it certainly is in the close personal relationships that are important to you. If you persist in avoiding vulnerable feelings, you are inherently limiting the extent to which you can grow in a relationship.

3. **Express anger as it arises,** or as soon as you can while maintaining appropriate self-control.

4. **Use good communication skills.** Communicate your anger assertively, not aggressively. Remember that no matter how "right" or "important" your message may be, if it is expressed in a way that is perceived as demeaning or provocative, you will probably not get very far in this endeavor.

Anger Is Energy

The highest and most constructive purpose of anger is to act as an agent of change. Anger is energy. It is a powerful motivating force. It can sharpen focus and provide the determination and power to change. While you may have minimal control over the fact that you experience anger, you have almost total control over how you choose to express that anger. You can spend that energy unskillfully, like a child with a garden hose, or you can channel it in healthy, positive, and constructive ways.

In a recent study from 2010, participants were asked to stare at screens showing pictures of items preceded by angry, fearful, or neutral faces. They were asked to squeeze a trigger when they saw an item they wanted. Results showed that they squeezed harder for items preceded by an angry face, leading to the conclusion that people use anger as fuel in competitive environments.

Anger can be a motivating force that can also make people feel more optimistic and confident. Acknowledging anger can help lower stress on the heart and manage pain. Research also shows that anger can make you push toward your goals despite problems and barriers. When you see something as beneficial, you want it more when you're angry.

The energy of anger, when wisely invested, can provide greater focus and intensity and lead to greater productivity. Martin Luther once wrote: "When I am angry I can write, pray, and preach well, for then my whole temperament is quickened, my understanding sharpened, and all mundane vexations and temptations gone." Researchers have discovered that the physiological changes brought on by anger increase blood flow in certain areas of the brain, stimulating what is called *motivational direction*. Anger forces you to get closer to whatever originally instigated the angry outburst. Then, by understanding its genesis, you can take measures to eliminate it altogether. This means resolving your issues, not knocking out the boss!

Anger can sometimes lead to newer, higher-level goals, possibly fueled by the desire to prove others wrong. This is an adaptive use of anger. One of the most famous examples of anger used in this way is provided by Joseph Jordan, widely recognized as the greatest basketball player who ever lived. Famously, Jordan was known to have a long memory for perceived slights. But rather than using this anger to hurt people or to wallow in self-pity, he channeled it to motivate himself to strive for higher and higher levels of excellence. Ironically, from this perspective, getting cut from his high school basketball team may have been a gift in disguise. That's the power of anger: Used correctly, it can help you transform failures, disappointments, and setbacks into the raw energy with which to resolve problems and achieve goals.

The highest purpose for resolving anger can only be found in action, the channeling of that powerful energy into a positive outcome. For example, many social activists are motivated by their anger at a perceived injustice, and their normal reaction is to fight anger with more anger. This approach only compounds the problem, by leading to more anger and without any action to change the situation. The better solution is an essentially assertive one: to channel that anger peacefully into a determination to change, and then to act with love and empathy to make the best progress.

Constructive Use of Energy

To use anger constructively as a source of energy and motivation, follow these steps:

- **Step 1. Determine to make the most of your anger.** This is a basic but important step. Harnessing anger as an energetic and motivational force is primarily an act of will. You have to *decide* to do it. Better yet, you have to commit to it. If you can generate a clear intention for how you would like to channel your anger, you will be in a good position to succeed. If that clear intention involves something that is personally *meaningful* to you, all the better. Directing the energy of your anger toward a goal that you are emotionally invested in will enhance your ability to maintain a consistent focus.

One positive way to respond to frustration and anger is to adopt an "I'll-show-you" attitude. Such a response can be effective as long as it is not volatile. Resentment can become a motivator as well. For example, if you have a teacher or supervisor who is critical or overly demanding, your resentment might motivate you to be perfect.

Not to be overlooked, many frustrations that people face in their day-to-day lives can be connected to their own personal shortcomings and failings. That is, people create a lot of their own frustrations. You may as well. Although this anger is often directed toward people who trigger their insecurities, the deeper issue is with themselves. Anger can be a powerful motivator in this arena as well. You might, for example, use the anger and embarrassment that you feel regarding your poor financial situation to energize yourself to pursue a better job, go back to school, or even start a business.

Anger prevents people from passively accepting societal wrongdoings and instead ignites action. Many of society's most important changes have come about because people grew angry with the way things were and set out to correct the injustice. If you experience frustration regarding social injustice, consider using that anger to motivate yourself to take action. Anger used in this way can be highly productive and satisfying.

- **Step 2. Plan carefully.** You are much more likely to achieve a goal if it is supported by planning. Remember that emotions increase the strength of the strongest response tendencies. Without careful planning, anger might prompt aggression, anxiety might lead to avoidance, and self-doubts might lead to paralysis. Anger is a highly motivating emotion, but if that energy is not thoughtfully directed, it will not be of much use to you—and might actually cause problems. You will be more likely to engage in constructive, goal-supporting behaviors, and your engagement in those behaviors will be more productive if you have a detailed plan.

With a careful plan, your effort to use your anger to increase your motivation should benefit both you and your loved ones. Break your major goal into smaller objectives that are required to achieve the larger goal. Then, map out exactly what you need to accomplish to achieve these individual objectives. These are your "action items." Once you have reached this level of planning, the final step is to create a structured daily and weekly schedule that integrates these action items into your calendar.

- **Step 3. Use your anger to keep yourself motivated and sharp in carrying out your plan.** Whenever you become emotional, think of your schedule and the plan you have for coping, and use the energy to accomplish your goals.

CHAPTER 17
The Power of Acceptance

Acceptance is a frequently misunderstood concept. Many people don't realize that acceptance can be extremely powerful not only as an antidote to anger, but as a means to maximize their overall happiness and well-being. People who practice acceptance are better equipped to cope with pain, frustration, and anger, and to flow through life with greater ease and effectiveness.

Anger Management: Acceptance Can Play a Big Part

When working on anger management, you have to get to the root of your anger and to think seriously about the issues and people that make you angry. While it's good to consider how you can change certain circumstances, it's also important to understand that some things just won't be changed.

In addition, it may be important to reflect on your job, or your home life, or even your past. Many people are angry with their spouses for conflicts in their marriage or are angry at the way their boss treats them. Often they're encouraged to consider what changes they can make in their life, such as hunting for a new job or communicating better with their spouse to alleviate tension at home. However, while making changes is a part of anger management, so is acceptance.

Too often, people are very angry at things that they just cannot change or really have no business even trying to change. Acceptance acknowledges such realities for what they are. The beauty of acceptance is that it not only allows you to manage anger, it allows you to prevent anger from happening in the first place.

The emphasis on acceptance has deep roots in both Western and Eastern intellectual traditions. The Stoics of the Roman Empire emphasized the importance of learning to embrace things as they are, rather than as you wish they would be, in order to maximize inner harmony. In the Buddhist tradition, acceptance is emphasized as a pathway to liberation from suffering.

Imagine that your spouse makes you angry because he is messy around the house. You get angry when you see a shirt tossed over the back of a chair. Traditional anger management approaches, such as have been reviewed so far in this book, will help you to cool the anger you are feeling, to rethink the situation more clearly, to effectively communicate your concerns to your spouse, and to take other forms of decisive action. But what if your spouse is unable, or unwilling, to change? Does your anger have to start over every time you find a dish left out or a bed unmade?

Here's a radical idea: Perhaps you need to be more accepting of your spouse's habits. He's an adult and doesn't need to feel as if he answers to you like a child. No doubt you have your own habits and quirks that irritate him, and yet you expect him to accept those, don't you? In cases like this, learning acceptance rather than demanding things be done *your way* is an important part of anger management.

What You Resist, Persists

The idea of "acceptance" initially strikes many people as weak or wimpy. They worry that if they truly accept aspects of themselves or circumstances that they don't like, then somehow they won't be motivated to change them in a positive way or, worse, they will become resigned to the way things are.

Even though it can be frightening and counterintuitive, acceptance is the first step in transformation. It's difficult and stressful to try to change things that you don't accept. Acceptance is not resignation, failure, or agreement; it's simply telling the truth and allowing things to be as they are. When you accept yourself, others, and life, you can create a real sense of peace and let go of much of your suffering. From this place of peace and truth, you're more able to appreciate life and to manifest the kind of circumstances, relationships, and outcomes you truly want.

Carl Jung once said, "What you resist, persists." Most people constantly "resist" the way things are. Whether it's their body, their work, their spouse, their family members, their friends, their coworkers, their finances, or the state of the world and the economy—they constantly find themselves arguing with reality instead of accepting it on its own terms.

The Basic Principles of Acceptance

Here are the basic principles of acceptance:

- **Accept things as they are, not as you want them to be.** The essential component of acceptance is making peace with reality, exactly as it . . . *because* it is. Acceptance is for yourself. It is a path to creating peace in your life that transcends the vicissitudes of fragile, changing circumstances. The common everyday phrase, "It is what it is" captures the spirit of acceptance very well. Instead of holding yourself in opposition to things that you cannot control, cultivate a mindset where you allow the natural flow

- **Accept others as they are, and as they are not.** They are who they are. Influencing someone to make positive changes in their life can be very supportive and meaningful. Acceptance does not prevent you from attempting influence. But in any particular situation, the only sensible approach is to work with the person as they are right now, not as they might be some day, or as you might think they should be. You can seek to encourage, instruct, and inspire, but ultimately you have to let go and allow the other person to live their life. In the spirit of acceptance, you will find that your dealings with people are more pleasant as you are able to appreciate interpersonal differences in areas such as values, interests, and beliefs. Cultivate within yourself an understanding, compassionate attitude toward others. Recognize your own humanity in other people. The differences might be many, but, like you, they are complex, vulnerable, emotional beings who love and fear and want.

- **Accept that all things are impermanent.** The only certainty in life is change. Good things come and go; bad things come and go. This is the nature of life. When you are too strongly attached to impermanent things and situations, you are setting yourself up for frustration. However, accepting the inevitability of loss and change in your life brings peace. More than that, it highlights the precious nature of every moment. Use your awareness of impermanence to embrace your moments fully, rather than pointlessly holding on to pleasant experiences and dreading what might be around the corner.

- **Don't fixate on unanswerable questions.** Many people trap themselves with unanswerable questions. Why am I so short? Why couldn't I have had loving parents? Why aren't I as smart as everyone else? These kinds of questions can be blind alleys. The real problem, though, is that they nourish a sense of unfairness that puts you at odds with the realities of your life. They reify a "poor me" attitude that traps you with feelings of resentment and hopelessness. Asking unanswerable questions moves you away from acceptance, not toward it. Instead of charging down the well of unanswerables, look at the specific situation you are in and work with it on its own terms.

The Importance of Gratitude

They say that medicine goes down easier with a spoonful of sugar. Something similar can be said for acceptance: It's easier with a spoonful of gratitude. Gratitude offsets the difficulty of accepting undesirable realities by focusing your attention on the positive aspects of your life, and, in an even bigger sense, on the wonder and beauty of the world itself. From the perspective of gratitude, it is easier to accept the negatives when you are eyeball-to-eyeball with the positives. This is easy to understand. Gratitude gives you the strength to embrace what you have in life, rather than focusing on what you have not. By giving you reasons to believe that life is worth living, gratitude fosters a balanced, positive outlook that allows you to more readily accept the good with the bad.

The Logic of Acceptance

To accept means to see things clearly. You don't have to walk around feeling like a victim in order to protect yourself. Acceptance doesn't mean passivity. It means freedom. The freedom to see the world as it is, with its dangers and its gifts. If you practice voluntarily accepting frustration, you can maintain a calm mind even when experiencing unpleasant circumstances. On the other hand, if you allow yourself to dwell on unhappy thoughts, there will be no way to prevent anger from arising.

There are two complementary perspectives that capture the logic of acceptance. On the one hand, if it is *possible* to remedy an unpleasant or difficult situation, what point is there in being unhappy? The sensible response isn't to remain mired in anger, but rather to focus on creating the changes you want to see. On the other hand, if it is *impossible* to remedy the situation or to fulfill your wishes, there is still no reason to get upset. How will resisting an irresistible reality and being unhappy about the situation help you in any way? This kind of response only adds to your woes, creating surplus suffering—in the sense that you not only have to come to terms with an unpleasant reality, but you are now additionally burdened by the anger and stress resulting from your refusal to accept the situation. By training your mind to look at frustrating situations in a more realistic manner, you can free yourself from a great deal of unnecessary mental suffering and anger.

ALERT

A big part of acceptance is teaching yourself to willingly tolerate unpleasant experiences. If you stay with your experience, in the present moment, whether that experience is "positive" or "negative," internal or external, you can find a place of deep healing and peace.

Acceptance does not mean that you do not take practical steps to improve your situation. If it is possible to remedy a situation, then, of course, do so. Just remember that becoming unhappy and impatient in the process will only cause unnecessary frustration.

Instead of reacting blindly through the force of emotional habit, the mindset of acceptance tells you to examine whether it is helpful or realistic to become angry in this situation. You do not need to become angry just because things do not go your way. Once you recognize that anger does not work, you are free to respond in a more realistic and constructive manner.

Acceptance and the Unfairness of Life

Life is not fair. Take a deep breath and read that sentence again: Life is not fair. Accepting the reality of a situation is the first step toward tolerating it. Marsha Linehan, the psychologist who created dialectical behavior therapy (DBT), observed that most people react to crisis situations in one of four ways: They try to change the circumstances, they try to change how they feel about the circumstances, they continue to be miserable about the circumstances, or they accept the circumstances. Linehan found those people who accepted the reality of their circumstances "radically"—wholly and from the depths of their very souls—suffered less and healed faster.

Acceptance means that you understand that bad things do indeed happen to good people, but it does not mean convincing yourself that things are okay, or that you are not negatively affected by crises in your life, or that things will never change. You can reduce suffering and anger with acceptance just by acknowledging the reality for what it is: *reality*. Too often, people fill their self-talk with *should-haves* and *shouldn't-haves*, but what is done is done. If you accept reality for what it is, you will stop dwelling on things you have no control over. Instead, you will be free to focus your time and energy on the actions you can take to create a beautiful and meaningful life for yourself and those you love.

Acceptance, Negative Emotions, and Suffering

Everyone seems to be able to relate to the word *suffer* in some form. You probably do not have to try too hard to think of someone you know who is, in your view, suffering. Stress. Anger. Fear. Hurt. Shame. Anxiety. All of these emotions can be linked through the core concept of suffering, and there are so many apparent causes: pain, illness, family, health or job issues, and, the big one, financial stress.

ESSENTIAL

Resistance (also called *willfulness*) is the opposite of acceptance. When you psychologically resist something that cannot be resisted, you are essentially guaranteeing that you will experience ongoing frustration, which is arguably the most potent source of anger. With resistance, you are actively investing your emotional energy in a goal that is unobtainable.

You may be in a life situation that you are not happy with, but there is no need to suffer. You can accept what is and go from there. If you are in a situation you describe as "horrible," "sad," "hard," or "unbearable," it is this belief that makes you suffer. The situation is what it is. Why add labels and meanings that make it feel worse? Acceptance is the key. Suffering is not the same as pain. Pain will happen. It keeps you focused on distress for the purpose of relieving it. When pain intensifies and generalizes over time, it becomes suffering, which is described as the repeated failure to act successfully on the natural motivation of pain to do something that will heal, repair, or improve the core wound. Nonacceptance, or what might be called *pointless resistance*, is a primary cause of suffering.

When you label something as "horrible," you are adding suffering to it. Your ego wants you to see your situation as suffering because it feeds off these thoughts. It wants you to be a victim. Your ego also thrives on getting others' attention. Instead of backing away from negative emotions, accept them. Acknowledge how you are feeling without rushing to change your emotional state. Many people find it helpful to breathe slowly and deeply while learning to tolerate strong feelings or to imagine the feelings as floating clouds, as a reminder that they will pass. A thought is just a thought. A feeling is just a feeling.

Acceptance and Pain

Few things can be more difficult to accept than raw, physical pain. Is it possible? Yes. Is it beneficial? Absolutely. A recent study showed that acceptance of pain can reduce the experience of suffering by as much as 40 percent. Even more impressive, this result was achieved after less than two weeks of acceptance training, which consisted of a modified form of mindfulness meditation performed for only ten minutes each day. Take a moment to let that sink in. Merely accepting pain reduced the experience of pain by *almost half.*

Researchers at the National University of Ireland in Galway tested the ability of student participants to cope with unpleasant electric shocks of increasing duration. The students were tested before and after they received training in distraction or acceptance techniques. Following their training, the students who had been taught acceptance were able to endure more electric shocks than they had in the first part of the experiment, but no such difference was observed for the students who were taught distraction. Even students who were taught acceptance based only on very brief instruction (less than what you've read in this chapter) showed greater capacity to endure shocks.

These results are impressive because people fear and avoid physical pain to an even greater extent than the "psychological pain" of anger, hurt, and fear. The ability of acceptance to blunt the impact of physical pain is arguably the ultimate testimony to its efficacy.

Accepting Others

Many of your anger problems can likely be conceptualized as a failure to accept things as they are. This basic problem comes up repeatedly in relationships. After some reflection, for example, you may realize that many of your relationship problems arise because you do not accept your partner as she is. It is not who she is that frustrates you; rather, it is your inability to accept who she is. In a situation like this, the solution is not to change your partner but to accept her on her terms.

There are levels of acceptance. Perhaps you already try to tolerate your partner's idiosyncrasies, refrain from criticizing her, and go along with her wishes much of the time, but have you in the depths of your heart given up judging her? Are you free from covert resentment and blaming? Do you still believe that she ought to be different than she is? True acceptance involves letting go of these thoughts. Once you fully accept others as they are, there is no further basis for dissatisfaction and anger. You simply respond to situations as they arise. Problems do not exist outside your mind, so when you stop seeing other people as problems, they stop being problems.

In relationships, as in other areas, this kind of acceptance should not be confused with complacency or passivity. If your spouse is making choices that are hurtful to you or that in some way jeopardize the family (e.g., overspending), you have every right to confront that behavior. Similarly, if you are concerned that your spouse is making choices that might harm herself (e.g., eating poorly, alienating friends), you have every right to confront that as well. But even here, in the context of addressing such difficult issues, you will find that your mind is clearer and your interventions are more skillful when you are coming from a place of acceptance, respect, and compassion, and when your communications are assertively expressed. Accept the reality of the other person as she is, and, if you believe that change is possible, pursue creating that change at the same time. These are not mutually exclusive behaviors. It's much like taking an analgesic while working to accept the pain that you already have.

Patient acceptance not only helps you, it also helps those with whom you are patient. Being accepted feels very different than being judged. When someone feels judged, they become tight and defensive. When they feel accepted, they can relax, which allows their good qualities to surface.

People are much more open to feedback, suggestion, and even outright confrontation when they feel accepted and respected. Acceptance solves many of your inner problems, but often it solves interpersonal problems as well.

Willingness Versus Willfulness

Another way to think of acceptance is as willingness. Willingness is being open to your whole experience while actively and intentionally choosing to move in a valued life direction. Willingness means you can accept, fully and happily, whatever occurs.

It is always possible to be willing. Willingness implies a commitment to actively work with what life offers you. It's when you allow the world to be what it is, and, no matter what it is, you agree to participate in the world. Think of being in front of a pitching machine in a batting cage. Life is like that. The machine is throwing balls at you, one after the other. You're standing there with a bat. If the balls keep coming, what are your options? You can take your bat, pull it back, and try to hit the ball. You can stand there passively, perhaps even allowing the ball to hit you. You can throw a tantrum. You can scream, "It's coming too fast. I don't like it. I'm not doing it. I'm not hitting that ball anymore. Stop!"

Do you think the balls would stop coming if you did that? You can get as upset as you want about life, but life just keeps coming, one moment right after the next. Willingness is trying to hit the ball.

Facing Willfulness

Willfulness is the opposite of willingness. It's saying no to reality.

What do you do when willfulness shows up? The first thing is just to notice it. First, you can say to yourself, "Willfulness has shown up." Then observe it, identify it, describe it. Second, accept willfulness. Accept the fact that acceptance is hard. That is real, too. Third, turn your mind toward willingness, toward acceptance, toward participating in reality just as it is.

If you're having trouble getting yourself to turn your mind (you want to, but your mind isn't turning), try assuming a willing posture. Sit or stand, open your hands, and relax your body. Breathe deeply and slowly for a few minutes, and open yourself to a willing state of mind. Be patient, and remember that this is a process. Developing a willing mindset takes time and a consistent focus; it doesn't happen all at once.

In those situations where your willfulness seems almost immovable, there is bound to be a reason. Ask yourself, "What's the threat?" Usually immovable willfulness has to do with some sort of threat—something you're afraid you will lose, or something you're afraid will happen. Adopt an open and inquisitive posture toward this deeper fear, and, in time, it will reveal its secrets to you.

Finding the Lesson

Part of the beauty of life is that it's unpredictable. Nothing is permanent, everything changes; and of course, a lot of things can happen that will have an impact on your life. Developing the ability to truly accept whatever comes can be difficult. Life brings many challenges, and it's not easy to embrace them when you're in pain and wishing those things had never happened. However, if you start cultivating acceptance in your life right now, you'll likely cope with future crises in a different way and view them from a different perspective. You will accept instead of resist.

One thing that facilitates the process of acceptance is to find the lesson or meaning that is implicit in the situation you are facing. Connecting with a sense of meaning in the midst of hardship and frustration makes acceptance much easier to accomplish. A good way to start is by listing all the possible explanations for why you're experiencing something.

Finding the lesson or purpose behind every challenge will help you embrace life, instead of fighting it.

Connecting with Values

A recent study looked at whether including a "values" component when teaching people about acceptance helped them better cope with pain. In the study, subjects were taught to endure pain while imagining their most valued area of life. Pain was simulated using a "cold-pressor task," in which the participants put their hands in ice-cold water. This task quickly becomes painful, so the researchers had created a situation in which their subjects could use acceptance exercises to try to tolerate this discomfort. The researchers found that when the participants were taught about using values, as well as acceptance, they tolerated pain better.

The acceptance skills the subjects were taught included:

- You don't need to control pain.
- You don't need to like the experience.
- You can tolerate negative thoughts ("This ice water is really hurting me").
- You can tolerate pain (feeling pain is okay).
- Thoughts ("This ice water really hurts") and feelings (distress about feeling pain) don't have to determine your behavior. You can make a decision to keep your hand in the ice water, even though it's unpleasant. Even if you think "I can't stand this another second," you don't have to act on that thought.

The values component focuses on leading a life consistent with your values, despite having pain. If playing with your kids is one of your top priorities, and it sometimes causes manageable physical pain due to arthritis, do that. If going to work is one of your top priorities, do that. Using values to cope with pain means letting your values determine what you do—*doing what's most valuable to you*—even if this increases your pain.

ALERT

Imagine you're climbing a mountain and you're halfway up. Suddenly, the clouds roll in and it starts to rain. You have two choices: Head back down or carry on. If you carry on, it's not because you like being cold and wet. It's because you value reaching the top and you've evaluated the risks. You are *willing* to experience *some* difficulties to do what you value.

The Key Steps of Acceptance

Follow these three steps to integrate greater acceptance into your life:

- **Step 1. Do your best to recognize the point at which nothing further can be done.** A person can only do so much. If you to try to push yourself past a certain point, there are diminishing returns. If you find yourself reaching the point in your life where things are just too hectic, and your vision of how your life should be (after you've done everything you can) isn't working out, consider accepting that it's time to acknowledge that nothing further can be done. Just accept where you are that moment. Try to become accurate at identifying where this point is, for you, in the things you do in your life. Don't keep pushing yourself past this point. Be willing to accept your life at that moment.

- **Step 2. Let go of the reins of control.** Control is often an illusion, and a self-defeating one at that. Although you can work hard and plan for contingencies, what you find when you're out and about in the world is that life is indifferent to your desires to control it. The more you try to control everything, the more difficult it becomes to keep your life balanced. It's kind of like to trying to preserve a handful of sand by squeezing it—the more you squeeze, the more you lose.

The moment you acknowledge that you can't control everything and you loosen up a little bit on the reins of control, it's a relief. Stress is much less likely to control you. Be willing to just let go, to let things be as they are. This is the kind of acceptance you need to have if you really want to get rid of stress and anger.

- **Step 3. Just let go.** After you discover that you've reached your breaking point with anger and frustration, and you've dropped the reins of control, the next step of acceptance is to just let go. You have to let the chips fall where they may.

When you let go, you are letting go of your attachment to the outcome. It is difficult to let go of the outcome completely. Yet, once you've done your best and put all of your effort into an endeavor, it doesn't do any good to beat yourself up if the outcome you intended doesn't happen. It can definitely be a learning experience. Focus on that because resisting the situation or fighting reality won't help you a whit. You can reassess your approach, make a commitment to strive harder, or vow to do things differently the next time.

Practice on the Small Stuff

When patience is present in your mind, it is impossible for unhappy thoughts to gain a foothold. There are many examples of people who have managed to practice patience even in the most extreme circumstances, such as under torture or in the final ravages of a terminal illness. Although their body was ruined beyond repair, their mind remained at peace. By learning to accept the small difficulties and hardships that arise every day in the course of your life, your capacity for patient acceptance will gradually increase and you will come to know the freedom and joy that true patience brings.

CHAPTER 18

Mindfulness and Meditation

Mindfulness is the quality of being fully present and "living in the moment." By practicing mindfulness, you can effectively neuter two of the more common precursors to anger: rumination about the past, and rumination about the future. The practice of mindfulness meditation can teach you how to be more calm and mindful in every aspect of your life. It is also the single, most powerful method available to develop your innate capacity for acceptance.

Mindfulness and Anger

One of your greatest strengths for preventing and managing anger is basic awareness, or what is often referred to as *mindfulness*. Mindfulness means maintaining a moment-by-moment awareness of your thoughts, feelings, bodily sensations, and surrounding environment. It also involves *acceptance* of the totality of your experiences, thoughts, and feelings, regardless of whether they are good or bad, pleasant or unpleasant. This means paying attention to them without judging them—without believing, for instance, that there's a "right" or "wrong" way to think or feel in a given moment. When you practice mindfulness, your thoughts tune in to what you're sensing in the present moment rather than rehashing the past or imagining the future.

To be mindful is to be more conscious, more awake, more informed about how you live your life. Your words and actions are mindful when you are anchored in the here-and-now, rather than caught up in ruminative thought, knee-jerk reactivity, and blind habit. Mindfulness teaches you to recognize anger before it becomes explosive, before you lose control or suppress it, so that you can release it and return quickly to a calm, rational state.

Focusing the Spotlight of Attention Using Anger Mindfully

Anger used mindfully can be quite powerful. Anger has a strong energetic component, and you always have a choice as to what to do with that. People are sometimes afraid to feel anger's raw power; they fear that expressing it will make them seem unkind. Others are all too willing to express their anger, but do so clumsily, with little thought of the consequences. In contrast, using anger mindfully awakens your compassion and self-awareness.

ALERT

The problem with labels is that they are imprecise, often exaggerated (the cashier was "awful"), and quickly take on a life of their own. When you identify with your labels, they can exercise enormous power. Mindfulness encourages you to step back and observe your experiences objectively, on their own terms.

Anger in its pure form, without the "additives" of concept and labels, has the potential to focus a considerable amount of energy. An effective way to harness that energy is through mindfulness, which enables you to recognize your anger without simply reacting to it—without either spitting it against another, or turning it against yourself. By looking at anger with an objective, accepting mind, you can choose to use that anger productively.

The following suggestions will help you use anger mindfully:

- **Notice how anger manifests in your body.** Is it a burning sensation in your heart? A cold tight clenching in the pit of your stomach? A flush of heat in your face or hands? Become familiar with your "early warning signs," so you can catch the energy without reacting to the anger.

- **As soon as you notice the physical sensation of anger, stop and breathe.** Allow the energy of anger to wake you up to what is actually happening at that moment.

- **Give yourself permission to feel angry, hurt, abandoned, scared, frustrated, or sad; have compassion for yourself.** Breathe in light, peace, and compassion, and breathe out the dark, heavy sensations of anger without judgment, accepting it just as it is.

- **If you notice the anger turning inward, continue to breathe it out more forcefully.** Use your body to keep the energy outward—shake it off your hands into the air, stomp it into the ground with your feet—whatever it takes not to turn that energy against yourself.

- **Be curious.** Ask yourself, "What is this feeling? What is it telling me?"

- **Trust your body to tell you the appropriate course of action.** Is there something you need to say to someone who has hurt you, in a way that will help you heal and contribute to the growth of the other person and your relationship? Is it something you can simply let be, making sure not to turn the anger inward?

Mindfulness Meditation: Developing Awareness and Acceptance

Mindfulness is a centuries-old practice usually cultivated through meditation. It is experiential, meaning that you must experience it to understand it. Just talking about mindfulness gets you only so far. This is why meditation is so important in cultivating a more mindful and accepting life. Meditation is the formal practice of cultivating the qualities of mindfulness and mindful acceptance. Daily life gives you plenty of opportunities for applying the practice.

The more you experientially understand mindfulness meditation—that is, the more you experience being more awake in every moment—the more of yourself you will experience, and the more awareness you will have about what your internal experience really is. Mindfulness meditation is not goal-oriented; it is process-oriented. The focus is not on reaching some future point; the focus is on being here in the present moment, being with whatever your experience is in the here-and-now.

You may be thinking, "Well, I already know most of the time (or all of the time) what my experience is, but so what? How is that going to help me when I'm angry?" Mindfulness meditation increases your awareness and slows the pace of things so that you have greater clarity; it opens up new possibilities, new choices. For instance, you may already know how you go from point *A*, totally calm, to point *Z*, totally enraged. With applied mindfulness, you will start to see the subtle shifts that bring you through points *B* to *C*, and *C* to *D*, and so on. This increased awareness is a powerful antidote to reactive anger.

Living in the Moment

At its core, mindfulness meditation helps you quiet your mind so that you can be completely present and accepting in the here-and-now. You've probably noticed all the repetitive thoughts that course through your mind during the day. It's like a running commentary on your life. Meditation quiets your mind, so it begins to focus only on one thing: the present. In the now, there are no concepts, no fears, and no problems. Fears and worries come when your mind is working, going from the past to the future, thinking about what has been and what could be. When you make your mind quiet, fears and worries go away. That's one of the beautiful things about meditation: It frees you from the concepts and thought structures you have accumulated that cause anxiety. It gives a respite from anger and worry and the burdens of the day.

Besides meditating your worries and fears away, you can practice being in the present all the time. If you are in the here-and-now during your daily activities, you are thinking about and focusing on the one thing you are doing at that moment. You're keeping the thoughts of the past and future from entering your mind. If you get up and wash the dishes, you simply wash the dishes; if you sit down to write an e-mail, you just concentrate on writing that e-mail. Of course, during these times, other thoughts will arise, but meditative living involves getting back to being present and focusing only on that. Athletes sometimes refer to this as being in "the zone."

FACT

By grounding yourself in the reality of moment-by-moment experience, mindfulness can help you see beyond the shadow of beliefs, assumptions, and cognitive biases when you need to analyze yourself objectively. A study in the journal *Psychological Science* shows that mindfulness can help you conquer common "blind spots," which can amplify or diminish your flaws in an unrealistic way.

As you learn through meditation to ground yourself in moment-by-moment awareness, this mindfulness will gradually extend throughout your everyday life. When your mind wanders or when worry overtakes you, simply go back to what's happening right now. Don't get upset that you've allowed your mind to stray, simply come back to focus on the present moment. In doing so, you learn to be more gentle and compassionate with yourself, and with others.

Keeping Grounded

Meditation helps you see that all things are well and going the way they are supposed to. You are doing your part, others are doing their part, and the world is a beautiful place for everyone to live in. In subtle and yet profound ways, meditation brings you to the point of discovering the beauty of the world around you simply by forcing you to slow down and recognize it.

But, of course, in this beautiful world, there is pain and suffering. There is injustice. When faced with it, you have two choices: Either, you can get stuck in your pain, just marinate in it. Or, you can work through your pain, accept it, come to terms with what it means for your life, and grow from it. Mindfulness helps at every stage. Mindfulness meditation is particularly helpful in terms of understanding what your pain is really telling you.

Because of life's challenges, it is important to stay grounded, to stay close to the center of what life is all about: the beauty and wonder of it all. Challenges will come; they're a part of living. They help you grow and become stronger. Meditation keeps you on an even keel so you can face these challenges with an inner flexibility and stability. Grounded, you face life with everything you have inside, because you know who and what you are through meditation. You are prepared for anything. When challenges come, you are able to face them with calm and understanding. You engage life's challenges with equanimity and peace, knowing that in the end, all will work out for the best.

Meditation teaches you to live in the here-and-now. No matter what's happening in the moment, there's always something beautiful. Meditation also teaches you that when you focus on the now, you lose the fear of what could be and the anger over what has been, because there is nothing you cannot handle one breath at a time. You learn to ask, "What do I need to do right now to get over this hurdle in this moment?" Then you can approach the challenge with calm capability.

The Scientific Studies

In the late 1960s, Dr. Herbert Benson, of Harvard Medical School, conducted studies to test the health benefits of meditation. He determined that meditation could be used successfully in treating physiological problems such as high blood pressure, heart disease, migraines, and certain autoimmune diseases. During their meditation, his test subjects had slowed heartbeats and breathing; their blood lactate levels were lowered; and their brains had increased alpha activity, which is a sign of relaxation. Dr. Benson later found that meditation was helpful in stopping or slowing obsessive thinking, anxiety, depression, and hostility. These early findings marked the opening of a new field of scientific inquiry.

Since Dr. Benson's time, more than 400 peer-reviewed scientific studies have substantiated the wide-ranging benefits of meditation. These findings can be summarized as follows:

- **Meditation improves your health.** Meditation has been shown to increase immune functioning, decrease cellular inflammation, and decrease pain.
- **Meditation improves your happiness.** Meditation has been shown to increase positive emotions, while simultaneously decreasing depression, anxiety, stress, and anger.
- **Meditation improves your social life.** Meditation has been shown to increase social connection and emotional intelligence, increase compassion, and decrease loneliness.
- **Meditation improves your self-control.** Meditation has been shown to improve your ability to regulate your emotions and to self-reflect.
- **Meditation changes your brain.** Meditation increases gray-matter brain volume, as well as brain volume in areas related to emotion regulation, positive emotions, and self-control. It also increases cortical thickness in areas related to attention and focus.
- **Meditation improves your productivity.** Meditation has been shown to increase focus and attention, improve memory, and improve your ability to be creative and think of novel solutions.

A number of studies have looked specifically at the relationship between meditation and anger. One study examined whether meditation could moderate the physiological expression of anger and fear. Because of the fight-or-flight response, people experience a range of physical symptoms when they are angry or fearful, including muscle tension and increased blood pressure and heart rate, resulting in potential medical problems and even violent behavior. Very few drugs can counteract this effect, but meditation has been shown to consistently ameliorate this reaction. Other research has looked at the effect of meditation on hardened criminals. Strikingly, inmates who are taught meditation during their imprisonment are 40 percent less likely to return to prison, compared to their counterparts who don't meditate.

This is just a small sampling of the research that has been done on the physical and mental benefits of meditation. Because there so much evidence that meditation is beneficial, and virtually no reason that people shouldn't try it, doctors practicing traditional Western medicine are now recommending it to their patients with cancer, AIDS, infertility, and attention deficit hyperactivity disorder (ADHD).

How to Meditate

There are many ways to meditate. The key to meditation and why it works so well is that it literally changes brain-wave patterns. Meditation is based on a system of focus. All day long, our minds are creating thoughts and ideas. We are seldom attentive to one thought or idea at a time. We mentally bounce all over the place and rarely focus on one thing for very long. Some people refer to this mental gymnastics as *monkey mind*. Meditation quiets the mind, stills it, by creating a rhythm, a pattern the mind can follow. When the meditator does that, brain waves start to slow and he or she becomes more peaceful and relaxed.

How Long Should You Meditate?

Beginners should start at twenty minutes per day, preferably in the morning (advanced meditators will often practice for between one to two hours per day). This is short enough to be realistic for most beginners, but long enough to have a beneficial impact. One well-known study looked at the impact for beginning meditators of meditating for twenty-three minutes per day (average) over an eight-week period. At the end of eight weeks, their brain activity had measurably changed, and they showed much higher activation of the parts of the brain associated with feelings of well-being and less activation of the parts associated with stress. They were found to have an improved immune response as well.

Meditating twice each day, morning and night, will help transform your experience of life in positive and permanent ways. You'll start each morning with a more peaceful outlook, and you'll wind down in the evening with a meditation that purges your body and mind of any stress that you may have collected during the day. Your evening meditation will help you sleep more deeply, and you'll awake feeling rested, at which time you are ready to begin your morning meditation again.

QUESTION

How should I sit when I meditate?
The two most common postures are to sit cross-legged, usually with a pillow or cushion placed under your sit bones to support better posture, or to sit on the edge of a chair or sofa with your back unsupported. In either posture, try to sit straight with your spine slightly arched and your eyes closed.

Basic Meditation: Using a Silent Phrase

This first technique utilizes a mantra that "follows the breath." Most forms of meditation are based on following the breath. When you pay attention to the breath, both your mind and your breathing slow down. Sounds easy enough, but people generally find it hard to do this. Their mind bounces around so much that they forget to focus on their breathing. That's why the first technique presented here adds something to the breath-observing method—something to help anchor you further in the present moment. This is the "I am peaceful" meditation.

The "I am peaceful" meditation involves breathing in while mentally saying "I am," then mentally saying "peaceful" as you breathe out. Your mind may wander, but you'll find that if you direct your mind back to that phrase, you will begin to stay more focused on your breath. Do not strain or force your attention on the words or on your breathing. Just gently redirect your mind to the phrase and to your breathing any time your attention wanders.

Begin the session with a few deep breaths. Then begin thinking the phrase, and just let yourself breathe normally. Don't try to control the rate of your breathing, whether it's deep or shallow. Let it be whatever the body wants it to be. As your mind slows down in meditation, you will likely begin to feel very relaxed. If your mind wanders, don't be critical of yourself; simply go back to your mantra: "I am peaceful." With time, as you continue this practice, you will find it easier and easier to quiet the mind and to remain in the quietness. Even if your mind wanders, you will find that you still feel the effects of the meditation. It takes time and patience to meditate each day. With practice, it becomes increasingly easier to stay focused on your mantra and to follow your breath.

You will eventually find that you can enter the world of meditation quite easily. Find a comfortable place to relax. Sit up and keep your spine straight (back support is fine if you need it). Don't worry about fidgeting, but if you can stay still, it's better. Meditation is about being present and relaxed. If you remain gentle with yourself and don't become harsh when your mind does not stay focused, you'll get better at falling into meditation easily and quickly.

Breath Meditation

The most widely used form of mindfulness meditation is *breath meditation*. It is one of the most powerful, yet one of the easiest, meditations to learn. Although the steps are simple and straightforward, it is not always easy to do.

In this form of meditation, you simply "follow your breath." Your breath functions like an anchor, grounding you in moment-by-moment awareness. Observe your breathing without using a mantra or prayer, just quietly notice the breath. Begin by taking a few deep breaths. Then allow yourself to breathe normally, without concern whether the breath is becoming deeper, shallower, or staying the same. As you sit there, notice your breath. Breathe in, breathe out, breathe in, and breathe out. Try to breathe through your nose if that's not uncomfortable, otherwise breathe through your mouth. Either way, let your attention be with your breath. Notice what it feels like, its temperature, the subtle sensations as it enters and exits your nostrils.

If something distracts you, simply come back to your breathing. When strenuous or uncomfortable thoughts arise, don't try to ignore them or push them away. Instead, acknowledge them, accept them, and return to observing your breathing. Allow your attention to focus on that. Acknowledge and accept any distractions, without being annoyed by them, and simply direct your awareness back to your breath. One of the aims of meditation, over time, is to diminish reactivity.

As you progress with breath meditation, you can experiment by switching your attention from your breath to your body. Allow your focused awareness of physical sensations in your body to ground you in the present moment. A great practice is to take notice of your body when your meditative state starts to take hold. Once your mind quiets, focus all your attention on your feet and then slowly move your way up your body (include your internal organs). With time, you will find that your awareness becomes sharper, so you are aware of subtler sensations. This is very healthy and an indicator that you are on the right path.

CHAPTER 19

Holistic Health

The word "holistic" means that the emphasis is on the whole, or the complete system, rather than on an isolated part. Holistic health is about the big picture. It's about understanding the many facets of your life in order to experience an overarching sense of health and happiness, free from unhealthy anger. When you are living a holistically healthy lifestyle, there is very little room for anger to take hold.

Living a Balanced Life

The phrase *holistic health* means creating a balanced lifestyle by adopting a whole-person perspective. The term was coined in the 1920s to describe the direct connection between physical illness and the mental, emotional, and spiritual self. For centuries, Eastern medical practitioners have embraced the belief that a person can't be truly well unless both the mind and body are working in harmony. However, it's only during the past several decades that the effectiveness of holistic health has been recognized by countless American health-care providers.

Why is striving to understand holistic health so important? If any one of the components that make up a healthy person breaks down, it affects the entire being, not just the disrupted part of the person. It's like a car. The parts have to work together in harmony to make it possible for the car to function. Start the engine, release the brake, and put the car into gear. If anything goes wrong with, say, the steering, the entire car is in trouble, even though that's only one component of the whole machine.

FACT

Ancient healing traditions as far back as 5,000 years ago stressed holistic principles. Although the term *holism* was introduced by Jan Christiaan Smuts in 1926, in his book *Holism and Evolution*, as a way of viewing living things as "entities greater than and different from the sum of their parts," it wasn't until the 1970s that *holistic health* became a common term in modern vocabulary.

Holistic health is like the example of the car. All of the parts of an individual, both external and internal, should be running smoothly, so that the person doesn't crash or break down. Of course, the physical body must be in tune, but the spiritual and emotional faculties that make up who you are must be kept "tuned up" as well. Otherwise, there will be disharmony in your life.

Nutrition

Nutrition is an integral part of holistic health. It is one of those important building blocks that make up the whole, healthy person. To be in total balance, you need to consider what you eat. The old adage "you are what you eat" is essentially true. If you eat mostly fried, processed, sugary foods, or fast-food hamburgers piled with cheese and bacon, you are more likely to clog your arteries, gain weight, and experience a multitude of health problems. On the other hand, if you eat organic, healthy foods, you're going to have minerals, vitamins, and antioxidants rushing into your bloodstream and into your entire body. Studies show that if you eat unprocessed, organic, raw plant-based foods, you will have an increased opportunity to live a longer, healthier life with fewer health problems.

Unprocessed foods should make up the bulk of your daily diet. When you are grocery shopping, focus on the foods that are stocked near the outer walls, where most of the fruits, vegetables, and fresh meat, fish, and dairy products are sold. Generally speaking, the interior sections of the grocery store are more likely to be stocked with frozen and processed foods that lack freshness, have low nutrient density, and are high in sugar and salt. Avoid refined starches—such as white bread, white rice, and white pasta—which have been associated with impaired blood-sugar control, overeating, weight gain, and the increased risk of gastrointestinal disease.

Remember, you are what you eat. Think about what you're putting into your body when you sit down for a meal. If you put good things into your body, your body is going to respond well. It will show in your complexion, how you feel, and how you age. You don't have to go from fast food to "health food" overnight. Instead, gradually improve your diet. Add more fresh fruits and vegetables, switch your bread, cereals, and pastas to unprocessed whole grains, and do so at a pace that is realistic for you. A practical approach for most people is to focus on eating healthy, nutrient-dense meals, with an occasional splurge on meals that are perhaps less than optimally healthy. This assures that you are eating well most of the time, without feeling deprived of a guilty pleasure now and then.

Exercise

A regular exercise routine not only helps to improve fitness, appearance, and energy level, but it has many psychological benefits as well. People who exercise regularly are more resilient in the face of stress, are better able to cope with unexpected challenges, and report a better overall mood. Other benefits include:

- Improved sleep
- A sense of achievement
- Focus in life and motivation
- Less anger or frustration
- A healthy appetite
- Better social life
- Improved self-confidence

There are three broad types of exercise that you should be doing to help your body stay healthy. Design your exercise routine so that you are doing each of the following:

- **Weight bearing.** This includes activities like lifting weights, resistance bands, plyometrics (e.g., jump training), or anything that requires you to lift or push against something to fight gravity. Weight-bearing exercise helps with osteoporosis and keeps your body strong. Many people have problems later in life if they don't do weight-bearing exercises.
- **Cardiovascular.** Exercises that get your heart beating faster, such as running, swimming, and playing tennis, fall under the category of cardiovascular exercise. This could mean participating in classes at the gym, going for a brisk walk, dancing the night away, or bicycling. Studies show that people who do regular cardio exercise to raise their heart rate actually have a slower heart rate the rest of the time. That means that marathon runners have a slower heartbeat than people who are sedentary. Getting your heart rate to a higher pace periodically is very healthy.
- **Flexibility.** Staying flexible is important, because having a limber body can head off injuries before they occur. Flexibility improves posture, adapts your body to physical stress, reduces joint and lower-back

pain, improves energy and vitality, and maintains a healthy range of motion as you age.

Your Job

Make sure that your job is something you enjoy doing. Your work should be something you're passionate about. How can you live a balanced, healthy life if you're in a work environment that makes you unhappy, bored, or constantly stressed?

Finding a profession that you enjoy is especially important for young people who are just starting their careers. Put a lot of thought into it, and find something that you're excited about, not just where you can make the most money. This is a well-researched area, and the conclusions are indisputable: Money alone isn't going to make you happy in the long run. Instead, find something you enjoy doing—a reason to get up in the morning with a positive attitude.

Work-Life Balance

Even if you're passionate about your work and look forward to going to the office each day, you still need to take time off. That means actually using up all of the vacation time you have accumulated throughout the year. Taking time away from work is very important. It's also important to maintain a balance between your work and your personal life. Work to live; don't live to work. Circumscribed periods of heavy-hour work weeks are acceptable, but if the overall trend is that your work time encroaches on other important activities, it can become a real problem.

ALERT

The lack of a work-life balance is a major source of dissatisfaction and of employee turnover in the modern work force. More than 39 percent of employees worldwide say they haven't got a balance. Research also suggests that, despite old stereotypes, stress and work-life balance issues are just as challenging for fathers as they are for mothers.

Let's say that you love Disneyland. You bought a season pass and go as often as possible. But if you had to go there forty or fifty hours a week, for about fifty weeks a year, you would likely get tired of the Magic Kingdom. It's like that for people who love their work. To have a holistically healthy and balanced life, don't work all the time, or you will eventually get burned out.

Changing Jobs

Let's say you studied finance in college and are a stockbroker. It's a stressful, high-power job and you make good money. But the stress has caught up with you, and you dread going into the office. Every Sunday night, you get a knot in your stomach anticipating returning to work the next morning.

If you're not happy with your work situation, give yourself permission to change jobs. It can be hard to give up those paychecks, without question. But if you've tried everything you can to make the most of your current situation, and it's still affecting you, your emotions might be telling you something important. Namely, that it's time to look into a new career path. Find something that makes you happy, and the money—at least enough money to live on comfortably—will follow.

Perhaps you're okay with the type of work you do, but someone at your office is the problem. Perhaps someone like your boss. To ensure your physical and mental health, make sure your workplace environment is positive and pleasant. If you work around people who are grumpy and negative, it will eventually take a toll on you. Try to be around people who are excited to work with you. People who like to be there, just as much as you like being there.

Burnout

What if you've been working at the same job for a long time? You have been happy, but now you've grown tired of it and would like a change. If that's the case, give yourself permission to do something else. It's better to change jobs than to suffer total burnout. If you're nervous about changing career paths, then think about doing the same type of job, but in a different setting. Find creative ways to work somewhere else, rather than staying at the same place. Otherwise, you could wind up hating the job you once enjoyed—and that's very bad for your overall health.

People in Your Life

One of the most important choices you make in life concerns the people you spend time with. They will influence every area of your life. Have you ever noticed that you may be having a wonderful day and feel very happy until someone who is being negative comes around? This is magnified when it is someone you know personally, especially if it is someone close to you. However, the opposite is also true. You could start out having a pretty awful day, but due to a random act of kindness, you may find yourself feeling more optimistic and joyful. There is great power in choosing positive and loving people to be in your life.

Keep or Toss

Every human being is valuable; however, not every relationship functions in a way that is beneficial to the parties involved. This is why you each need to take inventory of your life and evaluate which relationships you'd like to keep and which you'd like to toss.

Get rid of or minimize those dysfunctional relationships that sap your energy or add negativity to your life, but are not worth the investment of time and emotional energy necessary to improve them. Sometimes people outgrow their friends, or simply move on. This is a normal part of life.

Relationships that matter to you should be kept. A relationship may be important because of who the other person is to you, or because of what the association brings to you. A friendship that adds fun, joy, or some other great quality to your life is worth investing in. Just as plants in a garden need to be pruned and watered, these relationships need to be managed with healthy boundaries, good communication, and proactive scheduling. Too often, people fail to set healthy boundaries in their relationships. The long-term nature of these relationships may tempt you to take the attitude that "it is what it is" and never consider breaking out of old, dysfunctional patterns. Setting healthy boundaries is like pruning a shrub that has taken on an undesirable shape.

So often the significant relationships in people's lives go untended. When was the last time you went on a date with your spouse, or on a road trip with your best friend? When did you last have a heart-to-heart talk with Mom or Dad, or spend quality one-on-one time with your child? Investing in relationships gives them the water they need to grow.

Evaluate which individuals have the most positive or least negative effect on you. Make it a priority to schedule more time with these people, rather than spending that time with the people who drag you down. Don't fall into the trap of hanging out with someone who is a negative influence, simply because it is easier or requires less planning. Be sure to take time for the people who make you laugh, feed your spirit, and make life worth living. These relationships foster your growth and help you become your best self, which you can then offer to those you love and to the rest of the world.

Friends

Having people in your life who love and support you is an essential part of maintaining your overall health. Of course, your friends should also love and support themselves. Friends can help you celebrate good times and provide support during bad times. Friends prevent loneliness and give you a chance to offer needed companionship as well. They can also increase your sense of belonging and purpose, boost your happiness, reduce stress, and offer valuable advice and encouragement. You may not be able to choose your family, but you most certainly can choose your friends. Be particular.

QUESTION

What's a healthy number of friends to have?
Some people benefit from a large and diverse network of friends, while others prefer a smaller circle. There are also different types of friendship. Consider what works for you. Overall, the quality of your relationships is more important than the specific number of friends you have.

Friendship is a crucial element in protecting your mental health. You need to talk to your friends and you want to listen when your friends want to talk to you. They can keep you grounded and can help you get things in perspective. It is worth putting effort into maintaining your friendships and making new friends. Friends form one of the foundations for your ability to cope with the problems that life throws at you.

Marriage and Romantic Partnerships

If you are in a committed romantic relationship that is not healthy and loving, it can be very difficult to be holistically healthy. When there's a problem with one of your friends, you can take a break. But when your spouse or significant other becomes abusive or problematic, it's much more complicated to get out of the relationship. If there are problems with your spouse or partner, commit to working toward improving the situation. Until both of you are willing to dedicate yourselves to looking at the situation objectively and working to improve things, however, the situation is unlikely to improve on its own.

The key to having a loving relationship is being open and truthful. Be kind in all situations, especially when you disagree on something. Resolve conflicts without raising your voice, name-calling, or saying hurtful things that you'll later regret. If you are committed to this person and this relationship, it's well worth the effort to work things out. Make spending time with your significant other a top priority. He or she should be more important than your job or being with your friends or just about anything else. This can be hard sometimes. Keeping your relationship healthy can mean having to say no to lots of other commitments.

Make sure that both you and the one you love are doing things to build your relationship and make it last. Remember when you first fell in love. You worked hard on the relationship. Just because you're now in a committed relationship doesn't mean you can stop trying. If you don't keep doing the things that made you love each other in the first place, there's a very real danger of falling out of love. However, if you've done everything you can do to improve the situation and your life is still unbearable, you may need to think about moving on. Being emotionally healthy is more important than staying in a dysfunctional or abusive relationship.

Children

Most of what you learned about how to parent is based on the way you were brought up. If your parents were perfect, you're likely to be a pretty good parent. Of course, you have to factor in how your spouse was raised as well. The reality, however, is that no one is perfect, and your parents and your partner's parents likely made many mistakes. You probably will, too, and that's okay. You don't have to be "perfect" as a parent, but you want to be the best parent you can be. Both you and your child will benefit greatly.

Parenting is one of the most serious, challenging, and rewarding responsibilities you will ever have. If you are facing difficulties raising your children, move beyond the example of your childhood experiences and learn about being a good parent by taking classes or reading about the topic.

Three aspects of good parenting merit special emphasis:

1. **How you treat your kids.** How do you react when they make mistakes? How do you reward them? Do you interact with them on a regular basis? If you were to make a pie chart of everything you say to your kids, how much of it would be positive, and how much negative? Do you give them physical touch, such as hugs, kisses, back-scratching, or snuggling? Do you play with them?
2. **What you expose them to.** Now more than ever, numerous influences can affect your child's development and behavior—some good, some bad. While it's impossible to control everything, try to maximize the good and minimize the bad in terms of what your child is exposed to.
3. **Modeling.** So much of how your kids turn out is based on your example, rather than on what you tell them. For instance, if you want them to be healthy, set a good example by exercising, eating right, modeling healthy relationships, and so on. Teach your children to be good people by being a good person. Do you lose your temper? Do you have road rage? If so, realize that you're teaching your children to behave in the same way that you do.

Strategies for Managing Relationships

Here are some guidelines to help you maintain healthy boundaries and improve the quality of your interactions with others.

Disagreements

In every long-term friendship, things can hit a rough spot. You may have a disagreement or misunderstanding. It may be major or something minor. Are your friends the kind of people who are willing to work things through?

In other words, are they forgiving? Can you say to them, "We've had a misunderstanding. You hurt my feelings and I hurt yours. Let's talk about it. I'm willing to work things through. Are you?" They should be as eager to work things out as you are. That's what friendship is about. No one is perfect. Everyone has faults. If they say they are sorry, you need to forgive them. If you make mistakes, you need to say you're sorry. And if they are the type of friend you want to continue having in your life, they will forgive you. That's part of being in a healthy friendship.

Setting Boundaries

If someone you consider a friend is abusive, it may be time to walk away. If this happens, learn to set boundaries. For example, let's say that one of your closest friends makes a negative comment about your weight. She might say, "By the look of your hips, I can tell you're really enjoying cooking for your family these days." Of course, this snide remark is going to hurt your feelings, whether it's true or not. So you need to talk to your friend about how her comment made you feel.

Creating boundaries is about drawing a line in the sand and asking the person not to cross it. When someone does, this is an area where you can immediately apply the 3R method: Give yourself time to calm down and relax, then reassess the situation, and then respond.

Once you have made your boundary clear, see if your friend respects it. Often when you stand firm on your rules, people use the excuse that they were just kidding. If this happens, in a case like the weight comment, you still need to tell your friend not to joke about negative things. Sometimes, the person may say you are too sensitive. But again, you have to say, "Even if you think I'm too sensitive, this is my boundary, so please don't cross it." The bottom line is to make sure your friends are a positive force in your life. If they are not, then it's time to find other people who are better for you to associate with.

Abuse and Mistreatment

Far too many people have been treated poorly and even abused by family members, peers, and intimate partners. As a result, they have become accustomed to this sort of treatment, and often tolerate cruel and disrespectful behavior. In a sense, they don't know any better, and that's the real tragedy. Unkind and degrading behavior is not acceptable—from anyone. If you are being physically, sexually, or emotionally abused, remove yourself from the situation immediately and find a safe place to work on the changes you need in your life.

It is also possible for someone in your life to become upset and engage in negative, critical behavior that is not typical. When someone who cares about you has treated you badly, it is important for that individual to acknowledge the behavior, to show remorse, and to take steps not to repeat it. If the other person does not take the initiative to resolve the matter with you in this way, then you need to address the issue directly and assertively. Don't sweep problems under the rug; this might seem easier in the short term, but it is sure to create larger problems as time goes by.

Human communication is inherently imperfect. It is possible to misinterpret someone's intent in any given instance, either because of the way it was phrased or because of a bias you have. However, if you frequently find yourself feeling hurt or angered in a relationship, your emotions are probably directing your attention toward real issues that need to be addressed. Some people have a pattern of hurting others repeatedly, only to apologize and promise to change, which they do, only to repeat the behavior again and again. This is the classic cycle in dysfunctional relationships. If you are caught in this cycle, set a boundary by creating enough space between yourself and the abuser to gain some clarity and peace.

Gossip and Negative Talk

In an episode of the old TV show *Gilligan's Island*, Gilligan finds berries that allow him to read other people's minds. Gilligan shares the berries with his friends on the island, and soon they all hate each other because they can hear the negative things they are thinking. Gilligan burns all the berries and everyone becomes even angrier and asks why he did this. Gilligan says, "But look at how much damage it was causing!"

The moral of this story is that sharing all your negative thoughts with people causes damage to them and to your relationship. When you hurt others, you have to forgive yourself, and that is probably one of the most difficult things to do. Even when you only think mean things about someone else, it is not healthy for you. It can cause you to see yourself in a negative light, as cruel and unforgiving. At the very least, it robs you of your joy in experiencing the present moment.

The good news is that the reverse of this behavior is also true. When you focus on the beautiful traits of others, and cultivate the habit of sharing your kind observations with them, your world will change. People around you will feel your love and warmth and benefit from it. You will feel more loving, and perhaps, slowly but surely, you will start to fall in love with yourself. Kindness, gentleness, warmth, and love are the gems of life. Share them with others and yourself, and see how your world begins to change.

Time Alone

When considering the people you spend time with, don't forget yourself and the important role of solitude. Spending time alone can help you focus on the good and meaningful things in your life, and create the time and space for you to clarify your priorities and intentions. Many great spiritual leaders have embarked on solitary journeys through the wilderness before settling into their wisdom and beginning their ministry. You may not choose to wander for years, but how about half a day each month? Or twenty minutes each morning or night? Or both? For people who want to maximize their happiness and potential for growth, the value of alone time and self-reflection is difficult to overemphasize. Daily meditation can be particularly beneficial.

FACT

Spending time alone can have a number of benefits such as having an opportunity to discover yourself and find your own voice, to think deeply, to work through problems more effectively, to improve concentration and productivity, to replenish your mental energy, and to enhance the quality of your relationships with others.

Finances

Money can't buy happiness. Let's set that myth aside right now. It's also true that not having enough funds to pay the bills or take care of basic needs can create an enormous amount of stress. Resolving money issues is important to becoming holistically healthy. It's particularly relevant in difficult times, when so many people are out of work and losing their homes, their businesses, and their savings. Whether your financial woes are a result of overspending, or you've lost your job due to circumstances beyond your control, learning good money management skills is always beneficial.

Don't criticize yourself because of your financial mistakes, but do resolve to learn from them. One of the most important lessons you can learn is to live within your means. While you have to earn enough to meet your basic needs, too many Americans believe that "basic needs" include having a new car, a huge home, and other material possessions. Expensive things have their place, but they won't help you find happiness. In fact, quite the opposite can be true. Obtaining and keeping these objects can create a lot of stress.

Learn how successful people manage their money and live within their means. Read books on the subject. Get rid of your credit cards or learn how to use them appropriately. Staying out of financial trouble will eliminate a lot of stress on your body, mind, emotions, and spirit. If money is tight, you can still have a fulfilling and enjoyable life. You might not be able to eat out as much or go to the movies as often, but you can still have a great time.

Final Thoughts

All of the individual facets of who you are—physical, emotional, spiritual, and mental—are tied together. Each is a key component to your overall health and happiness.

You need to heal from your past, take care of yourself today, and prepare for the future. As you go about your daily life, be careful not to neglect important areas such as exercise, nutrition, the balance between work and leisure, your relationships, your finances, and keeping a positive attitude. Don't forget that your thoughts can affect your physical body. Negative thoughts that create stress can manifest as a multitude of health problems.

The quality of your life reflects a string of choices and responses to the hand you've been dealt. This is not static, but ever-changing. Where are you headed? Do you like the direction? If not, change it. It's a lot of work, but every change you make along the way will make a difference, and it's well worth the effort.

CHAPTER 20

Making Change Happen

The process of changing from what you are to what you would like to become can be either arduous and frustrating or easy and rewarding. The same effort is required for both paths. Choose the first, and you'll probably recycle yourself endlessly. But if you approach change with realism, consistency, and commitment, success is sure to follow.

Approaching Self-Change

Fundamentally, this has been a book about change—changing your relationship with anger. Change can be difficult, but it is possible, even in the realms of thought, emotion, and behavior. Change can be uncomfortable and frightening, but that's okay. The discomfort and fear will pass. An open, accepting attitude toward the process of change goes a long way.

If you are used to being bombarded by negative words and angry thoughts all day, and then you decide to cut that out and start listening to the birds and watching sunsets, it will probably be hard at first because you aren't used to it. You may start to make some of the changes suggested, but then find yourself wanting some of that "junk" back because you aren't used to having clear, open spaces in your mind. You might miss the drama. Don't conclude from this that you can't improve. Just notice your resistance with a spirit of mindfulness and acceptance, and keep moving in a positive direction, granting yourself some grace.

Consider yourself a work in progress. Change may come slowly, but keep at it. If you would like to speed the process along, working with a therapist who is practicing good self-care can be helpful. She can help you identify some of the unhelpful thoughts and self-talk that keep you from living life to the fullest and offering the world your best self.

When you decide to make positive changes in your life, you influence the people around you as well. Others may decide that they want to join you in leading a calmer, more controlled, positive lifestyle. Or they may not want to give up the negativity that they are accustomed to. You may find that this disparity shifts things in your relationships. People in recovery from substance abuse are the clearest example of this situation, since the break with their substance of choice often leads (often as a matter of necessity) to the dissolution of relationships in which the old way of doing things still occupies center stage.

When you break the existing patterns of interaction in a relationship, especially by setting healthier boundaries, a new pattern must emerge. When you change, the relationship will change, too. Unfortunately, it may not always be the kind of change you were hoping for. Every relationship takes two, and you cannot control the choices of the other person. The ways in which those around you respond can clarify the choices you need to make in order to lead a healthy and happy life. This may mean spending less and less time with certain people and perhaps even ending unhealthy relationships.

Genetics Versus Conditioning

There are two considerations that seem to dominate how people think about themselves and about the possibility for growth and change in their lives. The first is genetics—the genes you inherited from your mother and father determine things like your hair and eye color, how tall or short you are, and certain behavioral traits. The second factor is conditioning, which is the way you were brought up and influenced by your parents and other important people in your life.

There is a tendency to attribute an almost-deterministic power to genes. People believe that their personality, behavior, and health outcomes are largely a function of their genetic heritage, and there is only a small margin of change possible. This is a serious misunderstanding. Although genetics is important in shaping who you are, conditioning is a far more relevant concept when it comes to tackling behavior change. As much as 80 percent of the way you act is established by your conditioning.

Giving too much credence to genetics conveys the message that you can't change many of the things about yourself that you would like to change. You may have certain misconceptions about inherited traits—for example, thinking that because your father and grandfather had bad tempers, it's an inescapable family trait. You have heard this since you were a child and now believe that you have a short fuse because you inherited it. As a result, you excuse your behavior by thinking it's in your genes, right?

Wrong. First of all, it's possible that there is no genetic component to your temper issue. Much of who you are today was shaped by your upbringing. Second, even if there is a genetic predisposition to having a quick temper, the reality is that you can still change most things about yourself. It may be a lot of work, especially when a particular behavioral pattern has been deeply ingrained since childhood. But it is possible. Psychologists have known this for decades, and the evidence is now irrefutable. The science of epigenetics has demonstrated conclusively that genes are not destiny. Genes can be changed by habit, lifestyle, behavior, stress, even finances. Thanks to discoveries in the field of neuroplasticity as well, brains can be radically rewired well into advanced age.

By understanding your past and knowing who you are, you will be able to make effective and lasting changes. This is how you can get rid of those habits and characteristics that you don't like, and keep the positive things that you do like. A lot of people don't want to deal with their past. This is understandable, especially when they lived through unpleasant experiences. But if you don't address the negative things that happened to you, it's like stepping on a rusty nail and covering it with a Band-Aid. If you don't clean the wound out properly, it will get infected. If the wound is serious enough, it can fester to the point where it compromises the health of your entire body. Emotions work the same way. You may think that your old emotional wound no longer impacts you. Unfortunately, it can have a lasting effect on your life, unless you acknowledge it and heal it. For example, the old emotional wound you have tried to bury may have led to a negative habit. As strange as that sounds, it's true.

Another way to change old patterns is to bring new people into your life. That's a great benefit of finding ways to connect with new people, such as joining new organizations. Not that you have to disassociate yourself from everyone you know. But instead of seeing the same people you've seen consistently for years, bring new people into your life who aren't used to seeing you in your old environments and find new social outlets. That includes your family members, who may continue to treat you in the conditioned, dysfunctional ways they used when you were a child. So again, you are getting new conditioning and you're changing the old patterns.

Ten Rules of Change

In his blog on Psychology Today, Dr. Stan Goldberg, an expert on human change, tells the story of how, after his mother died, he counted fifteen self-help books on her bookshelves. Each one offered broad ideas but failed to discuss the practical mechanics of how to go about putting the ideas into practice. Based on his twenty-five years of researching how people change, Goldberg distinguished the following ten principles as decisive for successful self-change:

All Behaviors Are Complex

Behavior changes take place in stages, not all at once. Most behaviors can be broken down into different components. To bolster your odds of success, break the desired behavior into discrete parts and practice each part successively.

Change Is Frightening

People fear change. Therefore, they resist change. Work to overcome this obstacle by looking at consequences. What are the likely consequences of changing, and what are the likely consequences of not changing? Take your time to do this thoughtfully. Think about consequences in both the short- and long-term. Choose the behavior that has the most desired consequences and the least aversive consequences. Another good strategy is to "prepare for your observers," that is, for how the change you are making will affect the people who know you and have grown accustomed to the old way of doing things. New behaviors can frighten the people observing them, so introduce them slowly. Finally, be realistic. Unrealistic goals increase fear, and fear increases the probability of failure.

Change Must Be Positive

Reward—not punishment—is what is truly necessary for permanent change. Reward, or *reinforcement*, as psychologists call it, can be intrinsic, extrinsic, or extraneous. One type of reinforcement must be present for self-change, two types are better than one, and three types are better still. If possible, focus on approaching the change you would like to make in a way that you find enjoyable or rewarding. This provides an intrinsic reward. Alternatively, you can focus on the outcome. An act doesn't have to be enjoyable when the end result is extrinsically rewarding. You might dislike cleaning the kitchen, for example, but you persist because you like the sight of a clean kitchen. Finally, you can reward yourself, providing extraneous reinforcement that isn't directly connected to the act or its completion, such as dinner at your favorite restaurant.

Being Is Easier Than Becoming

To illustrate this principle, Dr. Goldberg tells the story of his karate class of twenty students. The teacher was notorious for yelling "No pain, no gain" during exhausting workouts. Within a short time, the class was down to only three students. People are not likely to persist in an activity where the perceived pain exceeds the reward. Rather than pushing yourself excessively at the beginning and exhausting your motivation, take baby steps. You will be more successful if your goals are realistic and more comfortably paced. Simplify the process as much as you can, and try to anticipate problems that might arise. Look for ways to cue yourself on a regular basis so that you don't lose sight of your objectives. The more you can anticipate and prepare, the better off you will be.

Slower Is Better

Slow, gradual change is usually better than dramatic, all-at-once transformations. Taking things slowly means taking the time to allow new behaviors to become automatic, and then layering on new elements as you become more proficient and skillful. Author Ursula Le Guin once said, "It's good to have an end to journey toward; but it is the journey that matters, in the end." Don't devise an arduous path; it should be as rewarding as the goal.

Know More, Do Better

Surprise spells disaster for people seeking change. Knowing more about the process allows more control over it. The first technique that will help you here is called self-monitoring—the monitoring of your behaviors, with an emphasis on the ones you want to change. Keep a scorecard or journal that tracks your progress over time. Second, try soliciting feedback from trusted friends and loved ones. Evidence suggests that taking the time to process important personal experiences, struggles, and goals with others can contribute to creating successful change in your life. Finally, take the time to understand the outcome, regardless of whether it is successful or unsuccessful. This knowledge can be a real asset as you move forward. Success is satisfying, and if you know why you succeeded or failed, similar strategies can be applied when changing other behaviors.

Change Requires Structure

Many people view structure as restrictive, something that inhibits spontaneity. While spontaneity is wonderful for some activities, it's a sure-fire method for sabotaging change. Take the time to identify what works best for you.

Classify all activities and materials you're using as either helpful, neutral, or unhelpful in achieving your goal. Eliminate the unhelpful ones, make the neutrals into positives, and keep or increase the positives. Revisit your plan regularly. Review every day how and why you're changing and the consequences of success and failure. Repetition increases the probability of success.

Finally, make sure that you have structured the change or changes you would like to make in a logical sequence. For example, when tackling a difficult behavioral change such as anger management, tackle the easier, more basic changes first, followed by the more difficult. This will enable you to establish a sense of momentum and confidence that will help carry you through any challenges that might arise later.

Practice Is Necessary

This shouldn't surprise anyone. It is only through practice that new behaviors can become automatic. Many failures that people experience in life can be attributed to a lack of practice and preparation. Don't try to cut corners on this one. There's no magic number or amount of time that will tell you when you've practiced enough, but you should be able to judge that by the results. If necessary, solicit help and feedback from a trusted friend. Also, try practicing the change in a variety of settings. This will help you generalize the new behavior across a range of situations.

New Behaviors Must Be Protected

Even when flawlessly performed, new behaviors are fragile and disappear if unprotected. One way to help support new behaviors is to control your environment so that it supports the change you wish to make. Environmental issues such as noise and level of alertness can interfere with learning new behaviors. Identify what helps you and what hinders you; increase what helps and eliminate the rest. Another helpful approach is to use memory aids. Because a new behavior is neither familiar nor automatic, it's easy to forget. Anything that helps your memory is beneficial.

Small Successes Are Big

Unfortunately, plans for big successes often result in big failures. Focus instead on a series of small successes. Each little success builds your confidence and self-esteem, while one big failure devastates it. Map out your successes in terms of distinct small missions, and savor the satisfaction of incremental gains. This process will eventually take you to your goal.

Setting Goals

Imagine you are the captain of a sailboat. Looking at the compass, you leave the harbor and head toward Hawaii. But after you leave port, you never look at the compass again, nor do you check the way the wind is blowing. You just keep going in the same direction without taking any necessary adjustments into account. Ocean currents and storms pull you off course, and you find yourself in the middle of the Pacific Ocean with no land in sight. Lost at sea versus lying on the beach in paradise—what a difference a few minor course corrections can make. Consider this: If you're traveling to Hawaii from the West Coast of the United States, being one degree off in your heading will result in missing your destination by 600 miles!

Life is like that. Most people have an idea about where they are headed with their lives. But circumstances can and do change along the way. So many things can distract your attention or throw you off course, such as going through a divorce, having children, losing your job, experiencing health problems. You are significantly more likely to succeed in any endeavor if you have defined concrete goals. You are even more likely to succeed if those goals are supported by a well-thought-out plan.

It is helpful to distinguish between ultimate goals and supporting objectives. The ultimate goal is what you want; the objective is a specific achievement that moves you closer to that goal. As circumstances change, you will need to modify your objectives in order to accommodate unforeseen circumstances. For example, you may desire to travel the world. You set the concrete objective of visiting two countries per year in order to move toward your goal. If life intervenes somehow and you're not able to travel for a year or more, remind yourself that the two-countries-a-year plan was just a means to a greater end. Make the course adjustment and continue on your journey.

Try to have goals that aren't only about making a lot of money or listing all the great things you're going to do when you retire. Have a variety of goals that come from different perspectives. Maybe you want to seek spiritual development, find a wonderful life partner, travel, or get your college degree. Some people create a bucket list filled with dreams and activities they want to accomplish before they die. Don't limit yourself. Taking the time to set goals will help you mentally clarify your targets so that you can eventually achieve them. Write down your goals and get started on the road to making them a reality.

The Long, Medium, and Short of It

You should have short-, medium-, and long-term goals. Naturally, short-term goals are what you want to accomplish today or in the immediate future. Making a to-do list can help you stay on track. Medium-term goals are what you hope to complete in around three to six months, while long-term goals extend out from a year or longer.

Write your goals down. People who write their goals out and share them with loved ones are more likely to succeed. Use a notebook, index cards, your computer, or whatever works best for you. Then, periodically update them, just as a skipper on a sailboat might periodically check her heading and make course corrections. While some people think they have to think about their goals constantly, it is actually better *not* to be looking at your medium- and long-term goals daily. To maximize your performance, mood, and clarity of mind, you need to live in the present moment as much as possible. If you're always thinking about the future, it's not possible to live a satisfying life now.

Find a balance between setting goals and letting go of them once they're written down. On a day-to-day level, it is primarily the short-term goals that you will want to focus on. This means knowing that your longer-range goals, like finishing a master's degree, require taking action in the present—namely, following through on the subsidiary activities that are necessary to reach the larger prize. Perhaps you will begin this journey by signing up for a night class. It's that way with most long-term goals. You must plan for them in the short term, while being careful not to obsess about the future.

Remember that it's the things you're doing in the now that can move you toward your goals. Each step is important. Say, you are currently forty-five years old, and one of your long-term goals is to be in good health when you reach sixty-five. To achieve that ultimate goal, your list of goals for today and at least two other days this week should include exercising. Other short-term goals might include healthy eating and reading a book on healthy aging.

Medium-term goals might be losing twenty pounds of excess body fat and learning to better manage stress. You get the idea.

Notice what you're not doing in this example: You're not obsessing every day on your long-term goal of being healthy at sixty-five. Instead, you are mainly focused on the steps you need to take to achieve that goal . . . step by step, day by day, week by week. You can set your daily goals to include walking, going to the gym, watching an exercise DVD, or whatever you enjoy. The important thing is that you're actively engaged in pursuing your goal while still very much living in the present.

You Can Do This

People can and do succeed, every day, in creating meaningful and important changes in their lives. So can you. Remember that all of the individual facets of who you are—physical, emotional, spiritual, and mental—are tied together. Each is a key component to your overall health and happiness.

Don't forget that your thoughts can affect your physical body. Negative thoughts that create stress and anger can manifest as a multitude of health problems.

You need to heal from your past, take care of yourself today, and prepare for the future. As you go about your daily life, be careful not to neglect such important areas as exercise, nutrition, the balance between work and leisure, your relationships, your finances, and keeping a positive attitude.

Your time on this earth is brief, so live each and every day to the fullest. Enjoy your journey. Make sure that each component of your whole self is strong and healthy. When you determine to give each area the attention it deserves and take care of your entire being, you have moved past simple anger management onto the path of holistic health.

APPENDIX

Top Ten Myths about Anger

1. **It's bad to feel angry.** Although anger usually makes you feel bad, it is simply an emotion and is not bad in itself. Anger serves as a warning to let you know when a situation is not right. Anger can also be a strong motivator to be assertive and to make changes.

2. **Other people and situations make me angry.** Not everybody gets angry at the same things. You make yourself angry by the way you interpret and relate to your experiences. In so doing, you allow circumstances outside yourself to control your peace of mind.

3. **Ignoring anger makes it go away.** This notion is misguided on two levels. First, anger is generally a response to a situation in which you feel threatened, frustrated, or both. Ignoring the situation will not make it go away and may mean that you won't stand up for yourself when you should. It can also lead to passive-aggressive behavior, lashing out, or stress and health problems. Second, emotions that are ignored or suppressed do not magically disappear. If you have a feeling that persists and you deny it, it will manifest in other, indirect, and usually more harmful ways.

4. **Anger is not controllable.** There is a shade of truth here, but little more. In the aftermath of a powerfully threatening event, emotions such as anger and fear can be difficult to control. Imagine being sucker-punched at a nightclub, or surprised by someone walking at night in an area where you feel unsafe. Your initial reactions would be hard to control indeed. However, very few of the situations that cause you anger are in any way like these examples. More often than not, these are situations involving people with whom you have established relationships (friends, coworkers, loved ones) and whose behavior hurt, annoyed, or frustrated you in some way. With effort, the frequency and intensity of anger is highly controllable in these situations. Moreover, you can exert complete control over how you respond in any situation.

5. **Anger is only a problem when it's openly expressed.** Expressing anger is not a problem; it only becomes a problem when anger is expressed poorly or at an inappropriate time. When people react with hostility or become angry in a way that is out of proportion to the situation, problems are likely. However, unexpressed anger can lead to serious problems as well—including health, emotional, and relationship difficulties. Instead of swallowing anger, or aggressively lashing out, there is a far more effective approach: firm, respectful, *assertive* communication.

6. **Anger is inherited;** there's nothing you can do about it. This is a common misconception. People sometimes view their personalities and behaviors as more or less "set in stone" because of their genetic inheritance. "I inherited my temper from my mom; she's even worse." People say things like this, and the situation seems almost hopeless. However, observations in the real world, along with considerable research evidence, demonstrate that this is not true. People are not born with set, specific ways of expressing anger. These studies show that, because the expression of anger is learned behavior, more effective ways of expressing anger also can be learned.

7. **Anger automatically leads to aggression.** It is commonly thought that anger builds and inevitably escalates to the point of an aggressive outburst. The experience of escalation toward aggression is common. For many people, moreover, this escalation can feel unavoidable or out of control. But it is controllable. Anger does not necessarily lead to aggression. In fact, effective anger management involves controlling the escalation of anger by learning diffusion strategies and assertiveness skills, changing negative "self-talk," challenging irrational beliefs, and employing a variety of behavioral strategies.

8. **Anger serves no purpose.** Anger has gotten a bad rap, and for understandable reasons. Anger is often irrational, displaced, and destructive to both the angry person and others. Throughout history, much harm has been done under the banner of anger. Despite these sobering realities, anger can serve a very important purpose. Anger is an informational signal that informs, directs, and motivates behavior. It can empower you to survive a life-threatening situation. If you didn't have anger, you would be much more likely to let people walk all over you. Just as pain causes you to pull away from a hot object, anger causes you to pull away from an unfair situation or to change it.

9. **Time heals all wounds.** Sometimes people avoid dealing with issues directly, thinking that "maybe it'll just go away." Rarely does that happen. Time does not heal emotional wounds—not unless you take steps to facilitate that healing. Unresolved anger is most likely to fester and reassert itself in disguised form. There are numerous examples of men and women of advanced age who are still very much weighed down by hurt and anger stemming from their youth.

10. **People respect you more when you are angry.** Engaging in brash, loud, angry behaviors might intimidate or annoy other people, but don't expect much more than that. Aggressiveness does not foster open communication, nor does it help other people to see your point of view, nor is it a particularly effective way to win friends and influence people. Quite the opposite, this kind of behavior pushes people away and hardens battle lines. There are times when using anger to impose your will on others can be an effective short-term tactic. However, in the long term, this approach tends to create more problems than it solves. Being a skilled communicator, having good ideas, and being able to approach disagreements objectively are all more likely ways to win the respect of others.

Index

We Have EVERYTHING® on Anything!

The Everything® list spans a wide range of subjects, with more than 500 titles covering 25 different categories:

Business	History	Reference
Careers	Home Improvement	Religion
Children's Storybooks	Everything Kids	Self-Help
Computers	Languages	Sports & Fitness
Cooking	Music	Travel
Crafts and Hobbies	New Age	Wedding
Education/Schools	Parenting	Writing
Games and Puzzles	Personal Finance	
Health	Pets	